Routledge Revivals

Human Documents of the Lloyd George Era

First published in 1972, *Human Documents of the Lloyd George Era* presents the years when Lloyd George was in his prime, and his career in peace and war may be seen as the frame in which the 'documents' find their proper place; but the book's real subject is not Lloyd George, it is the People, with whom he identified himself and spent his long life trying to serve. For the purpose of this book Lloyd George Era is taken as the period from 1905. The early documents enable us to reconstruct a vivid picture of life as it was lived 'before the war' by such people as London artisans, Middlesbrough ironworkers, Lancashire factory hands, Northumbrian pit-folk and farm labourers, while extracts from reports of the first 'Lady Factory Inspectors' and of the great Royal Commission on the Poor Law highlight the grim situation of the 'Pauper Host'.

With the outbreak of war, the mood changes, as Lloyd George leads the People in a massive war effort on the home front, producing munitions and trying to maintain normal industrial output. A glimpse is given of the various contributions made by women. Out of a vast mass of tiny details a picture emerges of an essentially peace- loving people joining forces to achieve what Lloyd George called 'the bloodstained stagger' to victory. This is an essential read for students of British history.

Human Documents of the Lloyd George Era

E. Royston Pike

Routledge
Taylor & Francis Group

First published in 1972
by George Allen & Unwin Ltd.

This edition first published in 2023 by Routledge
4 Park Square, Milton Park, Abingdon, Oxon, OX14 4RN

and by Routledge
605 Third Avenue, New York, NY 10017

Routledge is an imprint of the Taylor & Francis Group, an informa business

Publisher's Note
The publisher has gone to great lengths to ensure the quality of this reprint but points out that some imperfections in the original copies may be apparent.

Disclaimer
The publisher has made every effort to trace copyright holders and welcomes correspondence from those they have been unable to contact.

A Library of Congress record exists under ISBN: 0049420976

ISBN: 978-1-032-61509-7 (hbk)
ISBN: 978-1-032-61514-1 (ebk)
ISBN: 978-1-032-61512-7 (pbk)

Book DOI 10.4324/9781032615141

I. THE PHILANTHROPIC HIGHWAYMAN

Mr. Lloyd George : '*I'll* make 'em pity the aged poor!'

Punch (1908)

HUMAN DOCUMENTS OF THE LLOYD GEORGE ERA

BY

E. ROYSTON PIKE

London

GEORGE ALLEN & UNWIN LTD

RUSKIN HOUSE MUSEUM STREET

First published in 1972

ISBN 0 04 942097 6 Hardback
0 04 942098 4 Paper

Printed in Great Britain
in 10 point Plantin type
by Cox & Wyman Ltd.,
London, Fakenham and Reading

INTRODUCTION
THE LLOYD GEORGE ERA

David Lloyd George died at his home in Wales on March 26, 1945. Two days later Winston Churchill, the then Prime Minister, delivered in the House of Commons a characteristically Churchillian oration in honour of the man who for so many years had been his colleague in the high places of Government and his almost lifelong friend.

In his opening sentences Mr Churchill spoke of the time when, following upon their triumph at the general election of 1906, Lloyd George 'launched the Liberal and Radical forces of this country effectively into the broad stream of social betterment and social security in which all modern parties now steer'. He went on, 'There was no man so gifted, so eloquent, so forceful, who knew the life of the people so well.' Those were great days, 'when Lloyd George was in his prime, when his power, his influence, his initiative, were unequalled in the land, when he was the champion of the weak and the poor'. Health Insurance and Old Age Pensions were 'the first large-scale State-conscious efforts to set a balustrade along the crowded causeway of the people's life . . . to fasten a lid over the abyss into which vast numbers used to fall, generation after generation, uncared for and indeed, unnoticed. . . . The stamps we lick, the roads we travel, the system of progressive taxation, the principal remedies that have been used against unemployment – all these to a very great extent were part not only of the mission but of the actual achievement of Lloyd George . . . of the great, laborious, constructive work he did for the social and domestic life of our country . . .'

But there came a time when the 'calm, complacent, self-satisfied tranquillities of the Victorian Era exploded into the world convulsions of the terrible Twentieth Century', and then Lloyd George had another part to play. As Minister of Munitions in 1915 he 'hurled himself into the mobilization of British industry' and after he had 'seized the main power in the State and the headship of the Government' he 'imparted immediately a new surge of strength, of impulse, far stronger than anything that had been known up to that time, and extending over the whole field of war-time government'. Two achievements in particular Mr Churchill singled out for special mention – the adoption of the Convoy system, which Lloyd George 'enforced upon the Admiralty and by which the U-boats were defeated' and the establishment of 'the unified command on the Western Front which gave Marshal Foch the power to lead us all to victory'.

Of Lloyd George's record as Prime Minister in the four troubled years that followed the Armistice, Mr Churchill said nothing; nor did he refer to the succeeding years when Lloyd George, as an increasingly lonely figure, was still untiringly prolific in advancing schemes of national regeneration. But when he arrived at his peroration the Prime Minister struck again the note of high praise and generous acknowledgment. 'As a man of action, resource, and creative energy, Lloyd George stood, at his zenith, without rival. Much of his work abides, some of it will grow greatly in the future, and those who come after us will find the pillars of his life's toil upstanding, massive, and indestructible.'

* * *

Such was the tribute that Britain's captain in the second of the World Wars paid to his predecessor in the first; and having read it, we must surely feel that 'Lloyd George Era' is not only a fitting but indeed the inevitable designation for the period covered by the 'documents' in this book.

That period may be taken as being, approximately, the years from 1905, when the Liberals secured their great electoral triumph and embarked on an unparalleled programme of social reform, and 1919, when the Great War had been fought and won and the British people faced the harsh realities of the 'morning after'.

At the outset, it should be explained that this is not a biographical study of Lloyd George, although we shall meet his name on many of the pages, and even when he is not occupying the centre of the stage we may catch, coming from the wings, the echoes of his voice, that incomparable vehicle of passion and of power; perhaps it would be fair to say that his career forms a frame into which the 'documents' find their appropriate place. Nor is the book anything in the nature of a history of the Great War. True, rather more than half its pages are concerned with various aspects of that epoch-making conflict, but those aspects are almost entirely 'Home Front' in their composition; military events are altogether outside our purview.

To put it shortly, it may be said that this book is an attempt to show how the People 'lived and moved and had their being' in one of the most disturbed and disturbing periods of our history. Note the word, People. No more than in the earlier volumes of what has now become a series have I been concerned with the gilded minority; in making my selection of 'documents' I have always had in mind those 'ordinary' folk – the 'workers' – the working classes, the wage-earners and their families – who in those days constituted (as they have always constituted and still constitute today) the great majority of the population. (The sort of people, when you come to think of it, Lloyd George was most deeply interested in and spent his long life in trying to serve.) A second feature is the emphasis on the importance of women's work both in the activities of peace and those of war; and a third, and not least important is the constant endeavour to give pride of place to those 'documents' in which the 'human angle' is most clearly illustrated.

All the more than a hundred and fifty 'documents' are contemporary, reflecting the ardours and anxieties of the time, and (with the exception of an occasional cross-heading and some editorial explanations, etc., placed in square brackets) they have been left as their authors wrote them. They have been drawn from a great variety of sources (indicated at the foot of each extract) but in the main from Government or 'official' publications of one kind or another, which have never been reprinted and are hard to come by outside the State Paper Room at the British Museum. Of the other chief sources the London *Times* is pre-eminent. As regards the illustrations, they too are contemporary, drawn largely from *Punch* and the *Illustrated London News* and, so far as those of women war workers are concerned, from photographs taken under the auspices of the Ministry of Munitions and the War Office.

CONTENTS

ACKNOWLEDGMENTS

For permission to quote from Sir Winston Churchill's tribute to Lloyd George I am indebted to the Controller of H.M. Stationery Office; to the Carnegie Endowment for International Peace, New York, for permission to use extracts from Sir W. M. Beveridge's *British Food Control*, C. E. Fayle's *The War and the Shipping Industry*, and I. O. Andrews' *Economic Effects of the War upon Women and Children in Great Britain*; and to the following Publishers in respect of extracts from the books named, viz. Messrs. G. Bell & Sons Ltd (Pember Reeves, *Round About a Pound a Week*), Messrs. Edward Arnold Ltd (Lady Bell, *At the Works*), Messrs. Hutchinson & Co. Ltd (Monica Cosens, *Lloyd George's Munition Girls*) and The Bodley Head (Mrs Peel, *How We Lived Then: 1914–1918*). My thanks are also extended to the Editors of many periodicals, and in very special measure to the Editor of *The Times*, through whose courtesy I have been enabled to quote from a number of articles reflecting the contemporary scene during the period of the Great War.

ILLUSTRATIONS

PLATES

DRAWINGS IN TEXT

CHAPTER I

BRITAIN 'BEFORE THE WAR'

'Before the War' – the war of 1914–18 – the Great War, as it was originally, and very properly, styled – the population of Great Britain (England, Wales and Scotland) was about forty-one million. The great majority of these were poor, judged by whatever standard was adopted by the social investigators of the time.

This may come as a surprise to those who have been led to believe by nostalgic romanticists that the 'Edwardian Age' was one of comfortable enjoyment and elegant display. So, indeed, it was if you happened to have been born into the upper classes or that middle class to which those 'Forsytes' belonged who come to such vigorous life in the pages of John Galsworthy's *Saga*. But these were the Few – comparatively speaking, the very few.

Just what was the numerical composition of the various classes is impossible to determine with any certainty, since the science of social statistics was then in its infancy, and there were frequent and well-grounded complaints about the inadequacy of official information concerning the condition of the people, and of the wage-earning population in particular. All the same, a beginning had been made in the collection and evaluation of vital material by such pioneers as Charles Booth, B. Seebohm Rowntree, Professor A. L. Bowley, and Sir Leo Chiozza Money M.P., and there is a comforting significance in the discovery that all are in general agreement as regards their main conclusions.

From what may be gathered, then, the 'upper classes', the people at the top of the social scale – the men of wealth and status, the landed aristocracy and the larger landlords in town and country, the most successful men of business and in the professions, and those whose investment income was sufficient to relieve them of the vulgar necessity to work – may have numbered, with their families, something over a million persons.

Below these came those 'middle classes' which, with a throw-back to Gladstonian ideology, still liked to think of themselves as constituting the 'backbone of the nation'. Between 'upper' and 'middle' there was no such strict line of demarcation as was ruled in some Continental countries. Nor is it at all easy to determine just where 'middle' subsided into 'lower'. Any estimate, therefore, is likely to be invalidated by a difference in definition, but we shall probably be not very far out if we assume that the 'middle classes', composed of persons and their families with incomes between, say, £160 (the lower limit for income-tax) and £700 per annum, accounted for something between four and five million persons.

Taking even the larger figure, this still leaves us with some thirty-five million people to constitute the 'lower' or 'working classes'. This vast host of men, women and children, representing at least eighty per cent of the total population, cannot be regarded as anything else but *poor*. Taken all in all, they were poorly fed and poorly clothed, poorly housed, poorly educated, poorly attended in sickness and distress, poorly provided with leisure and opportunities for recreation and amusement. Thus there would seem to be not the least ground for challenging the conclusion arrived at by Sir Leo Money in his book *Riches and Poverty* (10th edition, 1910), that, 'In analysis, the United Kingdom is seen to contain a great multitude of poor people, veneered with a thin layer of the comfortable and the rich.'

All the 'documents' contained in this chapter are concerned with that 'great multitude'. Drawn as they are entirely from 'Official' sources, in particular reports of various inquiries instituted by the Labour Department of the Board of Trade, they provide a mass of carefully collected and well authenticated information concerning the 'facts of life' as experienced by the great majority of the people in Britain 'before the War'.

One of the 'documents' – No. 17 – deserves a footnote. Miss Margaret Bondfield (1873–1953) who told the Truck Committee of her own experiences as a shop assistant,was shortly afterwards appointed National Officer of the National Union of General and Municipal Workers, in which capacity she served for thirty years. A Labour M.P. from 1923 to 1931, she was Minister of Labour in Ramsay MacDonald's Labour administration in 1929 and thus had the distinction of becoming the first woman Cabinet Minister and Privy Councillor.

I

Cottage Homes of the Working People

Of the dwellings most commonly occupied by the working classes one type is prevalent, with few exceptions, in all the towns of England and Wales. This is a small self-contained four- or five-roomed cottage, containing a front parlour, a kitchen, a scullery, and two or three bedrooms. Varieties of this type are numerous. The front parlour is usually entered direct from the street; the stairs are built between the front and the back room, parallel with the line of frontage; and access to the third bedroom (where such exists) is obtained through one of the other bedrooms. In the larger houses there are usually entrance passages, while each of the bedrooms has a separate entrance from the landing.

In the Southern, and also to some extent in the Eastern Counties, bay windows and small forecourts are common, even in the cheaper houses of this type, whereas in the Midlands these features are found only in the better class of house, the ordinary workman's cottages rising with flat fronts directly from the pavement line.

Houses of six rooms are occupied by the working-classes in a number of towns, e.g. Cardiff, Chatham and Gillingham, Coventry, Northampton, and Portsmouth; but in general the proportion of six-roomed houses in working-class occupation is low. At the other end of the scale, dwellings of three rooms are frequently found in the Northern Counties, in Yorkshire and in Lancashire and Cheshire, and dwellings of two rooms in the Northern Counties and in Yorkshire, as well as in Plymouth and Devonport.

In the towns in the West Riding of Yorkshire, houses containing three or four rooms, built on the 'back-to-back' principle, are of great importance. Although it is true that this type of house occurs in towns in other parts of the country (e.g. in Birmingham) it can no longer be regarded as a representative type elsewhere. The Lancashire towns have also a distinctive type of working-class dwelling, viz. a square building containing two or sometimes three bedrooms on the first floor, and downstairs a front and back kitchen, the back kitchen serving also (in some cases exclusively) as a scullery. The 'Newcastle' or 'cottage flat', which is found in the Tyneside towns, consists of one floor of a two-storied house, and is entirely self-contained, having its own separate entrance.

Report of Board of Trade Inquiry into Working-Class Rents and Retail Prices in Industrial Towns of the United Kingdom in 1912; Cd. 6955 (1913), pp. xvii–xviii.

2

The Rent They Paid

The predominant weekly rents of working-class Dwellings in May 1912 in a number of provincial towns in England and Wales and Scotland, and in London (Middle Zone) were:

Number of Rooms per Dwelling	*E. & W. and Scotland*	*London*
2 rooms	2s 6d – 3s 9d	4s 0d – 7s 0d
3 rooms	3s 9d – 5s 0d	5s 6d – 9s 0d
4 rooms	4s 6d – 5s 9d	7s 0d – 10s 6d
5 rooms	5s 6d – 6s 6d	8s 6d – 13s 0d
6 rooms	6s 9d – 8s 0d	10s 0d – 15s 0d

Cd. 6955 (1913), p. xxv.

3

Scottish 'Flats'

There is little in common between the usual working-class dwellings in England and Scotland. In Scotland the typical residence of a working-class family is a flat of two or three rooms, in a stone-built tenement-block, two, three or four stories high. The building is entered by a passage leading to a stone stair, which gives access to the upper floors. Two, three, or four flats are usually found on each floor, and the door by which each is entered from the landing, or 'stairhead', generally opens into a lobby of fair size, from which entrance into the various rooms is obtained.

The rooms are large, and frequently provided with a bed-recess, which provides accommodation for a double bed. These recesses occur in one or two or more of the rooms, and the bedstead is sometimes a permanent fitting provided by the landlord. Generally each block of flats has a common wash-house and drying-ground.

The most obvious disadvantages of a Scottish tenement are the lack of a private yard or garden, the necessity for washing and drying clothes in a semi-public back green, the frequency of common sanitary arrangements, and the fact that the majority of the dwellings are situated at the head of one or more flights of stairs. This feature of the stairs involves many inconveniences and disadvantages, as, for example, the inability of a mother to supervise her children when they are playing out of doors, the danger which it presents for very young children and the difficulties which it imposes on the aged and infirm. In addition, the ascent and descent of several flights of stairs must often prove an obstacle to providing infants with a proper amount of fresh air.

With regard to the arrangements within the dwelling, the provision of the bed recess to compensate for the small number of rooms involves the use as sleeping apartments of living-rooms in which the air is, of necessity, more or less polluted. The small number of rooms also means that there is less facility for the separation of the sexes in a growing family, and less opportunity for isolation in cases of sickness; there is also the disturbance of young children who go to bed early.

On the other hand, this type of dwelling possesses several distinct advantages. It is as a rule exceptionally well and strongly built, the rooms are large and lofty, and the workman can live nearer to his work and so avoid travelling expenses.

Cd. 6955 (1913), p. xix.

4

Predominant Retail Prices Paid by the Working Classes in October 1912

Beef, per lb		Eggs, per 1s	
British	8d – 10d	Irish	8 – 10
Frozen	5½d – 6½d	Foreign	10 – 14
Mutton		Cheese, Canadian	
British	8d – 9½d	or American	
Frozen	4½d – 5d	cheddar, per lb	8d – 9d
Pork (British)	8½d – 9½d	Butter	1s 3d – 1s 4d
Tea	1s 4d – 1s 6d	Potatoes, per 7 lbs	3½d – 4½d
Sugar	2d – 2½d	Flour, per 7lbs	10d – 11d
Bacon	10d – 11d	Bread, per 4 lbs	5½d – 6d
		Milk, per quart	3½d – 4d
		Coal, per cwt	1s 0d – 1s 3d

Estimated average weekly consumption of a family consisting of 2 adults and 3 or 4 children:

Meat	6½ lbs	Butter	2 lbs
Tea	0·6 lbs	Potatoes	17 lbs
Sugar	5⅓ lbs	Flour	10 lbs
Bacon	1½ lbs	Bread	22 lbs
Eggs	12	Milk	10 pints
Cheese	¾ lb	Coal	2 cwt

Cd. 6955, p. xxxvi.

5

25s-a-week Railwaymen

The number of workpeople in respect of whom returns of wages, earnings and hours of duty in 1907 were obtained was considerably over 400,000, and included practically all those employed by Railway Companies in the Coaching and Traffic, Goods, Locomotive, Carriage and Wagon, Permanent Way departments. Station-masters, booking clerks, and officials on the salary list were not included.

The great majority were male workers in regular employment [who] may be regarded as the normal type of railway servant. Nearly all were 'six-day workers', i.e. their rate of pay was for a working week of 6 days, Sunday duty when taken being paid for as overtime or an equivalent time off being given in lieu of payment. The average actual weekly earnings in certain of the principal grades were as follows:

Engine drivers	45s 11d	Platelayers	21s 2d
Guards:		Porters:	
Goods	31s 2d	Goods	21s 10d
Passenger	29s 3d	Traffic	19s 9d
Signalmen	27s 6d		

The earnings quoted include a certain amount of cash bonus (on the average 2d per man and 1d per lad and boy). Other additions to the nominal rate of wages took the form of allowances for uniform or partial clothing or of a house rent free or at a reduced rental; the value of these allowances, however, has not been included in the rates of wages and earnings stated. In the case of adult workmen the allowance for uniform or partial clothing was valued at an average of 7d per week per recipient. The housing allowance averaged 1s 10d weekly per recipient.

A considerable number of railway servants were entitled to sick pay, pensions, etc. under contributing pension or provident schemes to which the railway companies also contributed. In a few cases sick pay or pension were given by the companies.

The average annual earnings of all workpeople (including piece workers and casual workers), as estimated from the total wages bill for the year, was nearly £65.

The hours of duty for a full week were given in the majority of cases exclusive of mealtimes; for adult workers ('6-day workers') such hours averaged 58, and for lads and boys 58·9.

Report of Earnings and Hours Inquiry: VII, Railway Service, Cd. 6053 (1912), pp. ii-iv.

6

A Million Men in the Building Trades

The Building Trades give employment to about a million workpeople, and form one of the most important groups of industries affording occupation for males. They include a large proportion of skilled workmen, many of whom have served an apprenticeship of from 3 to 7 years.

In the building trades practically all the workpeople are paid by time. In a large number of towns standard time rates, mutually agreed upon between representatives of employers and workpeople, are recognized both for skilled men and for the chief classes of labourers.

Much time is lost by workpeople on account of the number of engagements for short periods, and further, during the winter months shorter working hours prevail, the average number of hours being 45·9 for a period of 14·3 weeks in winter as compared with 52·9 in summer ... The rate of wage per hour was rather more than 8¼d for the great towns and rather less than 7d for the smaller. In the London district the rate was over 9d.

The average earnings of men who worked full time in an ordinary week in the summer of 1906 were: London, 38s 8d; Northern Counties, 33s 6d; Yorkshire, Lancashire, and Cheshire, 33s 1d; North and West Midland Counties, 31s 10d; rest of England and Wales, 30s 3d; Scotland, 33s 9d; Ireland, 27s 9d.

Earnings and Hours Inquiry: (III) Building and Woodworking Trades, Cd. 5086 (1910), pp. ix-xiv.

7

Skilled Workmen's Wages in London: October 1912

Building Trades	*per hr*	*Engineering Trades*	*per week*
Bricklayers	8d – 10d	Fitters	35s – 37s
Masons	8d – 9½d	Turners	do
Carpenters and Joiners	do	Iron moulders (sand)	38s – 40s
Plumbers	do	Labourers	19s – 22s 6d
Labourers	5d – 6½d	*Printing Trades*	
		Compositors	30s – 35s

Cd. 6955, p. lvi.

8

Badly-paid Labour of the Factory Women

The number employed in the Textile Trades are about 1,171,000, of whom 482,000 are males and 689,000 females. The average weekly earnings of Women in the Textile Industries in the last pay-week of September 1906 were:

Cotton	18s 8d	Silk	11s 2d
Woollen and Worsted	13s 10d	Hosiery	14s 3d
Linen	10s 9d	Lace	13s 5d
Jute	13s 9d	Carpet	13s 8d
Hemp	10s 11d		

The most noticeable fact brought out by this Table is that, with the exception of operatives engaged in the cotton industry, the majority of women employed in these industries earn considerably less than 15s a week, while, again with the exception of those in the cotton industry, comparatively few earn more than 20s.

In textile factories . . . the maximum number of hours which may legally be worked in a week, exclusive of mealtimes, by women and young persons under 18 years of age, is 55 on any manufacturing process, and 55½ on any purpose whatever. Throughout the cotton, woollen and worsted and carpet industries the regular working hours are identical with the maximum limit for textile factories above mentioned.

Earnings and Hours Inquiry: Textile Trades; Cd. 4545 (1909), p. xvii.

9

Living Conditions of Agricultural Labourers

The average earnings per week (including the value of all allowances in kind) of adult agricultural workers in 1902 were: England, 17s 5d; Wales, 17s 7d; Scotland, 19s 5d; Ireland, 10s 9d. The earnings were highest near the large industrial or mining districts.

The highest average weekly earnings in England were in the county of Durham (22s 3d), and the lowest in Oxfordshire (14s 6d). The average rate of weekly cash wages in this [latter] county, according to returns from farmers, was 12s, and the lowest rate usually paid in any Rural District was 11s.

Cottage rents Though it may be stated generally that in the greater number of counties [in England] the ordinary agricultural labourers do not get free cottages, it would no doubt be true to say that in every county there are numerous instances in which they are held on low or almost nominal rents. In the purely rural districts the usual rents paid in 1904 were from 1s to 2s 6d a week, 1s 6d being the most common. The landlords invariably do all the repairs, and usually pay the rates and taxes. Rents of cottages near industrial or residential centres, where other classes of workmen compete with the farm labourers for them, are frequently higher, and range from 2s to 3s 6d or 4s a week and sometimes higher.

Income and expenditure Reviewing the available information as to income and expenditure of farm labourers, their estimated average weekly earnings, including all classes (ordinary labourers and also men in charge of animals), are 18s 3d exclusive of earnings of wives and children, and of any profits derived from the sale of home-grown produce. The estimated weekly value of food consumed by farm labourers' families, comprising two adults and four children, is 13s 6½d, this value being based on ordinary retail shop prices. The rent most usually paid in purely rural districts is 1s 6d a week. Estimating the cost of firing and light at about 1s 9d a week, clothes (say) 3s a week, and club 6d, there is a deficit of 2s 0½d, if the cost of food, rent, firing, light, clothes, and club is compared with the earnings of the head of the house (without allowing for any expenditure on beer, tobacco, and household requisites). The labourer's garden produce, however, may be valued at 6d to 2s a week, 1s a week might be received from poultry keeping, and 3d to 4d a week from keeping a pig. In addition, the men's earnings would be supplemented by the earnings of wives and children.

It might be of interest to give some examples of the class of food eaten in various localities by farm labourers.

Oxfordshire

Breakfast – Tea, coffee, bread, sometimes bacon. *Dinner* – Boiled bacon, vegetables, tea, sometimes a glass of beer (Sundays – butcher's meat, currant or jam pudding). *Tea* – Bread and butter, tea. Sometimes cocoa or coffee. *Supper* – Bread, cheese, perhaps a glass of beer (on Sundays, some fresh meat). Most of the men keep pigs. All have gardens or allotments, and many have both. Nearly all the men belong to Benefit Societies, and some to coal and clothing clubs.

Durham

Breakfast – Bread, bacon, tea. *Dinner* – Beef or bacon, potatoes, pudding or tart (Sundays, generally beef). *Tea* – Tea and bread and butter or treacle. *Supper* – same as tea.

Employment of women The practice of employing women and children on the land largely declined in the seventies, and in the early eighties it had almost entirely ceased in many districts. But on small farms, particularly in the Northern districts, the wives and daughters of the owners or tenants frequently assist in the fields, especially at busy times. There are, however, districts, besides those in the North, where women are employed for wages at certain outdoor work, such as hoeing and weeding and picking stones, potato lifting, and during hay and corn harvest. In the fruit- and flower-growing districts, and also in the hop districts, they are often employed at certain seasons. Unmarried women are frequently engaged for farmhouse and dairy work.

WALES

In many parts of the country the farms are small ones, with a small proportion of arable land, and are entirely farmed by the occupier and his family. On numerous other farms of a rather larger size only one or two hired men are kept, who assist in the general work of the farm, the farmers and their sons working on the farm as hard as, or perhaps harder than, the labourers. In such cases the farm labourers are treated much as if they were members of the farmer's family.

Women employed in agriculture are mainly unmarried women engaged by the year or half-year, and lodged and boarded in the farmhouse. Generally, their employment consists of work in or about the farmhouse premises and sheds, such as dairy work, milking, feeding cows and calves, pigs and poultry, and domestic work.

Cottage rents are generally from about £2 12s to £5 per annum. Wages are governed to a considerable extent by the proximity of mines and quarries. In seven out of the twelve counties the estimated weekly earnings are between 16s and 18s; in Caernarvonshire, Brecknockshire, and Flintshire between 18s and 19s; and in Glamorganshire over 21s.

Food eaten by farm labourers in Cardiganshire
Breakfast – Tea, bread and cheese or butter. Boiled milk with oatmeal in it. *Dinner* – Broth and salted beef or bacon. *Tea* – Bread and butter, tea. *Supper* – Scalded milk with bread and cheese.

In almost every case, the labourers have gardens and in many cases allotments. They frequently have a cow and a pig or two. The pigs are fed with the skim milk and 'wash'; fattened with meal and killed and salted, the bacon being kept for the family consumption. Very little fresh meat is consumed by the family of a Welsh farm labourer.
Drink The regular farm labourers in Wales, whether married men or unmarried men boarded and lodged in the farmhouses, are said, generally speaking, to spend little on drink. Many men do not take any alcohol during the year, except on special occasions, and it is a frequent practice for none to be given by the farmer at harvest. In some of the agricultural districts near the mines there is said to be more drinking.

SCOTLAND

In Scotland nearly all farm servants are engaged by the year or the half-year, and given continuous employment and a regular wage, payable if they are prevented from working owing to weather or absent on account of illness. The highest average weekly earnings in 1902 were in Renfrew and Lanark (22s 3d), and the lowest in a group comprising Shetland, Orkney and Caithness (13s 7d).

The married farm servants, who are generally shepherds, men in charge of cattle, and first horsemen [ploughmen], usually live rent free in cottages which are let with the farm to the farm tenant. The smaller farmers more usually employ unmarried men, lodging and boarding them in the farmhouse . . . or in a bothy adjacent to the farm buildings.
Employment of women In all parts of Scotland women are frequently employed at farm work, taking part in the ordinary work of the farm. The women workers are generally the daughters, sometimes the wives,

of the men living in the cottages and working on the same farm. Near towns and collieries they are, however, sometimes the daughters of artisans and colliers. A number of young women are also hired for farmhouse and dairy work. In the Border counties and the Lothians . . . the number of women workers is nearly equal on many farms to the number of men, and, on some farms where potatoes are largely grown, there are sometimes more women than men. It will readily be understood that it is a great advantage to the Scottish employer to be able to secure the service of a considerable body of strong and active young women for field work at about half the wages of the men.

The following return is from a foreman ploughman in Fifeshire: *Breakfast* – Oatmeal porridge and new milk. *Dinner* – Scotch broth in winter, potatoes . . . pork and beef in cold season. Rice, sago, cornflour, tapioca, with rhubarb and wheaten bread in summer. *Tea* – Wheaten bread, with butter, cheese, jam, treacle or syrup; occasionally porridge with skimmed milk and a cup of tea. *Supper* is not recognized as a meal.

Agricultural Labourers' Wages, Earnings, and Conditions in the United Kingdom (A. Wilson Fox), Cd. 2376 (1905), pp. 2–4, 12, 24–5, 69–71, 85–7, 230–1, 238, 245.

10

Social Circumstances on the South Wales Coalfield

There is no part of the United Kingdom, with a population at all comparable in numbers with that of the South Wales Coalfield, where the surface is so broken up by deep and narrow valleys . . .

With the dwellings and other buildings ranged in streets that run along the length of the valleys in monotonous terraces, instead of approximately radiating from a common centre as would be possible on fairly level sites, the civic and corporate life of the community has suffered owing to the absence of 'town centres' and of any conveniently centralized institutions. For instance, dignified municipal buildings are extremely rare; not a single municipally maintained public library is to be found in the central Glamorgan block of the coalfield. . . . The Rhondda has an abundance of cinemas and music halls, but not a single theatre.

In several of the valleys, most of the houses have been built on the less sunny side, often, indeed, in positions where it is impossible for any sunshine to penetrate the houses. Of recent years the houses in the valleys and on the lower slopes are still further overshadowed by the huge coal-tips which are being piled on the breasts and upper slopes and which, besides making the landscape hideous, will in time endanger the very lives of those dwelling in the valleys below. Subsidence owing to mining operations prejudicially affects the habitable conditions of the houses owing to the injury to the gas, water and sewerage systems.

Land of a suitable kind, available for gardens and allotments, is extremely limited. Similarly there is a great scarcity of recreation grounds for adults and of open-air playgrounds (other than asphalted ones) for children . . .

Commission of Enquiry into Industrial Unrest; No. 7 Division, Wales & Monmouthshire, Cd. 8668 (1917), pp. 12–13.

II

The Miner's Beer Ration

Our attention has been called to the practice of giving intoxicating drink to workers in the mining industry. . . . It is the custom in the thick coal mines of South Staffordshire for the mine owners or contractors ('butty' men) to give a daily allowance of beer to their men. . . . We have had evidence as to this practice from Mr H. Johnstone, H.M. Inspector of Mines for the Staffordshire District. It seems that the practice is of very old standing. He said that it had prevailed for at least 150 years and that the reason for its introduction was probably to be found in the special physical conditions under which the work in the South Staffordshire mines was carried on. Owing to the mode of working the mines, the workings tended to become very hot, and the heat and dust induced perspiration and a violent thirst. The pit water is warm and unpalatable, and the men were accordingly allowed a certain quantity of beer which was sent down the pit at stated intervals. The men who worked in the thick seams were allowed two quarts a day and those who worked in the thin seams one quart, this allowance being halved in the case of boys.

The practice is still maintained in the great majority of collieries in the Black Country, but nowadays owing to the shortening of the shifts from twelve hours to about nine, only one drink per day is given instead of two. The workmen are in favour of a continuance of the practice. The Inspector estimated that about 5,000 men are at present receiving beer allowance out of 6,800 men employed. Mr Johnstone was in favour of the practice being stopped; the special conditions which gave rise to it have largely disappeared – the ventilation of the mines has much improved and the heat is not so great. ... We think it should be stopped . . .

Report of the Truck Committee, Cd. 4442 (1908), p. 64.

12

How a London Typist Spent Her Wages

An Invoice Typist living at home with parent in London. Period covered by the accounts – 52 weeks ending April 28, 1910.

Income	£	*s*	*d*	*Expenditure*	£	*s*	*d*
Wages (25s per week)	65	0	0	Board and Lodging	26	0	0
Overtime		3	0	Extra Food	17	2	9
Xmas Box from Firm	1	10	0	Fares	8	6	9
Present		5	0	Dress	5	9	2
				Medicine		3	2½
	£66	18	0	Holidays and Picnics	2	15	4½
				Amusements	2	18	4½
				Educational	1	11	1
				Books and Papers		15	2½
				Stamps and Stationery		14	10½
				Presents and Collections	1	16	6
				Insurance		—	
				Miscellaneous		17	8½
					£68	11	0

Board and lodging A fixed sum of 10s a week was paid for board, lodging, and washing at home, except during absence for a fortnight's holiday when no payment was made.

Extra food The midday meal and tea had to be obtained away from home, and the cost of this, including a small outlay on sweets, averaged 6s 7d.

Fares A train and bus journey to the city and back, costing 2s 4¾d a week for the railway season ticket and 9¾d a week for the omnibus.

Dress The material for a winter blouse was bought and made up, and a

Illustrated London News (1909)

1. BIRTHDAY OF THE WELFARE STATE. 'Veterans of Labour's Army' making application at the post office on the first day of Old Age Pensions.

Drawn by Otto Gerlach; Illustrated London News (1907)

2. A NOVEMBER DAY IN LONDON. A traffic jam near the Gaiety Theatre, the busiest point in the Strand.

dress was dyed. No new dresses or skirts were bought. A new coat was bought and two hats. All the underclothing was bought ready made. One pair of walking boots, one pair of shoes and a pair of sandshoes were bought, and boots were repaired three times during the year at a cost of 2s 3d altogether. Shampoo powders, hairdressing, toilet soap, dentifrice, etc., cost 7s 3½d. The following prices were paid:

	s	*d*		*s*	*d*
Winter blouse (material and			Stockings	2	1½
making)	7	5	Undervests	1	1½
Braid for skirt		6	1 pair walking-boots	8	11
Dress shields		6	1 pair shoes	5	0
Dress dyed	4	0	Sandshoes	2	0
Coat	21	0	1 pair kid gloves	2	0
Felt hat	5	6	1 pair woollen gloves	1	0
Hat	3	6	Gloves		8¾
2 flannel petticoats	7	10	Neckbow		3
Underbodices	1	5½	Tie		8
Corsets	2	0	Stock collars	1	2½
2 pairs knickers	8	9	Frilling		8½
2 chemises	8	9	Collar supports		11½

Recreation and amusements Full wages were paid during the fortnight's holiday. The expenses on this holiday included 18s for return fare and cab, £2 10s for board and lodging for 2 weeks, 20s 2d for pleasure trips, etc., and 2s for tips.

The expenditure on amusements included the cost of tickets for a companion at the threatre, as well as on programmes, picture-gallery catalogues, and fares to and from the place of amusement. Thus theatres account for 29s 10d for 8 visits; concerts for 4s 4d, but in five cases out of eight no expense was incurred except for the programmes. Rinking [roller-skating], including fares and admission, accounted for 10s 4½d. Records for a 'talking machine' cost 9s 8d.

Education The expenditure under this head was almost entirely for music lessons. A subscription of 2s 6d was paid for the winter season of a literary society.

Books and magazines The following books were purchased: *Elizabeth and her German Garden* (7d), *A Tale of Two Cities* (1s), Grote's *History of Greece* (8 vols bought on different occasions at 1s each), and *Eothen* (1s). The *Windsor Magazine* was taken in regularly. 'Fines on Library book' show that the local Free Library was utilized.

Presents and collections Eleven birthday and other gifts cost 22s 3d; one shilling was subscribed to the fund for relieving the employees of a firm whose premises had been burnt down, and another to the Paris floods relief fund. Christmas cards, cost of entertaining visitors for a week-end, a subscription for a funeral wreath and undescribed collections account for the remaining expenditure under this head.

Miscellaneous Flowers were bought 8 times, costing altogether 3s 4d; the mainspring of a watch was repaired for 4s 6d; a photograph of the late King (6d), a picture frame (1s 4d), a fountain pen (3s 3d), picture cards (1s 6½d), smelling salts (6d), and 'office sweepstakes for the Derby' (6d) are the remaining items of interest.

Insurance and saving Nothing was paid in the way of insurance. The expenditure for the year exceeded income by £1 13s. At the beginning of the year there was a balance in hand of 14s 3½d; 4s more was drawn out of the Savings Bank than was put in to it during the year; and at the end of the year a debt of 20s incurred a week before had not been repaid.

Accounts of Expenditure of Wage-earning Women and Girls (Board of Trade, Labour Department), Cd, 5963 (1911), pp. 25–8.

13

Juvenile Street Traders

The Employment of Children Act 1903 gives local authorities power to make bylaws 'with respect to street trading' by persons under 16. . . . Of [the occupations carried on] much the most important is the hawking of newspapers. Over 16,000 persons under 16 are licensed to sell newspapers in England and Wales. In London the number having badges is 6,780, and everywhere this occupation was found to predominate, many of the girls also being engaged in it. Though some boys are employed by retail newsagents, a far greater number trade on their own account, often employing younger lads than themselves.

The Committee collected some detailed and interesting information concerning the system existing in London. The boys deal directly with the newspaper proprietors, buying from the offices or from travelling vans. A quire of 26 copies of a halfpenny evening paper is purchased for 8½d on the 'sale or return' system, and is sold for 1s 1d, with the possibility of a penny or two extra received from purchasers who do not demand their change.

The sale of flowers or matches engages a smaller number. The latter, the sale of which was represented to us as being largely a cloak for begging, are dealt with by both boys and girls. Shoeblacking appears to be a declining industry. The number of boys engaged in the delivery of goods, chiefly milk and newspapers, is considerable. Another small class is that of children assisting costers, or at work in recognized markets.

We have come to the conclusion that the effect of street trading upon the character of those who engage in it is only too frequently disastrous. The youthful street trader is exposed to many of the worst of moral risks; he associates with, and acquires the habits of the frequenters of the kerbstone and the gutter. If a match-seller, he is likely to become a beggar – if a newspaper-seller, a gambler. . . . The occupation is one which sharpens the wits without developing the intelligence. It leads to nothing permanent, and in no way helps him to a future career. There can be no doubt that large numbers of those who were once street traders drift into vagrancy and crime.

So far as girls are concerned . . . again and again, persons specially qualified to speak, assured us that, when a girl took up street trading, she almost invariably was taking the first step towards a life of immorality . . .

On the physical side, the evidence emphasizes the obvious danger to health arising when young children, and especially young girls, often very inadequately clothed, are exposed for long periods to inclement weather. . . . On the other hand, some witnesses expressed the view that the open-air life of street traders was not unhealthy . . .

The evidence dealing with the money earned was often striking. In Liverpool we were told that such sums as 3s 6d could be earned nightly; and in Edinburgh the figure given was 8s to 10s per week, running up to 20s for older, smarter boys. However, in Birmingham a weekly sum of 5s to 6s seemed to be usual, and the returns furnished by the Committee on Wage-earning Children indicate that many newspaper-sellers do not make more than 1s or 1s 6d a week. . . . This money, so readily made, is spent with equal dispatch. The children spend it on sweets and cigarettes, and in attending music-halls, and in very many cases, only a portion, if any, of the daily earnings is taken home . . .

Report of the Departmental Committee on the Employment of Children Act 1903, Cd. 5229 (1910), pp. 5–12.

14

Physical Condition of School-children

Impossible though it is to make any numerical statement as to the percentage of children . . . who might be classified as well-nourished or as below normal or of poor nutrition . . . it is clear from the reports that there is a considerable number (rising in poorer districts to a serious proportion) who exhibit evidences of malnutrition. Such children, though found in greater numbers in the large industrial centres, are by no means confined to them.

Cleanliness of the body There is reason to believe that the condition of the children in regard to cleanliness is far from satisfactory, more especially in the large manufacturing districts. There seemed a tendency to adopt too low a standard and to consider it inevitable that children should attend school in a more or less dirty condition.

The influence of the teacher in promoting and encouraging cleanliness is great, and perhaps indeed supreme. In some districts, however, if the children are to attend school in a clean condition, it would appear to be necessary to supplement the efforts of the home. Experience has shown that, in the poorer districts of the larger cities and towns especially, the conditions of the home and the home life, due largely to a somewhat low idea of hygienic living, do not permit of a high or even a reasonable standard of cleanliness. Recognizing this fact, many towns have made some degree of public provision for bathing in connection with the public swimming-baths.

In this connection the following paragraph from the Report of the Medical Officer of the London County Council is of interest: 'The St Pancras children make great use of the baths, and the teachers speak very highly of the improvement of the children in school, both as regards their health and their attention to their work. It is certainly remarkable to see what a difference can be made in the aspect of a child by such a weekly cleansing bath and clothes free from vermin – the skin and colour improved, brighter eyes and a more intelligent look, and a disappearance of the horrid fidgeting, the result of irritation. There is no question of the popularity of such a bath with the children; often it is their first acquaintance with the joys of immersion in hot water, and the feeling of well-being that the use of it with soap brings about.'

It may be said in a general way that of the children examined approximately one-half of the girls in urban areas, and one-quarter of those in rural areas, have verminous heads. Ringworm has been found to be more widespread than was supposed. It is commonly found that from twenty to forty per cent of all school-children examined, have four or more decayed teeth. Enlargement of the tonsils associated with adenoid growths at the back of the nose is a very prevalent condition. In regard to the children examined who were about to leave school, approximately ten per cent were in need of treatment for visual defect. Ear disease occurring during childhood is a comparatively frequent complaint, and one which is especially likely to follow some of the infectious diseases, particularly scarlet fever. Defective hearing of a degree noticed by the teachers exists in approximately five per cent of school-children.

Board of Education's Chief Medical Officer: Report for 1908, Cd. 4986 (1910), pp. 44–63.

15

Provision of School Meals

The Education (Provision of Meals) Act, 1906, has now been in operation for more than two years, and the time has arrived when the information which has been collected with regard to the operations of Local Education Authorities under the Act can usefully be summarized.

The limits of variation of the sum determined by the authorities as the charge to be recovered from parents are but small; in 12 cases it was as low as 1d, and in one case only ½d; 22 Authorities fixed it at 1½d, 21 at 2d, and only seven at a higher sum, which in no case exceeded 3d. Within the limits mentioned, it has, however, been found possible to achieve considerable variety in the bill of fare. The *Bradford* Local Education Authority, who fixed the charge at 2d, prepared a list of 17 dinners, each of two courses. A week's dietary is given as a specimen:

Monday Lentil and tomato soup. Currant roly-poly pudding.
Tuesday Meat pudding (stewed beef and boiled suet pudding). Ground-rice pudding.
Wednesday Yorkshire pudding, gravy, peas. Rice and sultanas.
Thursday Scotch barley broth. Currant pastry or fruit tart.
Friday Stewed fish, parsley sauce, peas, mashed potatoes. Cornflour blancmange. All these meals included bread.

A midday dinner appears on the whole to have been regarded as the most useful meal. In the areas of 43 Authorities dinners only were provided; in 28, breakfasts only; in 36 both dinners and breakfasts were provided. At *Aston Manor* the breakfast dietary is as follows:

(1) Hot bread and milk. (2) Oatmeal porridge with milk and syrup or sugar. (3) Bread with butter or beef dripping or lard. (4) Bread and jam. (5) Currant bread. (Nos 3, 4, and 5 with cocoa.)

The advantages of treating the provision of meals as a part of the educational system and of connecting it with the training in conduct which every public elementary school tries to give are obvious. To many of the poorest children a well-ordered meal, with its accompaniments of clean tablecloths, clean crockery, and seemliness of behaviour, is almost unknown; and it is hoped, with some confidence, that the object lesson supplied by the meals, which have been provided either by private benevolence or by money derived from the rates, will have more than a transitory effect upon the behaviour of the children who have received them.

Report on the Working of the Education (Provision of Meals) Act, 1906, up to March 31, 1909 (Board of Education), Cd. 5131 (1909), pp. 7–21.

16

Beer for Baby

From my personal observation in Birmingham, I can state that the practice amongst women of taking infants and young children into public-houses at all hours from early morning until late at night is general and very extensive. I have seen women giving infants a portion of their beer to drink; and I am told that they do this as it makes the children sleepy and quiet. In the lower quarters of Birmingham women resort to the public-houses shortly after 10 o'clock in the morning in large numbers, when they are supposed to be doing their shopping, and on these occasions they take the younger children and infants. The same thing occurs late at night, especially on Saturday nights. *C. H. Rafter*, Chief Constable.

* * *

This practice undoubtedly does exist in working and poor neighbourhoods, particularly on Saturdays. It is evident that the women are attracted by the warmth and glitter of the public-houses, which afford a contrast to the houses in which they live, and in a number of cases they are unable to leave their young children at home as there is nobody to take care of them. *E. R. Henry*, Commissioner of Police for the Metropolis.

* * *

It is a common practice in the low-class districts of this city for women to take infants and young children into public-houses. A few of the larger brewery firms instruct the licensee to discourage – and in a few cases refuse to serve – women accompanied by children. The objectionable practice principally prevails in the low-class beer-houses, where women with young children mingle in the vaults with the men of the neighbourhood. On many occasions women have been seen to dip their fingers in the intoxicating liquor and by that means give an infant a taste for the liquor. *R. Peacock*, Chief Constable of Manchester.

Women and Children in Public Houses, Cd. 3813 (1907), pp. 4–10.

17

A Shop Assistant's Day

[*Miss Margaret G. Bondfield*, assistant secretary of the National Amalgamated Union of Shop Assistants, giving evidence to the Truck Committee, was invited by the Committee's chairman to give 'a twenty-four hours' history of one of those assistants – an adult woman in full employ who lives in'.]

In the morning she would be expected to get up at half-past seven if she is an adult assistant who has finished her period of squadding. Squadding is that part of the work that is done before the shop is properly open to customers; it consists of going down to the shop and taking off wrappers, dusting fixtures and counters, and putting the place in readiness for the people who come to dress out with goods. In addition they are expected to watch the sweepers, the people who come to clean the floors and windows and so on, and see that they do not pilfer any goods.

At 8 o'clock they go to breakfast. Breakfast consists of bread and butter and tea or coffee; in many houses the assistants get nothing else at all, but in some houses they are given permission to purchase an egg for 2d, or fish for 2d, or a rasher of bacon for 1½d, or some jam for 1d, from the housekeeper. The young people cannot afford to purchase extras for breakfast. The bread is almost invariably stale; the butter is of indifferent quality. The tea is made in an urn and very frequently is quite undrinkable.

The assistants who are not squadding commence their work at half-past eight. The intervals between serving customers are filled up with keeping stock tidy; sometimes they are ticketing new goods ready for putting into stock . . . but they must be doing something all the time; if there is nothing to do they make work for them. It is one of the principles of the business that all young people shall look busy.

At 1 o'clock the first party go to dinner, usually for half an hour, probably eighteen or twenty in a party sitting down at a narrow table. Their food is carved at the sideboard; their plates are thrown in front of them haphazard. The food is usually of very poor quality and very indifferently cooked . . . the noise and confusion and rush all the time to get one's food, makes the dinner-time perhaps the most disagreeable interval of the day.

From half-past one till five again the business of serving customers, looking after stock, dressing windows, and so on. At five they have an interval of twenty minutes for tea. . . . In a long business experience I have never yet had a properly made cup of tea. Then they go up again to business at twenty past five, serving customers . . . till closing time . . . seven o'clock as an average. In many cases the shops are understaffed, and it means they are serving right up to the time the shutters go down, and then they are probably delayed half an hour or three-quarters of an hour clearing up . . .

The assistant is released from duty at 7.30. If she wants supper, she gets bread and cheese, and milk or water to drink. Some houses provide a glass of beer. In many houses they have a sitting-room set apart for the use of the assistants . . . usually a most dreary place, very much like the waiting-room of a railway station. . . . The great majority of assistants either go out for a walk in the street, or go for a bus ride. Frequently they are too tired for walking, and if they can afford it they take a bus ride. An assistant will probably share the sleeping-room with three or four other girls.

Truck Committee, *Minutes of Evidence*, Cd. 4444 (1908), vol. iii, pp. 113–22.

18

'Physical Degeneracy'

It may be as well to state at once that the impressions gathered from the great majority of witnesses examined do not support the belief that there is any general progressive physical deterioration. The evidence of Dr Eicholz [one of H.M. Inspectors of Schools] contains a summary of his conclusions on this point: 'With regard to physical degeneracy, the children frequenting the poorer schools of London and the large towns betray a most serious condition of affairs. . . . Nevertheless, even in the poorer districts there exist schools of a type above the lowest, which show a marked upward and improving tendency. . . . In the better districts of the towns there exist public elementary schools frequented by children not merely equal but often superior in physique and attainments to rural children. And these schools seem to be at least as numerous as schools of the lowest type.

'While there are, unfortunately, very abundant signs of physical defect traceable to neglect, poverty, and ignorance . . . there appears to be very little real evidence on the pre-natal side to account for the widespread physical degeneracy among the poorer population.

'There is, accordingly, every reason to anticipate RAPID amelioration of physique as soon as improvement occurs in external conditions, particularly as regards food, clothing, overcrowding, cleanliness, drunkenness, and the spread of common practical knowledge of home management . . .

'The apparent deterioration in Army recruiting material seems to be associated with the demand for youthful labour in unskilled occupations, which pay well, and absorb adolescent population more and more completely every year. . . . The aimless wastrel population at the bottom of the intellectual scale . . . unfortunately becomes more and more the material available for army recruiting purposes.'

Testimony is almost unanimous as to the improving conditions under which the denizens of large towns are called upon to exist. Rookeries are being dispersed, enclosed yards opened out, cellar dwellings and back-to-back houses are disappearing. One-roomed, and three-roomed tenements, with more than two, four, and six occupants respectively, are diminishing. With an increase of wages a fall in the price of food, coal, and clothing has taken place, more than counterbalancing the rise in rent, which, in itself, is largely due to the higher wages paid in the building trade.

Further, the water supply has been enormously improved, both in purity and quantity; under the Public Health and the Housing Acts wide powers have been placed in the hands of local authorities for cleansing unhealthy areas, closing insanitary houses, preventing overcrowding, abating nuisances and enforcing generally a high standard of sanitation . . . pauperism has diminished, better accommodation is provided for the sick poor, the conditions of labour touching young persons and women, in factories and workshops, have been greatly ameliorated, and all the children of the State in workhouse schools, reformatories and similar institutions, are started in life under better auspices than formerly.

On the other hand, in large classes of the community there has not been developed a desire for improvement commensurate with the opportunities offered to them. Laziness, want of thrift, ignorance of household management, filth, indifference to parental obligations, drunkenness, largely infect adults of both sexes, and press with terrible severity upon their children.

Report of Interdepartmental Committee on Physical Deterioration, Cd. 2175 (1904), pp. 13–15.

19

'Tea-poisoning'

In a statement furnished to the Committee relating to the physical condition of the working-class children in Ancoats, one of the poorest districts of Manchester, these words are used: 'Another fruitful and one of the most unexpected causes of deterioration lies in the long ingrained habit of tea drinking at breakfast and other times in the factories and foundries of the City.'

Tea drinking, if it really were so, might not be harmful, but unfortunately the mixture drunk can hardly be called tea at all. More frequently than not boiling water is poured on to too large an amount of poor tea-leaves and is left to stand until the tea has become almost a stew, and this dark and nasty mixture is drunk, sometimes three and four times a day, by hundreds of young lads. . . . We were informed by the late Chief Recruiting Officer in Manchester some time ago that a very large proportion of young men rejected for the Army had been refused on account of ailments brought about by this practice.

Dr Hawkes' experience of female workers employed in factories and workshops in Finsbury pointed to the same abuse of tea. In the case of many of these, tea is the only thing consumed before starting to their work from places in remote parts of the suburbs. During some years' work at a large Metropolitan Dispensary, he found that 80 per cent of women and girls who came under his notice never touched solid food till the middle of the day: pickles and vinegar were then often the staple of the 'solid' meal with tea, and tea again in the afternoon; three or four pints of 'tea poison' being thus absorbed in the course of the day. An enormous amount of dyspepsia is thus set up which rapidly assumes acute forms, with the result that alcohol, at first taken to allay pain, is frequently the final refuge.

Cd. 2175 (1904), p. 41.

20

Evil Consequences of 'Urbanization'

There is reason to fear that the 'urbanization' of the population cannot have been unattended by consequences prejudicial to health.

(I) *Overcrowding* stands out, with its attendant evils of uncleanliness, foul air, and bad sanitation. The evil is, of course, greatest in one-roomed tenements, the overcrowding there being among persons usually of the lowest type, steeped in every kind of degradation and cynically indifferent to the vile surroundings engendered by their filthy habits, and to the pollution of the young brought up in such an atmosphere. . . . Surely the time is ripe for dealing drastically with a class that, whether by wilfulness or necessity, is powerless to extricate itself from conditions that constitute a grave menace to the community.

(II) *Pollution of the atmosphere* In dealing with the Manchester district one witness said, 'The foulness of the air contributes much to that general gloominess of the town which led Mr Justice Day to say in explanation of the prevalence of drunkenness in the town, that to get drunk "is the shortest way out of Manchester".'

The chief causes of this pollution are alleged to be the non-enforcement of the law for the prevention of smoke from factories, the imposition of inadequate penalties, the neglect to limit works which produce noxious vapours to special areas . . . and the absence of any provision in the law compelling the occupants of dwellings to produce the least possible quantity of smoke. On the point of prosecutions, it was stated that there are people in Manchester who systematically pollute the air and pay the fine, finding it much cheaper to do so than to put up new plant.

(III) *Conditions of employment* No one will deny that great amelioration has taken place in the circumstances of labour, but . . . it seems to be the case that the advance has been more in the direction of combating the effects of dangerous trades, which, after all, only affect a comparatively small section of the working population.

Describing the life of a boy of fourteen in a textile district, Mr Wilson, H.M. Inspector of Factories, said: 'The hours will be long, 55 per week, and the atmosphere he breathes very confined, perchance also dusty. Employment of this character, especially if carried on in high temperatures, rarely fosters growth or development; the stunted child elongates slightly in time, but remains very thin, loses colour, the muscles remain small, the legs are inclined to be bowed, the arch of the foot flattens and the teeth may decay rapidly.'

He continues: 'The girls exhibit the same shortness of stature, the same miserable development, and they possess the same sallow cheeks and carious teeth. At an age when girls brought up under wholesome conditions usually possess a luxuriant growth of hair, these factory girls have a scanty crop which, when tied back, is simply a wisp or "rat's tail".'

Cd. 2175 (1904), pp. 16–27.

CHAPTER 2
HOMELY INTERIORS

When it is said that a working man's weekly wage was 20s or 25s or 30s or any other figure, what did it mean in real life? How did a woman manage who had to keep a home going for a husband and two, three or four children? The 'documents' contained in this chapter go some way towards providing an answer.

The first comes from *Round About a Pound a Week*, by Mrs Pember Reeves, wife of William Pember Reeves, one-time Cabinet Minister in New Zealand who in 1905 became New Zealand's High Commissioner in London and from 1908 to 1920 was Director of the London School of Economics. On coming to London, Mrs Pember Reeves joined the Fabian Society and her book, published in 1913, was based on investigations carried on over four years by members of the Fabian Women's Group in the densely populated working-class district of Vauxhall, in south London.

'North Country Pit-folk at Home' and 'All in the Day's Work in Lancashire' are drawn from articles that appeared in *The Englishwoman*, an admirable monthly which was 'intended to reach the cultured public and bring before it, in a convincing and moderate form, the case for the Enfranchisement of Women'.

'Middlesbrough Ironworkers' has for its source *At the Works: a Study of a Manufacturing Town* (1907) by Lady (Florence) Bell, wife of the ironmaster Sir Hugh Bell. At the beginning of the last century Middlesbrough was an obscure village, but by the time Lady Bell wrote her small classic it had developed into a roaring, restlessly thriving centre of the iron manufacture, with a population in excess of a hundred thousand.

I

Round About a Pound a Week in London

They are not the poorest people of the district. Far from it! They are some of the more enviable and settled inhabitants of this part of the world [the Vauxhall district of Lambeth]. The poorest people – the river-side casual, the workhouse in-and-out, the bar-room loafer – are anxiously ignored by these respectable persons whose work is permanent, as permanency goes in Lambeth, and whose wages range from 18s to 30s a week.

They generally are somebody's labourer, mate, or handyman. Or they may be fish-fryers, tailors' pressers, railway-carriage washers, employees of dust contractors, carmen for Borough Council contractors, or packers of various descriptions. They are respectable men in full work, at a more or less top wage, young, with families still increasing, and they will be lucky if they are never worse off than they are now. Their wives are quiet, decent, 'keep-themselves-to-themselves' kind of women, and the children are the most punctual and regular scholars, the most clean-headed children of the poorer schools in Kennington and Lambeth.

The streets they live in are monotonously and drearily decent, lying back from the main arteries, and with little traffic other than a stray barrel-organ, a coal-lorry selling by the hundredweight sack, or a taxicab going to or from its driver's dinner at home. At certain hours in the day – before morning school, at midday, and after four o'clock – these narrow streets become full of screaming, running, shouting children. Early in the morning men come from every door and pass out of sight. At different times during the evening the same men straggle home again. At all other hours the street is quiet and desperately dull.

The houses are outwardly decent – two stories of grimy brick. The roadway is narrow, but on the whole well kept, and on the pavement outside many doors there is to be noticed a semi-circle of hearthstone, which has for its radius the length of the housewife's arm as she kneels on the step. Districts of this kind cover dreary acres – the same little two-story house, with or without an inconceivably drearier basement, with the same kind of baker's shop at the corner faced by the same kind of greengrocer's opposite. The ugly, constantly recurring school buildings are a relief to the spirit oppressed by the awful monotony.

The homes are kept in widely different states of order. There is the rigidly clean and tidy, the fairly clean and tidy, the moderately clean but very untidy. The difference depends on many factors: the number of children, the amount of money to spend, the number of rooms, the personality of the husband and the personality of the wife.

A man who loves order has a great influence for order, and a man who likes to go to bed in his boots and spit on the floor has an almost overwhelming influence in the other direction. He may be an equally good fellow in all other respects, but his wife, if she has a tidy nature, may quarrel bitterly with him; whereas if she is more easy-going she may remain his good friend. It is a fact that a woman the law of whose being is cleanliness and order at all costs may, to a slovenly man, make a most tiresome wife. The mother who is not disturbed by a little mud on the floor has vitality left to deal with more important matters.

How does a working man's wife bring up a family on 20s a week? The chief item in every poor budget is rent, and on the whole and roughly speaking it is safe to say that a family with three or more children is likely to be spending between 7s and 8s a week on rent.

The ordinary housing for 8s a week consists generally of three rooms out of a four-roomed house where the responsible tenant pays 10s or 11s for the whole and sublets one small room for 2s to 3s, or of three or four rooms out of a five- or six-roomed house where the whole rent might be 14s or 15s, and a couple of rooms may be sublet at 6s to 7s.

On the whole, the healthiest accommodation is usually to be found in well-managed blocks of workmen's dwellings. This may be as dear as three rooms for 9s, or it may be as cheap as three very small rooms for 5s 6d. The great advantages are freedom from damp, freedom from bugs, light and air on the upper floors, water laid on, sometimes a yard where the children can play, safe from the traffic in the street. But there are disadvantages. The want of privacy, the tendency to take infection from other families, the noise on the stairs, the inability to keep a perambulator, are some of them. Then there is no such thing as keeping the landlord waiting. The rent must be paid or the tenant must quit.

The question of vermin is a very pressing one in all the small houses. No woman, however clean, can cope with it. Before their confinements some women go to the trouble of having the room they are to lie in fumigated. In spite of such precautions, bugs have dropped on to the pillow of the sick woman before the visitor's eyes. The mothers accept the pest as part of their dreadful lives, but they do not grow reconciled to it.

It is difficult to say whether more furniture or less furniture would be the better plan in a house consisting of three rooms. Supposing the family to consist of eight persons, most people would be inclined to prescribe four beds. As a matter of fact, there will probably be two. In a double bed in one room will sleep father, mother, baby, and ex-baby, while in another bed in another room will sleep the four elder children. When a new baby is born, the mother does not get her bed to herself. There is nowhere for the others to go, so they sleep in their accustomed places.

The women, when asked why they do not relieve the pressure in the family bedroom by putting a child or two in the kitchen, explain that they have no more beds and no more bedclothes. Each fresh bed needs blankets and a mattress. They look round the tiny room, and ask, 'Where'd I put it if I 'ad it?'

The rest of the furniture is both as insufficient and crowded as is the sleeping accommodation. There are not enough chairs, though too many for the room. There is not enough table space, though too much for the room. There is no wardrobe accommodation other than the hook behind the door, and possibly a chest of drawers, which may partly act as a larder, and has in the visitor's experience been used as a place in which to put a dead child.

Living in One Room

To take an actual case of a one-room tenement. There are four children, all living. The man is a dusky, friendly soul who usually addresses an elderly visitor as 'mate'. On first making his acquaintance, the visitor was so much struck by the brilliance of his teeth shining from his grimy face that she ventured to express her admiration. 'Yes, mate, an' I tell yer why: 'cause I cleans 'em', he answered delightedly, and after a short pause added, 'once a week.'

The single room inhabited by this family is large – 15 feet by 13 feet – and has two windows. Under the window facing the door is the large bed, in which sleep mother, father, and two children. A perambulator by the bedside accommodates the baby, and in the further corner is a small cot for the remaining child. The second window can be, and is, left partly open at night. At the foot of the bed is a small square table. Three wooden chairs and a chest of drawers complete the furniture, with the exception of a treadle sewing-machine purchased by the mother before her marriage on the time-payment system. The small fireplace has no oven, and open shelves go up each side of it. There are two saucepans, both burnt. There is no larder. On the floor lies a loose piece of linoleum, and over the fireplace is an overmantel with brackets and a cracked looking-glass. On the brackets are shells and ornaments. Tiny home-made window-boxes with plants in them decorate each window. The whole aspect of the room is cheerful. The overmantel was saved for penny by penny before marriage, and is much valued. It gives the room an air, as its mistress proudly says.

Drawn by H. H. Flere; Illustrated London News (1908)

3. THE REAL HEAD OF THE HOUSE – BUT SHE HAS NO VOICE IN THE NATION'S AFFAIRS! Appearing at a time when the 'wild women' of Mrs Pankhurst's following of militant Suffragettes were arousing intense hostility by their rampaging, this drawing is yet a powerful exposition of the opinion that 'there are thousands of cases, such as that which our Artist has illustrated, where the wife is far better fitted to exercise the suffrage than the husband.'

Drawn by Otto Gerlach; Illustrated London News (1908)

4. ON THE BEACH AT BRIGHTON: a German artist's spirited representation of a crowd of 'trippers' making the most of the few hours beside the sea that, for most of them probably, will be the only holiday break in the year's round of toil.

Another family with eight children, all living, rent four rooms – two downstairs and two up. Downstairs is a sitting-room 10 feet by 12 feet. In it are a sofa, a table, four chairs, and the perambulator. A kitchen 10 feet by 10 feet contains a tiny table and six chairs. The cupboard beside the stove has mice in it. A gas-stove stands in the wash-house beside the copper. By it there is room for a cupboard for food, but it is a very hot cupboard in summer. One bedroom with two windows, upstairs, has a large bed away from the window, in which sleep mother and three children. The baby sleeps in a cot beside the bed, and in a small cot under one window sleeps a fifth child. One chair and a table complete the furniture. In another bedroom, 10 feet by 8 feet, sleep two children in a single bed by night, and the father, who is a night-worker, and any child taking its morning rest, by day. The remaining child sleeps on the sofa downstairs, where the window has to be shut at night.

Washing Arrangements

It will be noticed that in none of the bedrooms are any washing arrangements. The daily ablutions, as a rule, are confined to face and hands when each person comes downstairs, with the exception of the little baby, who generally has some sort of a wash over every day. Once a week, however, most of the children get a bath.

In the family of eight children mentioned above, the baby has a daily bath in the washing-up basin. On Friday evenings two boys and a girl under five years of age are bathed, all in the same water, in a washing-tub before the kitchen fire. On Saturday nights two boys under eleven bathe in one water, which is then changed, and two girls of nine and twelve take their turn, the mother also washing her hair. The mother manages to bathe herself once a fortnight in the daytime when the five children are at school, and the father goes to the public baths when he can find time and afford twopence.

In another family, where there are four children in one room and only a very small wash-tub, the children get a bath on Saturday or Sunday. The mother manages to get hers when the two elder children are at school. The father, who can never afford a twopenny bath, gets a 'wash-down' sometimes after the children have gone to sleep at night. 'A bath it ain't, not fer grown-up people,' explained his wife; 'it's just a bit at a time like.' Some families use the copper when it is built in the kitchen or in a well-built scullery. But it is more trouble to empty, and often belongs to the other people's part of the house.

All of these bathing arrangements imply a great deal of hard work for the mother of the family. Where the rooms are upstairs and water is not laid on, which is the case in a great many first-floor tenements, the work is excessive.

Cooking Arrangements

The equipment for cooking is as unsatisfactory as are the arrangements for sleeping or bathing. One kettle, one frying-pan, and two saucepans, both burnt, are often the complete outfit.

Another difficulty which dogs the path of the Lambeth housekeeper is either that there is no oven or only a gas oven which requires a good deal of gas, or that the stove oven needs much fuel to heat it. Once a week, for the Sunday dinner, the plunge is taken. Homes where there is no oven send out to the bakehouse on that occasion. The rest of the week is managed on cold food, or the hard-worked saucepan and frying-pan are brought into play.

The certainty of an economical stove or fireplace is out of the reach of the poor. They are often obliged to use old-fashioned and broken ranges and grates which devour coal. They are driven to cook by gas, which ought to be an excellent way of cooking, but under the penny-in-the-slot system it is a way which tends to underdone food.

Table appointments are never sufficient. The children hardly sit down to any meal but dinner, and even then they sometimes stand around the table for lack of chairs. Some women have a piece of oilcloth on the table; some spread a newspaper. So many plates are put round, and the mother helps each one as quickly and as fairly as she can.

If her husband is not there, she may put aside his portion to be warmed up and eaten later. She does not attempt to eat with the family. She is server and provider, and her work is to see that everyone gets a fair share. She may or may not sit down, but perhaps with the baby in her arms she feeds the youngest but one with potato and gravy or suet pudding, whichever is the dinner of the day, for fear it shall waste its food and spoil its clothes.

When the family have finished what she sets before them, she sees to the washing of hands where the age of the washer is tender, and thankfully packs them all off again to afternoon school, having as likely as not called back the one who banged the door to tell him to go out again and 'do it prop'ly'.

Cleaning

The cleaning of the house is mostly done in the afternoons, when dinner is disposed of. Scrubbing, grate-cleaning, bed-making, are attended to after the return to school and to work of the children and the husband. The baby and ex-baby are persuaded to sleep then, if possible, while the mother, with due regard to economy of soap, cleans out her little world. She has hardly finished before the children are back for tea, and after tea the washing-up.

Two pennyworth of soap may have to wash the clothes, scrub the floors, and wash the people of a family, for a week. It is difficult to realize the soap famine in such a household. Soda, being cheap, is made to do a great deal. It sometimes appears in the children's weekly bath; it often washes their hair.

Shopping

The regular shopping is monotonous. The usual plan for a Lambeth housekeeper is to make her great purchase on Saturday evening when she gets her allowance. She probably buys the soap, wood, oil, tea, sugar, margarine, tinned milk, and perhaps jam, for the week. To these she adds the Sunday dinner, which means a joint or part of a joint, greens, and potatoes. The bread she gets daily, also the rasher, fish, or other relish for her husband's special use. Further purchases of meat are made, if they are made, about Wednesday; while potatoes and pot herbs, as well as fish, often come round on barrows, and are usually bought as required.

When she has put aside the rent, the insurance, the boot-club money, and spent the Saturday night's five or six shillings, she keeps the pennies for the gas-meter and the money for the little extras in some kind of purse or private receptacle which lives within reach of her hand.

In households where there is but one room there may be no storage space at all. Coal may be kept in the one cupboard on the floor beside the fireplace; or there may be such hordes of mice in the walls that no place is safe for food but a basin with a plate over it. In such cases it is necessary for the housekeeper to buy all provisions other than tinned milk, perhaps, day by day. She probably finds this more extravagant – even to the extent of paying more for the article. Tea, butter, and sugar by the ounce may actually cost more, and they seldom go so far.

Clothing

Clothing is, frankly, a mystery. In the budgets of some women 6d a week is set down opposite the item 'clothing club'. This seems meant to provide for underclothing – chiefly flannelette. One shilling is down, perhaps, against 'boot club'. In the poorer budgets items for clothes appear at extraordinarily distant intervals, when, it is supposed, they can no longer be done without. 'Boots mended' in the weekly budget means less food for that week, while any clothes which are bought seem to be not only second-hand, but in many instances fourth- or fifth-hand.

The women seldom get new clothes; boots they are often entirely without. The men go to work and must be supplied, the children must be decent at school, but the mother has no need to appear in the light of day. If very badly equipped, she can shop in the evening in the Walk, and no one will notice under her jacket and rather long skirt what she is wearing on her feet. Most of them have a hat, a jacket, and a 'best' skirt to wear in the street. In the house a blouse and a patched skirt under a sacking apron is the universal wear.

Some of the women miraculously manage to look clean and tidy; some do not. The astonishing difference made by a new pink blouse, becomingly-done hair, and a well-made skirt, on one drab-looking woman who seemed to be about forty was too startling to forget. She suddenly looked thirty (her age was twenty-six), and she had a complexion and quite pretty hair – features never noticed before. These women who look to be in the dull middle of middle age are young; it comes as a shock when the mind grasps it . . .

MRS PEMBER REEVES, *Round About a Pound a Week* (G. Bell & Sons, 1913), chaps. 1–4, 8.

2

North-country Pit-folk at Home

The wit and pathos of the north-country miners, or pit-folk, their cheerful acceptance of danger and fear as a part of their daily existence, their love for whatever kind of sport they can realize, goes far to balance the thriftlessness, coarseness, and that almost heathen nonchalance in face of danger, which is what strikes an outsider first of all. The recklessness which lights a match in a forbidden place leaves us aghast.

It is this recklessness which causes superficial critics to describe a body of workers (in reality as fine as any in the kingdom) as a brutalized, hard-drinking people, willing to live in conditions of hopeless ignorance, always ready to strike for more than their fair share, and constantly lacking in self-control and decency. There may be isolated instances of squalid tragedy in outlying pit-villages, and it is true that even women and children have taken part in the senseless riots set going by annoyance at the regulations of the Eight Hours Bill, but the average 'Geordie', as he is locally called, is no worse than his neighbours. The continual nerve-strain of his work, which seems to emphasize an emotional side to his nature, is especially noticeable among the women and children who have been 'pit-folk' for generations – an emotional side which, at the same time, fosters a ready pity, generosity, and affection.

The present writer can well remember the first introduction to a young pitman, and the surprise felt when he turned out to be a slight, silent man, spectacled and rather nervous, whose chief delight was to play the organ in the neighbouring village churches, and act as sacristan to the ritualistic church of his own parish. Indeed, the pitman is often a great reader; one man studied Richard Jefferies, another has taught himself to read German, and so on.

Geordie is not a great politician, except when labour questions touching his own 'Union' are concerned. He is not very Socialistic, and the famous story of the Pitman Socialist, who allowed of equal division of land, horses, and cows, but drew the line at pigs with 'Stop there, hinny; thou knaws I hev two pigs', is probably true to life. In trade matters he has his own well-grounded views; he hates change as a cat a new house, and has been known to favour the reopening of a dangerous pit, 'though she hev' killed a many', rather than starting a new one.

The quaint local names for pit-villages, such as 'Pity Me' and the 'Betty', seem to touch the great shaft with human feeling. As a sailor personifies his ship, so does the pitman endue his pit with a friendly living spirit, he gets to know from end to end her mazy passages, with all their tales of sudden death and patient heroism, and when that spirit is suddenly transformed to a roaring fire-fiend, or choking demon of the after-damp, it is the wives who curse the work and the pit, not he who knows it so fatally well.

It is the younger men, mostly, who cannot remember the great coal strikes of the past, who are anxious now for trade disputes; the old people remember when they were all turned out of their colliery houses, to lie in barns or shelter with neighbours; they, indeed, wish for peace, and say, 'A pitman's used to his meat; he can't starve, like some of the casuals can.' At the same time, the changes made by the new regulations have been most upsetting in ways our lawgivers can never realize. In households where the laddies follow in their father's steps, and 'go down' as soon as of age, it means that the women are continually cooking and serving meals, and are tied to the house, so that a night out or a walk with their husband is almost impossible.

A pitman's pay, too, is often exaggerated. The hewers cavil (in old English, to cast keevils) for a place, which they and their 'marrow' hold for six weeks or two months, and if the place is a difficult one from which to get out coal, they earn scarcely more than 18s a week, piece work, so that the women complain that 'unless he has better luck with his cavils they will scarcely be able to keep going'. Those who work 'at bank', the pony-men, and others, of course, get a fixed wage, but in any case the work is desperately hard, often done in cramped, wet places after a walk along the pit-bottom of two miles, or perhaps more. Is it a matter for wonder that when Geordie is 'playing' he likes plenty of stir and noise? It is a curious sight on pay fortnight to see him sitting on his haunches, watching the passers-by about Newcastle market and streets, his favourite dog between his knees.

A pitman's wife has a busy time, too: endless black garments to wash and baths to get ready, for Geordie is perforce a great washer, though it is said that he never washes between his shoulder-blades, lest next day an accident 'happen him'. In fact, as a woman once remarked to her visitor, 'Never you be a pitman's wife, hinny: you're always in the dirt.' If there is nothing else to be done, the women often undertake a little quiet coal-selling, a dirty job in itself.

They are full of interest in each other's welfare, and the banner carried the other day by a group of strikers, embroidered with the text, 'Love one another' was not as irrelevant as it seemed. The homes for aged miners, the yearly trips for miners' widows, and other charities, speak to this, apart from individual kindnesses to fellow-workers in distress, gifts of coal and bread, and the like.

You are always welcome to a meal in a pit-house, 'rough but hearty,' as the saying is, and it is surprising how many professional beggars realize the profit to be obtained from a trip down a line of pit-cottages. These cottages are very low, with a big front room, smaller back one, and an attic, perhaps, upstairs. Doors and windows are generally painted a bright 'pitman's green' and the whole is whitewashed outside and surrounded by a little wooden paling enclosing hen-house or pig-sty.

Pianos in the Parlour

The room is generally crowded with furniture. One such, known to the writer, has a piano across each of the two corners furthest from the fire, because Geordie 'felt a miss' when there was only one corner full, a beautiful brass bedstead inlaid with mother-of-pearl, a big desk or 'secret-bed' cupboard, a table and form, much hideous china and many bright-coloured pictures, and framed over the mantelpiece the usual card, 'What is home without a Mother?'

No one could play on these pianos, but, as the wife remarked, 'He was just in his hobby when he was buying them, and when I open the tops they do well for cooling the bread in.' There is generally a sofa in such houses, with one or two of the famous racing-dogs tied up to it, or lying full length on its cushions, and hens and geese run in and out unchecked – just like the bairns. The bed is rarely empty, it is 'one out, and another in' and an unaccustomed visitor gets a 'gliff' or shock, when a voice suddenly proceeds from the roll of clothes that looks so unlike a human being, to mix in the talk.

It is never safe to enter a pit cottage without waiting for an answer to your knock, unless you wish to see a black and stalwart form sitting in the bath in the centre of the room. Not that *he* is ever worried at the situation. He takes it like a gentleman, as a matter of course, and politely invites you to state your business, although if you are low-minded enough to depart hurriedly, you may hear, as you fly, a coarse comment and a query, 'What's the fool feared on?'

Geordie's Pets

The dogs are, as a rule, as important as the bairns in the house, and their health and beauty of as much, if not more care; it is funny to see a little whippet with his tail being put carefully into splits to 'shape it'. Nothing is prettier than to see a couple of these graceful dogs coursing – they go so proudly to the nearest fields in their smartly cut 'clothes', over which no expense is spared, and rush off at lightning pace, after a ball, when let loose to have their speed tried. Then there are Bedlingtons and Yorkshires, so small that they can be carried about in their master's pocket.

Besides these pets, Geordie often has a roomful of cage-birds, which he enters for singing competitions and prizes, or he keeps bantams, or grows leeks, for the popular leek shows, in his garden. The pit-folk are musical, too; each great colliery has its brass band just as it has its ambulance corps.

The love felt for your own village was quaintly uttered by the Geordie who dourly remarked, 'Hinny, aa'd rather walk to ma funeral at Hetton-on-the-Wall, than be carr'd to it at Ovingham' – and that was a good deal to say, for dearly does Geordie love a funeral and all its details. The walls are hung with white cloths tied with black bows, the 'death blind' goes up over the door, a plate of salt is laid on the breast of the corpse, on the curiously folded sheet, and all mirrors and bright steel articles are covered up, 'lest the soul go astray'. A plate of funeral cakes is placed for the visitors – the local grocers advertise that they always supply this dainty – and the relatives gather to receive all who care to come.

Of course, in case of accidents the 'pit is laid idle' but this is always an occasion for meeting old friends. This is one of the few occasions when the average Geordie troubles the Church, and likes to have his dead 'sung over' before the 'lift'. Baptisms are less important; he is often dragged rather unwillingly to church, and according to custom, he takes the packet of bread and sweet cake to be given for luck to the first fair man or dark woman the party meet, according to the baby's sex. We hear very little talk of divorce; if his wife is unsatisfactory, he takes the matter into his own hands, and 'brays her' a bit.

Geordie is very fond of the bairns as a rule. Many a pitman who has never denied himself saves for the bairns, and does wonders with his spending-money to get them on in the world, though they may be 'poor man's bairns'. Thrift in itself he has no mind to. He uses his language strong, although it is doubtful if he means much by his maledictions. It is said you can always tell if a lost dog is a pitman's, by seeing if it wags its tail when you swear at it affectionately.

Little Pit Laddies

Most of all, one feels for the little pit laddies, who, unless some kind folk give them a lift, often have to walk two hours to their work and back. One meets whole gangs of them trudging along between ten and eleven at night, with the iron hook for their lamps under their chin, and their short check breeches and heavy boots, with such tired little black faces, for they have been down below for eight hours, and had a two-hours' walk to work, 'and them but canny bit bairns!'

It is small wonder that a pitman's house has a constant undercurrent of fear; an unusual step down the path when one 'shift' is down and the other in bed brings every woman to the door with the query, 'Anything wrong?' Geordie is full of superstition, too, about lucky and unlucky days, dreams, and eerie tales about the evil eye. To return for a forgotten article when once started for work is absolutely to court disaster, and many are the narrow escapes from death told of from falls of stones or the like, because such warnings are disregarded. This silent strain seems to bring a curious, half-expectant look to the wives' faces, and it also produces a far-reaching sympathy for any sufferers in a mining accident, however far away.

'Pit-folk at Home', *The Englishwoman*, December 1910

3

'All in the day's work' in Lancashire

A glorious summer morning. Five sonorous strokes from the Town Hall clock. The stone-flagged streets of a factory town in North-East Lancashire already show signs of life. From the electric tram depot one car after another comes forth to carry its human burdens to their daily toil. Here and there a man may be seen carrying a long pole, having a kind of mop made of thin wires at one end. Up and down the long street he goes, stopping here and there, in some streets at nearly every house, and applying his mop to the bedroom window-pane. A rattling hail-storm of sound results, calculated to wake the dead.

Mrs Bolt lives in the middle of one of these long streets, and is fast asleep when the 'knocker-up' applies his instrument to her window-pane. Morning already! It's only a minute since she came to bed! But there is no time to lie; for there's a lot to do between now and six o'clock, when she is due at the factory doors.

'Fred,' says she, nudging with her elbow the sleeping man at her side, who has opened his eyes drowsily at the familiar noise on the window-pane, and then had turned over with a grunt. 'Fred, ger up! It's time to be off.' Another grunt from Fred . . .

Meanwhile she is dressing. She goes down the narrow, crooked stairs, leading into the back kitchen, which is about two yards wide and three yards long, in which is the set-pan (a boiler for washing clothes), the mangle, and the sink, which is of stone, like the flagged floor and the little back yard. On the slop-stone is a gas-ring, on which Mrs Bolt places the little enamel kettle. She then washes her face in the back kitchen, but she does not take out her curling-pins. What's the good of bothering with your hair to go to the factory?

She then goes into the front room, about four and a half yards square, which opens directly on to the street. It is Friday, the weekly 'siding-up' day; so she blackleads the bars of the grate, which is of the kitchen-range type, a large oven for bread-baking on one side and a boiler on the other. Next she lays the fire, ready to light at tea-time. By the time she has done this it is nearly half-past five, and after making 'a sup o' tay' she goes upstairs. Fred is summoned again from the land of slumber, and five minutes later follows her downstairs; yawning sleepily, as he, too, swills his face at the slop-stone.

A gill pot of tea, 'sugared and milked' is ready for him by the time he has donned jacket, cap, and the woollen scarf which he wears winter and summer alike. They stand – there's no time to sit – drinking the tea, blowing it till it cools. Then she pins her factory shawl under her chin, and takes up two other shawls which lie ready on a chair. She hands one to her husband, as they both go upstairs and into the back bedroom, over the scullery. In the bed in this room lie their two children. The five-year-old lies with arms stretched out above his head, smiling as he dreams. The two-year-old has kicked off every bit of clothing; he opens his eyes as his mother picks him up and wraps him in the shawl, but is asleep again in a moment. The elder boy does not wake as his father wraps him in the other shawl and follows his mother downstairs. As they pass through the front room the man picks up a square tin containing the food for their breakfast, and two tin cans in which to make their breakfast tea; and Mrs Bolt takes a bundle which contains the children's clothing. Her husband locks the door, and they hurry along the street, which now resounds with the clatter of clogs and is alive with old men and women, young men and maidens, boys and girls. Mr and Mrs Bolt meet many with similar burdens, on their way to the electric cars. On the opposite side of the main road is a street the exact replica of the one in which they live. They enter a door without knocking, and lay their burdens at each end of the sofa. Mrs Earnshaw, who 'minds' their children, is up, and of course expecting them, but there is no time to waste in words.

In this town the finishing stage only of cotton manufacturing is done, so all the factories are 'weaving sheds' and nearly all the operatives, men and women alike, are cotton weavers; there is almost no other industry in the town. Mr and Mrs Bolt work at the same factory, and both are paid at the same rate. Both 'mind' four looms, and therefore are doing exactly the same work. The factory is five minutes' walk along the main road and down a side street, and they arrive just as the last whistle blows. The engine has already started, and as they enter the factory a deafening roar greets their ears.

Mrs Bolt's looms are on one side of the factory and her husband's on the other. She threads her way through closely-packed looms, by a passage-way wide enough for one person only, and soon her shuttles are adding their quota of sound, and the lengths of sheeting in her looms begin their day's growth under her watchful eye. The machine needs continuous feeding, and Mrs Bolt's job is to replace, ever and always, the cops of cotton inside the shuttles. A cop lasts about three minutes, so Mrs Bolt has not much idle time in keeping her four looms supplied.

Breakfast-time, eight o'clock. The whistle blows. Each weaver releases the 'knocker-on' on each loom, the steam goes off, and a heavenly peace descends. Mrs Bolt joins others who are going to the copper boiler, for boiling water for breakfast, for which each operative pays a penny a week. She fills her own and her husband's can, in which she has already placed the milk and sugar, and carries them back to her looms, where she finds her husband awaiting her. They sit on turned-up weft-cans, and eat their breakfast of bread and butter, between the slices of which are fried ham and eggs. Mr Bolt announces that he has had a 'smash' (an entanglement in the threads of the warp) and that it has taken a full hour to 'get it reet'.

. . . How hot it is! The roof is half glass, because a good light is essential to the production of flawless cloth; and it is whitewashed to reduce the heat. But today's sun is fierce, and the temperature mounts higher and higher. The sleeves of Mrs Bolt's cotton blouse are already rolled up. She unfastens the neck, and wishes she could take it off altogether. Beads of perspiration stand out on her forehead, and ever and anon run down the sides of her face, and, between the momentary intervals of her cop-filling, she wipes it with her apron. It is impossible, even to the noise-inured weavers, to hear themselves speak, but they have invented a kind of finger-and-mouth action, and Mrs Bolt uses this language to convey to her neighbours her commentary on the heat.

The half-past twelve whistle blows at last. Mr and Mrs Bolt are at home by a quarter to one, being a little later today owing to Friday being pay-day, and their having to stop to get their wages before leaving the factory. The five-year-old meets them at the end of the street, and goes with them to dinner; but there is no time to bother with the baby, who dines with Mrs Earnshaw. Nor is there time for a tablecloth and an elaborate set-out for dinner. Mrs Bolt wipes the oilcloth, which covers the square deal table in the middle of the room, with the dishcloth; and brings out bread, butter, knives, forks, and spoons, and the milk which the milkman has left in the jug on the window-sill outside; and then goes to the 'eating-shop' at the end of the street, and brings sixpennyworth of hot potato pie, two twopenny custards, and a pennyworth of pickled cabbage. Some tea is made and poured into the gill-pots.

Whilst they are dining Mr Bolt gives his wife his wages, except what he keeps for his own manly needs. If, as this week, his wages happen to be twenty-six shillings, he keeps six shillings and gives his wife a pound; if, as sometimes happens, his wages are only a pound, he keeps four shillings and gives her sixteen shillings. The only unalterable condition is that he must have a minimum of four shillings for his own pocket. Mrs Bolt's wages this week are only a pound, because for four or five days she had in bad warps, and could not get on, owing to continual 'floats' and 'smashes'.

They leave the boy with Mrs Earnshaw on the way back, and Mrs Bolt has a look at her baby. The afternoon waxes hotter, till the temperature of the weaving-shed is up to a hundred. Four hours without intermission Mrs Bolt stands at her post, eyes and hands mechanically performing their never-varying tasks. At last the releasing whistle blows, and Mr and Mrs Bolt draw in the fresh air with relief, as they trudge home. Mrs Bolt calls for her boys on the way home, and by the time she gets there her husband has put the kettle on the gas-ring and is now resting, and having a look at the evening paper. Mrs Bolt puts a match to the fire. It's hot, but the childer'll have to be bathed, and can't be bathed without hot water. Then she makes tea, and fetches the chips and fried fish from the little shop never very far from the Lancashire factory home.

Tea over, she clears the table, and asks her husband to keep an eye on the children, whilst she, with a large carpet-bag and a basket, sallies forth to the co-operative shop in the main street. She joins a shopful of women all bent like herself on buying enough butter, bacon, cheese, flour, eggs, tea, cocoa, soap, potatoes, and numerous other articles, to last a week, and finds she has 'made a hole in half-a-sovereign'. Returning home with her load, she finds 't' Union man' waiting. Eightpence satisfies him – fourpence each for trade-union benefits. .. Now here comes the rent-man, and hard on his heels the Death Insurance man. Mrs Bolt declares that her hand is never out of her pocket!

Her next job is to blacklead and polish the grate in the living-room, before it gets too hot with the fire. It is nearly half-past seven now, and Mr Bolt, who up to now has been sitting on a chair in the open doorway, where it's cool, reading the cricket news, proceeds to wash himself, and to change into his 'second best' preparatory to spending the evening at the Working Men's Club and Institute.

At last the grate and fire-irons are shining enough to satisfy Mrs Bolt's critical taste, and she is glad to leave such a 'hot shop' and to go upstairs to make the beds. Coming down, she debates with herself as to the advisability of bathing the children, or first swilling the flags. The children both being happily at play outside, she decides on the flags. . . . She decides to do 'the front' whilst she is about it . . . finally, the doorstep. That finished, and Mrs Bolt's front is as nice as everybody else's.

It is after eight o'clock. The panful of water has been ready some time, and the two-year-old is soon in and out of the zinc bath which occupies the hearth. He is sleepy, and 'drops off' before his brother's bath is finished. By a quarter to nine they are both in bed and asleep, and Mrs Bolt is free to wash up the day's dirty pots, sweep the floor and scrub the oilcloth surround.

When she has finished the floor she goes to the little eating-shop for some potted-meat for breakfast, as she is too tired to cook anything tonight. When she comes back, her husband has arrived, and they have a bite of the meat and bread for supper, Mrs Bolt eating hers as she cuts up the food and packs their breakfast-tins. She makes some cocoa, and sits down to drink it, falling asleep before she has finished it, and having to be roused by her husband. One more job! The little clothes and shawls to place ready for morning, and then bed . . .

ADA NIELD CHEW, 'All in the Day's Work', *The Englishwoman*, July 1912.

4

Middlesbrough Ironworkers

Middlesbrough . . . a typical town in which to study the lives of those engaged in the making of iron, for it has come into existence for that purpose and for nothing else. It is obviously not a place that people would be likely to settle in unless there were very practical reasons for their doing so. There are no immediate surroundings, either of buildings or of country, to appeal to the aesthetic side of imagination, although five or six miles south of the town the beautiful Yorkshire moors begin. There is nothing to appeal to a sense of art or of beauty. There is no building in the town more than seventy years old; most of them, indeed, are barely half that age.

But yet imagination can be stirred – must be stirred – by the story of the sudden rise of the place, by the Titanic industry with which it deals, by the hardy, strenuous life of the North, the seething vitality of enterprise . . .

The whole town, as a place of residence, is designed for the working hours of the people who live in it, and not for their leisure. There are hundreds of little streets, in which lives a struggling, striving population of workmen and their families, some of them prospering, tolerably secure, some in poverty and want, the great majority on the borderland between the two . . .

Most of the houses consist of four rooms: two rooms on the ground floor, one of them a kitchen and living-room, which in many of them opens straight from the street, and in some cases has a tiny lobby with another door inside it – and another room behind, sometimes used as a bedroom, sometimes shut up as a parlour. A little steep dark staircase goes up from the kitchen to the next floor, where there are two more rooms. Sometimes there is a little scullery besides, sometimes a place hardly big enough to be called a room just big enough to contain a bed, off the kitchen. Such abodes are big enough to house comfortably a couple with two or three children, but not to house the families of ten, twelve, and more, that are sometimes found in them . . .

The wages of the ironworkers, broadly speaking, range from 18s to 80s per week. These wages can be supplemented in other ways, such as working overtime, etc. Some of the houses, about one-third, take in lodgers, who pay from 12s to 16s per week for lodgings, board, and washing, and the woman generally is supposed to make a profit of between 2s and 3s on each person.

These wages seem high, no doubt, and many of the men are well off and prosperous; but not necessarily always those with the higher incomes. Some of the most comfortable homes are those where the man is in receipt of about 30s more or less, and has a wife and children to provide for out of it.

The time when existence seems to press most hardly is during the first twelve or fourteen years after marriage, when there is usually a family of young children, who have to be provided for and who cannot earn; and the wife is constantly, before and after every birth, in a condition in which she cannot fulfil her duties with efficiency.

The income during these first years of married life being almost entirely dependent upon the health and physical condition of the one bread-winner, any illness or accident affecting him at once plunges them into difficulties. The men are constantly breaking down in health, either from conditions inherent in the work – the noxious fumes, the violent alternations of temperatures, to which they are necessarily exposed – or simply because they were not strong enough at the beginning to follow an occupation which, of all others, requires great physical strength. The man is thrown out of work: and then come the dreaded lean weeks in which the wages, which may just have sufficed before, when carefully administered, cease altogether, at a time when he is ill and probably requires some different, better, and therefore more expensive, sort of food.

'Unending struggle'

We may call those of the ironworkers absolutely poor who have actually not money enough to buy what are called the necessities of life – food, drink, fuel, and clothing, and a house over their heads. . . . Out of 900 houses carefully investigated, 125, in round numbers, were found to be absolutely poor, the people living in them never have enough to spend on food to keep themselves sufficiently nourished, enough to spend on clothes to be able to protect their bodies adequately, enough to spend on their houses to acquire a moderate degree of comfort. One hundred and seventy-five more were so near the poverty-line that they are constantly passing over it. That is, the life of a third of these workers is an unending struggle from day to day to keep abreast of the most ordinary, the simplest, the essential needs.

I give here a weekly budget of a household – father, mother, and girl of twelve – the man's income varying from 18s 6d to 23s 9d.

Mrs A. B.'s Budget

One Week	*Income 18s 6d*		*Family, Three*		
	s	*d*		*s*	*d*
Rent	5	6	3 oz tobacco		9
Coals	2	4	½ st. potatoes		3
Insurance		7	Onions		1
Clothing	1	0	Matches		1
Meat	1	6	Lamp oil		2
1 st. flour	1	5	Debt		3
½ st. bread-meal		4½			
1 lb butter	1	1		18	6
½ lb lard		2½			
1 lb bacon		9	*Summary*		
4 lb sugar		8	Rent	5	6
½ lb tea		9	Insurance		7
Yeast		1	Coal	2	4
Milk		3	House		8
1 box Globe polish		1	Food	7	5
1 lb soap		3	Clothing	1	0
1 packet gold dust (washing powder)		1	Tobacco		9
			Debt		3
				18	6

The woman is a skilful, competent manager . . . every penny has been considered, and laid out with wisdom and foresight, if we except, perhaps, one item, the 9d weekly for tobacco for the husband, as compared with the 3d which constitutes the weekly expenditure for milk. But this is the only item which can be called self-indulgent; there is absolutely nothing allowed for any form of diversion.

If we recapitulate the allowance for food for the week for these three persons, as it would appear to the eye, we should see on the table:

One dish of meat, tolerably full, not piled up, the dish about 10 inches long.
Seven and a half quartern loaves, about 15 inches long, 8 in height, and 6 inches wide.
Two wedge-shaped pieces of butter 5 inches long.
One piece of lard of the same size.
A piece of bacon about half the size lengthwise of a large octavo volume.
Ten teacups full of sugar.
Two breakfast-cups full of tea-leaves.
Four tumblers of milk.
A bag of potatoes 16 inches high and half as broad.

The amount of coal, 2s 4d, represents two sacks, each about 3 feet high and 1 foot across, and containing one hundredweight.

Rent

The rent, 5s 6d, always seems a considerable item for such an income. Out of 700 houses, 30 were under 3s 6d a week, 180 from 3s 6d to 4s, 254 between 4s and 5s, 76 between 5s and 6s, 62 between 6s and 7s 6d, 21 over 7s 6d, and three men had bought their houses, and were living in them. The difference in the rent of these houses is a difference in position as well as of the quality of the house. There are some quarters which are more crowded and more insanitary, that are on lower land near the river, and in case of bad weather are flooded. The houses at 7s 6d are nearly all in the newer quarters of the town, built in wide, airier roads, and with more accommodation.

Clothing

It is somewhat difficult to obtain much information about the important item of expenditure on clothing. The careful manager, the skilful needlewoman, turns and re-turns and adapts; the unskilful and extravagant one sometimes pays sums that are almost incredibly out of proportion to the income. Thus it was found that one woman in receipt of 42s a week paid 2s 6d a yard for the flannel out of which her husband's shirts were made (for these shirts it is absolutely no good buying inferior flannel), and then gave them out to be made by somebody else, and had to pay, of course, for the making as well . . .

The question of boots, both for children and grown-up people, is with the badly-off a constant difficulty, and one of the most serious that they have to face; and the miserable foot-gear of the women and children especially – the men are obliged to have more or less good boots to go to work in – is a constant source of discomfort and of injury to health.

One reason why so many of the poor women go about with skirts which drag about in the mud is that they do not want to display what they have on their feet by holding their skirts up. A working-girl said on one occasion that she thought the mark of a 'real lady' was that she wore a short skirt and neat boots, this last representing to the working-girl almost the unattainable.

Boiled-boot shops are still met with. 'Boiled' boots are old boots begged, found in the street, etc., picked up, patched, polished, and sold at a low price. There are various old-clothes shops, market stalls, hawkers' barrows, at which men's suits as well as women's clothes can be bought for a trifling sum . . .

Most of the women buy their clothes ready made, and pay for them and for their boots on the £1 ticket system. These £1 tickets are sold by men who buy them for cash down at certain shops in the town, getting the tickets for 18s or even less; and the women, who buy these from them in their turn pay 21s, payable in instalments of not less than 1s weekly, and usually 2s 6d for the first week. The advantage of this system over that of buying from the 'tallymen', or hawkers, is that, although in each case the woman has to make a weekly payment, in the case of the £1 tickets she goes to the shop in the town and can get the goods that she sees at the prices marked in the windows, whereas by the other system she is at the mercy of the tallyman . . .

Passing Round the Hat

There is a form of expenditure frequently met with which if it may not be wise, is generous and beautiful – the amount expended on charity by the very poor, who, with self-sacrificing kindness, seem constantly ready to help one another. It often happens that if one of their number is struck down by accident or sudden illness, a 'gathering' is made at the works, the hat is passed round, and each one contributes what he can . . .

Funerals

The expenditure on funerals – cabs, mourning, etc. – is usually greater after an accident, as it appeals to the public imagination more. Even when a man has been insured, and there should therefore be a small sum to tide over the first moment of great need, it often happens that nearly all the insurance money goes in the funeral. 'I put him away splendid,' you will hear a widow say, forgetting, or at any rate accepting, the fact that her house is nearly bare of necessaries, and that in a day or two she may not know where to turn for bread. Another said with pride after her husband died that she had 'buried him with ham', meaning that the assembled company who came to the funeral had had sandwiches of the best description.

A funeral, indeed, is one of the principal social opportunities in the class we are describing. 'A slow walk and a cup of tea' it is sometimes called, and the busy preparations in the house for a day or two before, the baking, the cleaning, the turning out, are undoubtedly often tinged with the excitement and anticipation of the entertainer. And after all we must not forget that to many women, at any rate, giving a party, having a great many people in the house at once, is in itself a stimulus and a pleasure, and that for those of the community who are debarred by their conditions as well as their habitations from giving an 'at home' or a dance, the justifiable crowding of the funeral means absolutely the only opportunity for keeping open house, and is accordingly eagerly seized.

Middlesbrough Wives

The position of the women of the working-classes in Middlesbrough is different from that which they occupy in the other big manufacturing towns, for the reason that what is practically the only large industry, the iron trade, offers absolutely no field for women in it. There are not, as in most manufacturing towns, large factories; there is, therefore, no organized women's labour.

Middlesbrough is one of the very few towns in the kingdom in which, from the constant influx of men in search of work, the males outnumber the females. Here the girl of the working classes, therefore, usually marries in her teens, or soon after. If she wishes to earn anything before this, when she is growing up, she either goes into a shop or into domestic service. A certain number go into the elementary schools as teachers, continuing, therefore, their schooldays without a break by passing from scholar to monitor and pupil-teacher.

The young man of the iron-working class usually has no misgivings about embarking upon matrimony early and without sufficient income. During their courtship he [and the girl] go about together in the streets. They 'walk out' together, they fall in love, they have their brief romance. Then these two young people go into housekeeping on perhaps 23s or 24s a week, or even less.

At first, perhaps, they get on pretty well. They buy their experience, as most young people do, but the price they have to pay for it in this walk of life is out of proportion heavy. The man's wages, which before marriage generally left him a margin after paying his lodging or contributing to his parents' expenses, need careful handling to make them go far enough for two. The young wife often does not understand how to do it. She does not know much about cooking, she is not skilful at sewing, she does not know how to organize. At first she may be able to encounter life with tolerable success. Then she has a child . . . and possibly before the first baby is able to walk, while she is still having to carry it about and look after it incessantly, another one is coming, or come – the mother herself, perhaps, being still in her teens.

It is not surprising that the mortality of infants in Middlesbrough is very high. In 1904, out of 2,072 deaths in the twelve months among the whole population 650 were those of children under one year. This high mortality is attributed by experts to overcrowding, bad atmosphere, bad air, maternal ignorance and negligence, unsuitable feeding, an inadequate or polluted milk supply. The cause of death in many of the cases is given as premature birth, and is accounted for partly by the mother being physically worn out and unfit for child-bearing owing to the short intervals between each birth. One woman had 6 children in 8 years, one 7 in 10, one 9 in 11, one 11 in 14, one 12 in 15, one 15 in 23, and one 17 in 25 years. One woman had had 17 children and 12 had died; another 14, of whom 8 had died; one woman had had 10 stillborn children, in addition to four more born alive . . .

I was told the other day a story which, if it had not been well attested, I should have declined to believe. A young married woman was living with her husband and two children on 19s a week, out of which they paid 5s 9d for their home. This means that the four of them had 13s 3d a week to live upon; 13s 3d with which to pay for food, coals, clothes, absolutely everything, and not one penny more. And somehow this woman actually managed to do it. She had so far pawned nothing; her surroundings, her person, her children, were all spotlessly clean . . . A young professional man, zealous for the welfare of the nation, and anxious about the decline of the birth-rate, seeing one day the tidy house and the respectable woman at the head of it, and wishing, no doubt, that it should be people of this admirable kind who should multiply their descendants, asked the woman how many children she had, 'Two,' she replied. 'And how long have you been married?' 'Six years.' 'Only two children in six years!' he said. '*You ought to be ashamed of yourself.*' And he passed on . . .

LADY BELL, *At the Works: A Study of a Manufacturing Town* (Edward Arnold, 1907), Chaps. 3, 8, 9.

CHAPTER 3

WHAT THE 'LADY INSPECTORS' FOUND

The first Factory Inspectors were appointed in 1833, following upon the Factory Act of that year. There were only four to begin with, but as their usefulness was demonstrated their numbers were added to. They were all men, although from the middle of the century there was a growing demand for the appointment of some women, in view of the ever-increasing number of women and girls who were employed (and often exploited) in factories and workshops and miscellaneous trades.

For long the demand was successfully resisted. As one Chief Inspector of Factories wrote, he doubted very much whether the office of Factory Inspector was one suitable for women. Factory inspection required the activity, acumen and stern authority of a man to enforce his interrogatories. It was not an agreeable duty for a man, and he could not conceive that its functions would commend themselves to a woman, or that a woman could successfully discharge them. Imagine a woman inspector having to conduct a case in a metropolitan police court, questioning witnesses and having to submit herself in the witness-box to the cross-examination of an astute attorney . . .

At length, however, a Home Secretary arose whose imagination was strong enough to bear the strain. In 1893 H. H. Asquith (the future Prime Minister), who was then Home Secretary in Gladstone's short-lived fourth and last administration, appointed two women to the factory inspectorate. The pioneer 'lady inspectors' (as they were designated: not until after the Great War were they allowed to become 'women') were Miss May Abraham and Miss Mary Paterson, both of whom had recently been chosen to serve as assistant commissioners on the Royal Commission on Labour. These were joined in the year following by Miss Adelaide Mary Anderson and Miss Lucy Deane, and then came Miss Rose Squire, Miss A. Tracey, and Miss Hilda Martindale.

Miss Abraham (1869–1946) was given the title of Chief Lady Inspector, and she held the post until 1897, when she retired on her marriage to H. J. Tennant, a Liberal M.P. and Asquith's brother-in-law. She was succeeded by Miss Anderson (1868–1936), who remained Principal Lady Inspector until her retirement in 1921, whereupon the men's and women's sections of the Factory inspectorate were combined into a single organization, in which all posts were open to men and women alike.

From 1896 to 1914 the reports of the Principal Lady Inspector formed a separate section of the annual report of the Chief Inspector of Factories. On the whole, what they 'found out' makes much more interesting reading than the accounts of the male inspectors. From the outset, these Victorian born and bred ladies showed the splendid stuff they were made of. The witness-box had its terrors, no doubt, and the 'evidence they had to give' may have made them blush, but they soon learnt how to make the nastiest little bully of an attorney know his place. When on their rounds of inspection, what a nose they had for smelling a rat (in more senses than one)! What a way they had with a slippery employer or works foreman! With what resolution (even though their stomachs might be turning over) they insisted on penetrating into places where no male colleague had ever ventured to set foot! Through evil-smelling workshops and accident-ridden factories went their trailing skirts, and the grubbiest scrap of 'annonamous' writing had its immediate response in the shape of a woman on the war-path.

I

A Working Woman's Life

Sometimes one feels that one dare not contemplate too closely the life of our working women, it is such a grave reproach. I went to a woman's house to investigate what appeared a simple, almost commonplace accident. She was a middle-aged, single woman living alone. Six weeks before my visit she had fainted at her work and in falling (she was a hand gas ironer) she had pulled the iron on her hand, that and the metal tube had severely burnt both arm and hand. She was quite incapacitated.

She told me she left home at 5.15, walked 2½ miles to the factory, stood the whole day at her work, and at 6, sometimes later, started to walk home again, and then had to prepare her meal, mend and do her housework. Her case is not so bad as many, for in addition to their own needs, a married woman or a widow with children has also to see to the needs of the family, meals, washing and mending and the hundred and one other duties that are required to keep a home going.

MISS TRACEY, *Factories & Workshops Report for 1913*, Cd. 7491 (1914), p. 93.

2

A Child Was Born

The investigation of one particular infringement of Section 61 [prohibiting the employment of mothers within less than one month after their confinement] occupied considerable time because, for some reason still unknown, all the persons concerned were obviously prepared with statements intended to baffle the Inspector. One of the witnesses – a contractor at the Works where the woman was employed – was found when visited, however, to be not sufficiently sober to adhere to the statement which he desired to impress on the Inspector, and his unguarded and contradictory admissions provided a clue by which the truth was eventually reached.

A.B., an unmarried woman, about 23 years old, had been employed for two or three years at these works. Her work was very laborious, that of setting and drawing kilns. The manager of the works ordered the contractor – under whose superintendence the woman was at the time working – to send her home, and discontinue her employment as she was obviously not in a fit condition to do the work, which was heavy.

Shortly afterwards her child was born, and during the time of her absence she was kept by her mother and sisters with whom she was living; the sisters were in work elsewhere. Ten days after the child's birth she was re-engaged by the same manager of the works who had ordered her to be sent home, and employed directly for the firm at the same place in loading wheel-barrows at the canal bank and other work. Sixteen days after its birth the child died, apparently from wrong feeding or neglect; she did not nurse it herself being employed too far from home. The poor woman was of a low type and seemed almost without natural feeling about the child.

I may add that a child was born last year, and died under much the same circumstances.

The feature in this, and all other cases which I have investigated, is the total lack of any sense of responsibility in anyone. A number of women of a very poor, very ignorant, very low type are employed, and though this Section was admittedly well known by occupier and manager, no steps of any kind were taken for insuring that it should be properly carried out – in no way was it brought before the ignorant, helpless creature as a matter of any importance to anyone. Not even in the poor woman herself did there appear the slightest regard for the life and welfare of her child. It is possible that had she attempted to care for it, the task – in the face of the callousness of everyone else concerned – would have been almost impossible. It was quite obvious that until the woman Inspector put the matter before them in what was evidently a new light it had not occurred to anyone that it was worth consideration, or that even a legal – let alone a moral – responsibility rested on anyone.

MISS DEANE, *Factories & Workshops Report for 1904*, Cd. 2324 (1905), p. 274.

3

Such Plucky Women!

I spent many days in visiting the cases which had been certified and in visiting the cases of illness which were not directly certified as due to lead. I visited these workers in their own homes and found them in different stages of illness and convalescence. Their pluck will always remain fixed in my mind; although many of them were unable to put into words the sufferings they had gone through, yet not one of them but was eagerly wishing to be well enough to go back to work.

When, as is so common now, women are accused of malingering, I often wish that complainants would accompany me on my investigation of cases of accident or poisoning at the workers' homes, for I know that, like me, these people would return in a humbled state of mind, recognizing courage and endurance under circumstances which would break many of us.

MISS TRACEY, *Factories & Workshops Report for 1913*, Cd. 7491 (1914), p. 89.

4

'So very cold in Manchester'

'Can anything be done for us sewing machinists in the Manchester warehouses to get us a little warmth this winter? It is so very cold we can hardly hold our work sometimes. We have the gas lit sometimes, but not for long unless it is a very dark day, but that does not warm us very much . . . There are many of us who have no parents or homes of our own, so are not very well fed or clothed in the cold weather. . . . We do not want anything unnecessary, only just to be warm enough to work.'

From a letter to Miss Squire, *Factories & Workshops Report for 1908*, Cd. 4664 (1909), p. 133.

5

Scalped in the Factory

There were eight cases of injuries received through unfenced shafting – five to women and girls and three to men – all severe except one. A girl of 14, picking up something under the table, received a severe lacerated wound of scalp and eyelid as the result of her hair being caught in the low shafting, which was only partially fenced. A woman, stepping over some low shafting temporarily uncovered, was caught by her dress and dragged to the ground, her foot going under the shaft. In their desire to help her, the 'too eager helpers' lifted her upwards before cutting her clear after the machinery was stopped and both bones of her leg were fractured. In another case, a woman fainted (having had no breakfast before coming to work) and a fellow worker jumped on a disused bench to open the window; in so doing, her fringe caught on some disused shafting, $7\frac{1}{2}$ feet from the ground, and her scalp was torn completely away. Similar accidents happened to girls of 14 and 16, when they were caught on the revolving part of the machine in leaning over it, and they both suffered considerable nervous shock and loss of hair. A girl of 17, putting the belt on her sewing machine, had her hair and clothing entangled in the shafting which was inefficiently fenced, and she was seriously ill with shock and injuries.

MISS TRACEY, *Factories & Workshops Report for 1909*, Cd. 5191 (1910), p. 139.

6

A Working Girl's Fingers

I find that injury to a finger is regarded as a very slight matter by those unthinking persons who fail to realize how terribly dependent working girls are on these members for their livelihood. The quickness and precision or the delicacy of touch on which so many hundreds depend is destroyed even by a stiff joint, or a maimed or enfeebled muscle; and though indomitable will and much practice may enable a girl to carry on her work under the altered conditions, it is at a lower wage. In addition there are the weary weeks and months of enforced 'out of work', for which the compensation (even if allowed, which is by no means always the case with women and girl workers) is generally totally inadequate. The sum of £20 cannot be held to compensate a working girl for the amputation of her right hand.

I was not surprised, therefore, when a girl explained to me that the loss of her whole foot would have seemed a less serious blow than the loss of her two first fingers, for 'I could ha' come to work in a bus with a crutch, but now I can't do my work at all.'

MISS DEANE, *Factories & Workshops Report for 1902*, Cd. 1610 (1903), p. 166.

7

'This annonamous letter'

Dear Madam, I am sure you will think it presumption on the part of a factory worker to write to you however as pen and paper refuses nothing I venture to write you this annonamous letter.

When you come to inspect a factory, does it ever strike you to look around and see if any of these weary women and girls have a seat to sit down on. I am a winder myself I have worked in a great many factories for the last 30 years one looks on their workshop just like their home why should we be denied a seat I suppose you think our work very light so it is we have no extra heavy lifts we have mettle cups that I suppose they would be 2 lb weight or more we are pushing these up continually the whole thing is tedious just look around you and you will see some winders have not so much as a lean for their backs.

I hope Dear Lady you see to this. You would never think of putting a servant to work in a kitchen without a chair in it, she would not stick it, the winders are an uncomplaining lot if you asked them would they like to be provided with seats they would smile and say they were all right, it would look to them like making complaints behind backs but don't ask us but think about us and do something for us and our children will rise up and call you blessed. I hold that rest is essential to Good Health.

Letter to MISS SLOCOCK, Lady Factor Inspector in Ireland, from a woman mill worker, *Factories & Workshops Report for 1913*, Cd. 7491 (1914), p. 76.

8

Plain Talk about 'Conveniences'

The outstanding defect of all others in this N.W. Division is the sanitary accommodation provided for women. It is impossible to describe in a public paper how low the standard has been, and still is in many places. I have been in repeated communication with Medical Officers of Health and Town Clerks on the subject, and the whole small staff have tried unremittingly to deal with the subject.

Absence of doors and screens, uncleanliness and insanitary conditions can all be remedied by the sanitary authority, and in the large towns at any rate notices of these matters have received prompt attention, but there still remains the question of unsuitability of position. Many examples might be given.

In a waterproof factory four or five girls were employed in an 'overflow' workroom of a large factory, and worked in an upper room; in the lower room about a dozen men and youths were at work. To reach the sanitary convenience it is necessary for the girls to walk across the men's room and through a narrow space between rows of machines at which men are sitting and a wall at the far end of which the sanitary convenience is situated. As it is only an auxiliary workroom, there is no foreman or manager in charge; this undesirable position is felt very keenly by the girls.

In another case in a large rubber works Miss Taylor found that five of the conveniences which were situated in the yard were never used. The rusted keys were shown her by the forewoman and on inquiry she found that all the women and girls refused to use them on account of the public position of the approach in the yard.

There is no doubt that glass panels in doors, commoner still, no doors, no bolts, no provision for privacy is all calculated to prevent 'waste of time', and it is a pathetic comment on employment that there should be this improper supervision and control of decent and respectable women. That they do sometimes stay longer than is actually necessary in these places is, of course, a fact well known to me, but to my thinking it only shows how great is the strain on the women and girls that they should desire rest so obtained.

When one thinks of the perpetual striving, the work which must never slacken, the noise which never ceases and of the legs which are weary with constant standing, of the heads which ache, because the noise is so great no voice can be heard above the din, one can understand that to sit on the floor for a few moments' talk, as I have often seen, is a rest which under even such horrid circumstances is better than nothing. Proper conveniences and the supervision of a nice woman would do away with all the drawbacks which employers foresee in complying with the standard laid down in the Order of the Secretary of State so long ago as 1903.

MISS TRACEY, *Factories & Workshops Report for 1913*, Cd. 7491 (1914), pp. 80–1.

9

Women who 'Follow the Herring'

No industry is so exempt from factory regulation as fish-curing in its many branches. No industry, I venture to think, requires definite regulation more.

In talking to the women who 'follow the herring' round the coast, I found the yearly round was Stornoway in May and June; Shetland, Fraserburgh or Peterhead in July and August; Scarborough and

Grimsby in September; Yarmouth in October; Hull in January for two months or more; then a short time at home until the season opens again at Stornoway.

Defects and discomforts are condoned by local authorities and employers because the season is a short one. It may be a short one in many of these places, but it is not a short one for the worker who, engaged by an agreement for which she has an almost superstitious reverence, takes things as she finds them, being usually able to recall to her memory, for her comfort, some time or place in which they were worse.

In Fraserburgh, last summer, where during the herring season, 3,445 women were employed, of whom 3,000 came from other parts of the kingdom, it is the custom for the employer to house the crews of women who work at fish-curing (gutting, salting and packing), for the foreign market. The majority of the yards have attached to them a shed in which barrels, etc., are stored in the winter. When these, or some of them, are removed in summer, the shed becomes lodgings for the girls, unfurnished save for a small fireplace or stove, and some rough deal boards nailed together to form a bedstead. There are usually two beds, one on top of the other, in the manner of berths on board ship, each to hold a crew of three women. The women bring everything – bedding, cooking utensils, and any furniture they need, although the large wooden trunks with which they travel serve as a rule for chairs, and not infrequently for table also. In this one room they eat, sleep, entertain their friends, and perform their domestic duties in what I can only consider marvellous harmony.

In Yarmouth, where the workers lodge throughout the town, great difficulty is often experienced in getting lodgings near work – a very important point when one considers the conditions of work there in wintry and stormy weather. The curing trade for the foreign market is carried on on a large plot of ground belonging to the town and rented to various curers. The farlins, or troughs, at each of which ten or fourteen women work, are scattered over this with the barrels. It is unpaved, undrained, uncovered. Working at great speed, as these women do, it is not possible to prevent some refuse or herring occasionally falling on the ground to be immediately trampled into it. The whole of the soil there seems to be impregnated with decayed or decaying animal matter which it is under present conditions impossible to get rid of.

In cold, in wind and in rain, in the darkness of the morning hours and the darkness of the night, with no shelter or care for their comfort, except some sanitary accommodation of the most insufficient and primitive kind, these women work on. There is no advantage to the fish (but rather the reverse) in being exposed in this way. 'The women are so hardy,' says the employer. The prevalence of lung and chest diseases in many districts from which the fisher people are drawn is very marked, and, even granting their hardiness, it is at least a pity to force on them the rheumatism from which so large a proportion of our fishing people suffers in any case.

MISS MARY PATERSON, *Factories & Workshops Report for 1900*, Cd. 668 (1901), pp. 388–9.

10

Outraged Modesty of Highland Women

In the Island of Uist a point calling for attention and intervention at the [fish-gutting] yards is the sanitary accommodation. In no cases have we found that the women use the accommodation provided, a fact not surprising to those who know the class of worker.

The difficulty of providing suitable accommodation at Balta is admittedly great, but it could scarcely have been more imperfectly met than by putting up for Highland women, whose shy sensitive feelings have been outraged by them, the little structures which we found here and there in the yards.

Sometimes what is nominally the women's accommodation is part of the same structure as the men's; sometimes it is separate from it, but in all cases it is placed on the edge of the yard, the structure overhanging the beach, and, no pan being provided, the scavenging is simply effected by the action of the sea at high tide. All necessity for any sanitary system is thus avoided by placing the structures in the most exposed position possible in the yards, where coopers and others are always working, and fishermen are constantly coming and going.

All occupiers and managers to whom we have spoken on this matter, as well as the local doctor and the sanitary officer, are agreed that no use is made of the accommodation, and that it is not to be expected that any use will be made of it by the women. It has to be remembered that the only alternative for the women, no provisions being made at their huts, is to go over the hill, as they say; that in this flat country it often involves a long walk to reach any place of privacy, and that this necessarily leads to delay and difficulty which cannot be without serious results to health.

The women, with their natural reticence, seldom say more than that it is very inconvenient, until one has got into friendly conversation with them, when one learns more of their feelings in the matter.

MISS MARY PATERSON, *Factories & Workshops Report for 1905*, Cd. 3036 (1906), pp. 304–5.

II

'Dirty Habits' of Tobacco Workers

[Following up complaints of smoker's heart among cigar-makers, Miss Squire visited a large number of cigar-factories, and found the practice of biting and licking the ends common in all of them.]

In each case the occupier or manager told me that it was not allowed, and in three of the factories my attention was called to notices prohibiting it on pain of dismissal in case of journey-women and fine in that of apprentices. When I pointed out that it was going on without interruption while the occupier or manager and I stood watching, the reply was: 'We can't prevent it; it has become a habit with the older hands, and the young ones do as the others do.'

All the occupiers and managers complained that it was a dirty habit, and I learnt from them and from the employees that it is usual to send up to the rooms before a visitor is taken round and warn the workers not to put the cigars in their mouths while he is there. 'Customers object to it' was said to me everywhere, and in some of the factories it was recognized by the employees as dangerous to health. Scissors and knives are provided for every worker to use instead of biting off the end of the cigar, but it takes longer to use these, and in practice it is seldom done. Pots of paste are found too on every table, one for each worker, but it is rare to see any means except the mouth used for moistening the edges of the leaves. The women say, 'We are taught the right way, but the other way is so much quicker that we prefer it, and it becomes such a habit that we don't know we do it.'

In cigar factories I have found little girls banding cigars, moistening the gummed labels, which are coloured and gilt, by mouth. They sit at this work all day and do about 3,000 daily. I have succeeded here in getting the employers to provide means of 'damping' in some cases; in others I have been unable to overcome the indifference displayed towards anything 'the Factory Acts can't compel us to do', as it is expressed.

Factories & Workshops Report for 1904, Cd. 2324 (1905), p. 267.

12

Women Who Like Working in 'Dust'

I visited during my inquiry dust yards owned by local authorities and by contractors. In the dust yards belonging to three of the contractors and to one local authority I found the process of refuse sorting in its most primitive form.

The women are arranged in a line down one or two sides of the yard, and each is provided with a large coarse sieve, and is surrounded by a number of baskets. As the carts bringing the refuse enter the yard they are emptied in front of each of the women in turn, and a man is employed to spade the refuse into the sieves. After sifting out all the dust the women sort the remainder into different baskets, separating carefully the ashes, wood, china, paper, tins, glass bottles, and 'soft core'.

The dust and breeze are usually taken to the brickfields where the dust is mixed with the clay for the manufacture of bricks, while the breeze is used for burning them. The china and other hard 'core' are used for making roads and filling up waste spaces, while paper and soft core are mostly sold to working gardeners to be used as manure. Tins are flattened and used as ballast for ships. Some of the glass is converted into emery paper, while brown cardboard boxes find a sale among boot manufacturers . . .

The wages vary from 10s to 15s a week, and in some yards women are allowed to carry [away] baskets of wood and cinders. The majority of the workers are old women, although I found a fair number of young women. I was informed that there has never been any difficulty in obtaining women to carry on the work; in fact, one manager informed me that he could easily get twenty additional if he could employ them. I believe this work is attractive to women (1) because they find that spending such a considerable portion of their day out of doors suits their health . . . (2) because they earn fair wages in most cases, and have the chance of finding valuables.

MISS HILDA MARTINDALE, *Factories & Workshops Report for 1902*, Cd. 1610 (1903), pp. 102–3.

13

A Hovel on the Slag Heap

Owing to the fact that during the course of the work carried on in iron mills the furnaces are subjected to continual stirring, a large amount of coal escapes with the ashes, and to separate the good from the useless material is the duty of the workers on the breeze banks.

The waste material from the furnaces is wheeled in barrows by men to the bank, and there it is spread out on the ground to cool. It is then 'carried in', i.e. raked in with large shovels by women and emptied into large coarse sieves, which are moved (by women) backwards and forwards on iron supports fixed into the ground. A wheelbarrow is placed under these supports, and into it the dust falls. The material which remains in the sieve is emptied into a large tub of water, in which it is thoroughly washed. It is the duty of the women to stir up the material in order to free the breeze, and then to catch it in a sieve, and after allowing the water to drain away, throw it on a heap at the side of the tub, whence it is carried or barged from the bank.

The work is always carried on out of doors, but in every case but one I found a roof shelter over the site where the washing and riddling took place; and on nearly every bank I found what is known as a 'hovel' – a small room of brick or galvanized iron fitted with fireplace and rough seats, where shelter is sought during the rain and mealtimes are passed.

It was most interesting to see how much the women appreciated these hovels. To obtain for them a new hovel, or have an existing one repaired, seemed to many of the workers to be the chief duty of H.M. Inspectors, and I was given on one bank the unasked for promise that if I would insist on the cleaning and repairing of a hovel it should be kept like a little 'palace'.

Considering the coarse and heavy nature of the work I did not find that the women belonged to a rough class; they seemed respectable women and good workers. I found workers related – in fact, it might almost be called a family industry.

MISS H. MARTINDALE, *Factories & Workshops Report for 1902*, Cd. 1610 (1903), pp. 182–3.

Illustrated London News (1912)

5. THE MINER'S TOIL: fixing pit props in a new seam in a coal-mine.

Illustrated London News (1909)

6. THE SIEVE IN THE WALL. To pay for his night's board and lodging, a 'casual' has to break a certain quantity of stone into pieces small enough to go through the grating in his 'cell'. In this drawing the artist has 'removed' one wall of the cell to enable both inside and outside to be seen. In the foreground are some unbroken stones.

14

Dirty Work for Welsh Girls

In one of the largest ironworks in Wales where hundreds of men are employed, and where it seems as if there could be no occupation for women and girls, I found one gang of twelve girls from 14 to 16 years of age working for the furnace-men as carriers of 'fish-plates' (the iron plates used for joining railway lines).

It is heavy, dirty work, and both it and the environment seemed most unsuitable for young girls. They seemed to be, however, healthy and well-behaved, and to like the work; they had, it appeared, only two grievances – one, which I took steps with all speed to remedy, the absence of any sanitary convenience; the other, a matter outside any Act of Parliament, a wage of 6s for a week of 48 hours' working, recently reduced to this amount by a few pence at a time from 6s 6d.

Other dirty work for women and girls I came across also unexpectedly in iron works in Wales, and in this case also there was only one small gang in the whole of the immense works. This gang of seven women was employed by a contractor, and under his superintendence they worked daily at unlading coal from railway trucks in a siding. The women stood in the trucks knee deep in small coal, shovelling it through iron gratings into a receptacle below. Clouds of coal dust rose as it was disturbed by the shovels and fell down from the height of the truck on to the gratings and down into the cellar beneath.

The women, although black as any miners, seemed strong and in good health; they were well-spoken and evidently self-respecting young women of 18 or 20 years of age; their hours of employment were from 7 a.m. till 5 p.m., with one and a half hours for meals, and they earned 14s a week.

The agility with which they leaped down from the trucks to speak to me and up again was amusing to see, and their evident pleasure in seeing a woman inspector, and their eagerness to converse, was great – as, indeed, I have always found it among women and girls of the roughest and least 'womanly' occupations.

MISS SQUIRE, *Factories & Workshops Report for 1901*, Cd. 1112 (1902), p. 185.

15

'So Disgusting an Occupation'

I have continued this year the inquiry commenced last year into the conditions of women's labour in gut-scraping, catgut, and similar work. The work is exceedingly disgusting, and, even under the most favourable conditions, it is offensive to the senses. Objection has been raised from time to time in the public press to the employment of women in these trades, on the ground of its having a demoralizing and brutalizing effect upon those engaged in so disgusting an occupation.

The repugnance with which one encounters the sights and odours of these places naturally makes one revolt against the thought of women's daily presence there, but experience among the employees themselves and careful consideration of all the aspects of the question, gives no support to the view that work in these offensive trades is *per se* demoralizing. The numbers of women at present engaged in this occupation are small, and very few young persons are employed. The employees are mostly middle-aged women of a rough type, although I have found as nice self-respecting young women in this occupation as in any other. The employers in most cases speak most highly of the capacity and steady behaviour of the women. The hours are short and the wages good.

Briefly, the work is as follows: the small intestines of pigs and sheep are used for sausage-skin making, and those of the ox for lard-bladders, etc. The muscular and mucous layers are not required for these purposes, and their removal is the work of the gut-scraper or cleaner, who leaves only the peritoneal covering for the purposes indicated above. The intestines of the pig average 72 feet in length; those of the ox, 147 feet. Women standing at benches scrape these long lengths of gut which are hung over pegs for the purpose. If required for catgut or gold-beater's skin, the guts are left lying in water for many days until the tissues have been so softened that their separation is easy; they are then placed on a table and rubbed with the back of a knife or a piece of wood. Catgut is made by sewing the ends together with a needle and thread while still wet, and spinning the ends together by an ordinary hand-spinning wheel. The catgut is then stretched in a drying-room.

The nauseating effect of the presence of so much animal matter, especially in warm weather, can hardly be exaggerated, and the necessity for minimizing to the utmost extent, by cleanliness and ventilation, the contamination of the air must, I think, force itself upon everyone whose business takes them to gut-scraping or catgut works, even for a short time. To wait in such cases as these for such definite evidence of actual illness among the employees as could be demonstrated to have been caused by inhaling the offensive odours before doing all that common sense dictates to remove or reduce them, seems little short of cruelty.

Bad as the conditions are which I have found in some of the places where women were working, these were as nothing compared to the abominable filth and stench (milder terms are impossible) of places where men only worked, and which I had to pass through to reach the women's processes, or into which I entered to enquire whether women were employed.

MISS SQUIRE, *Factories & Workshops Report for 1905*, Cd. 3036 (1906), pp. 176–7.

16

The Price of Irish Embroidery

The southern part of Donegal is the district noted for sprigging [embroidery]. During the last four or five years there has been a rapid development in this industry. The demand for embroidered skirts, blouses, household linens, bedspreads, cushion covers, tray cloths and fancy linens has been almost phenomenal.

The linen, which is usually made up into various articles with the pattern stamped on it, and the thread required for the embroidery, are sent down by rail from the large factories in Belfast and the neighbourhood to agents who distribute it amongst the outworkers. The agents are in nearly every case shopkeepers, and they often receive work from two or three firms. They are paid a commission of 10 per cent.

The prices paid for embroidering fancy linens and handkerchiefs are curiously uneven. Some linens entailing much work are paid for at a lesser rate than articles with a scanty design and which would take far less time to embroider. We found that 1s was considered to be a good day's wage; and we were informed that the usual wage was 9d a day, and many old women can earn only 3d to 6d a day.

It was difficult to arrive at a correct estimate of the number of hours worked. Many of the women and girls had their duties in connection with the farm, and it seemed almost impossible for them to tell us the actual number of hours spent by them in sprigging. They invariably replied to our questions regarding the number of hours worked by 'we sit constant' or 'we cannot sit constant'. I have come to the conclusion that work is seldom begun before 9 a.m. or carried on long after dusk, and intervals are taken during the day. Undoubtedly the universal introduction of oil lamps has made embroidering on winter evenings easier than it was in the days when the girls had to crouch over a 'bog' fire and do their sprigging by this flickering light. In stating the wages earned per day, I have as far as possible taken the day as meaning 'sitting constant'.

Handkerchiefs

Handkerchiefs	7d a dozen	(1 dozen per day)
Handkerchiefs	1s 4d each	(1 handkerchief in 2 days)
Monogram	8d a dozen	(1 dozen per day)
Initial	½d each handkerchief	(10 handkerchiefs per day)
Four corners	1½d each handkerchief	(3 handkerchiefs per day)

Fancy and Household Linen

Muslin tray cloth	10d	(2 days)
Muslin bedspread	4s	(nearly 1 week)
Bedspread	7s	(1½ weeks)
Cosy covers	3d each	(1½ per day)
Tablecloth	3s	(4 days)
Sideboard cloth	4d	(1 day)
Ladies skirts	5s each	(9 days)
D'Oyleys	3s a dozen	(1 dozen in 2 days)

The Truck Acts We found no evidence in support of the statement that the Truck Acts are being complied with in Donegal. There are two methods adopted to pay workers otherwise than in the current coin of the realm which we found especially prevalent. (1) Supplying only customers with outwork or giving the best paid work to customers. Continually we were told that unless the wages were left at the shop no work would be given. . . . It seems to be almost instinctive with the workers that it would be an ungenerous act to take their wages from the shop, and it was almost with indignation that I was met with, 'Indeed, and it's ashamed I'd be not to leave my wages at the shop.' (2) A customer is enticed into making extensive purchases for which she cannot pay cash, on the plea that the heavy debt so incurred can be wiped off by means of the outwork. In some cases the matter is put before the customer in such a way that she is made to think a benefit is being conferred on her . . .

MISS HILDA MARTINDALE, 'Truck in Donegal', *Factories & Workshops Report for 1907*, Cd. 4166 (1908), pp. 214–18.

CHAPTER 4

THE PAUPER HOST

(*Royal Commission on the Poor Laws and Relief of Distress, 1905–1909*)

When the present century opened, the only social services provided by the State were operated through the Poor Law system. In the main, this system was that which had been set up by the Poor Law Amendment Act of 1834. The whole of England and Wales (in Scotland and in Ireland the principles and the machinery were somewhat different) was divided into Poor Law Unions, each with its specialized institutions and staff, and under the control of a popularly elected Board of Guardians. On the national level, general oversight was exercised by the Local Government Board.

Every kind of distress fell within the purview of the Poor Law, and it was the responsibility of the Guardians to relieve it to the best of their ability. The guiding principle in giving relief was that the condition of the pauper ought to be, on the whole, *less eligible* than that of the independent labourer who was obliged to contribute to his support. This principle was based on the belief, almost universal in 1834 and still very widely held seventy years later, that the able-bodied worker, if he really tried, should be able to find a job and earn sufficient to maintain himself and those dependent on him. When relief was given it was either 'outdoor' (given to the recipient in his own home) or 'indoor' (in the workhouse or other Poor Law institution).

When the Poor Law was reformed in 1834 it was in the expectation that poverty, apart from that induced by accident, sickness, and old age, would be erelong brought within easily manageable limits. But in the event 'the poor' simply would not make themselves scarce; they insisted on constituting a problem which seemed to become ever more intractable as the years passed. So far from the pauper tide dwindling to a trickle it swelled to a menacing flood.

What had gone wrong? How had it come about that after seventy years of striving to make Poor Law administration as cheap and its effects as nastily deterrent as possible, something like a million and a half persons 'passed through the portals of the Poor Law' in the course of a single year? How was it that hundreds of thousands of men able and willing to work were unable to find employment? Bombarded by such questions, to which they had no satisfactory answers, Mr Balfour's Conservative government fell back on the time-honoured device of a

Royal Commission. This was on December 4, 1905, and a few hours later on the same day Balfour resigned, and the Liberal leader, Sir Henry Campbell-Bannerman was called upon to form a government.

The Commission's terms of reference were 'to inquire into the Poor Laws and Relief of Distress in the United Kingdom'. Eighteen commissioners were named in the Royal Warrant. The chairman was Lord George Hamilton, a younger son of the Duke of Abercorn, who had been a Conservative M.P. for many years and had held Cabinet office; and looking down the list of names we may note Charles Booth, author of the great survey of *Life and Labour in London*; Miss Octavia Hill, housing reformer and prime founder of the National Trust; Rev. H. Russell Wakefield, later Bishop of Birmingham; the Fabian, Mrs Sidney Webb and the Socialist, George Lansbury; and (the one Trade Unionist) Francis Chandler, former secretary of the Amalgamated Society of Carpenters and Joiners.

Altogether the Commission held 209 meetings, examined 452 witnesses, and asked more than 100,000 questions, while some of their number visited several hundred Poor Law Unions. At length three Reports were issued, one each for England and Wales (Cd. 4499), Scotland (Cd. 4922), and Ireland (Cd. 4630), but these were accompanied by such a great mass of supporting material that the Commission's total printed output takes up forty volumes.

To make matters more complicated, each of the main reports is in two parts: a Majority Report, signed by 14 of the Commissioners, and a Minority, signed by the four more or less socialistically-inclined (Lansbury, Mrs Webb, Russell Wakefield, and Chandler). On the whole, the Minority reports are the more informative, comprehensive, and penetrating in their analysis, and the bulk of the 'documents' printed in this chapter are taken from them.

As regards their proposals, both Majority and Minority agreed on many points, but whereas the former wished to improve Poor Law administration the latter were resolved on the break-up of the whole Poor Law system and the distribution of its functions among the local authorities. In the event, neither body of reports was accepted by the Liberal government, but this did not matter so much as the immediately practicable reforms (Old Age pensions, Trade Boards, Unemployment Exchanges, and National Insurance) were already being carried out. Thus it happened that the Boards of Guardians survived until 1929, and it was not until 1948 that the last vestiges of the old Poor Law system were done away with by the Attlee Labour government.

I

Doles and Allowances

So far as the orphans and deserted children, the aged and infirm, the sick and the mentally afflicted, and the widows with legitimate offspring are concerned – and these make up nine-tenths of the pauper host – the Boards of Guardians all over England and Wales . . . exercise unchecked their power of awarding doles and allowances under such conditions as seem fit . . .

The most frequent clause in the couple of hundred Bylaws that we have seen is one which makes the grant of Outdoor Relief dependent on the character and conduct of the applicant. This is expressed sometimes as excluding those who are actually of 'immoral habits', or 'habitual drunkards and bad characters', or merely 'known to be in the habit of frequenting public-houses'. Some Boards exclude 'common beggars' or 'persons known to be addicted to begging'; others disqualify anyone, whatever his present conduct, who 'has wasted his substance in drinking and gambling, or has led an idle or disorderly life'; or those who cannot satisfy the Relief Committee that their destitution has not been caused by 'their own vicious habits' or their improvidence or intemperance in the past.

Most Unions which have Rules prohibit Outdoor Relief to widows, whatever their legitimate family, who have had an illegitimate child; indeed, 'any person who may have given birth to an illegitimate child' is commonly excluded. Widows who have only 'a small family' or, if an able-bodied widow of the working class, not more than two children are made ineligible in some Unions. Far more usual is it to require the widow with only one child to keep herself and child without relief at all . . . at least, say some Boards, if the child is a year old, eighteen months old, two years old, or of school age.

Some Boards deny Outdoor Relief to applicants 'residing with relatives of immoral, intemperate, or improvident character, or of uncleanly habits'. There are even Bylaws in many Unions forbidding the grant of Outdoor Relief to 'married women (with or without families) whose husbands, having been convicted of crime, are undergoing a term of imprisonment'.

Many Boards of Guardians profess the enlightened policy of insisting on a sanitary home, refusing Outdoor Relief to anyone, whatever his character or conduct, who is living in a cottage or room 'kept in a dirty or slovenly condition' or in premises reported by the Medical Officer of Health to be unfit for occupation. . . . On the other hand, too good a home is as fatal a disqualification in some Unions as too bad a home is in others. Outdoor Relief is, in some places, refused to persons who 'live in cottages rented above the average rent of the neighbourhood'.

Many Unions require the applicant for Outdoor Relief to 'have shown some signs of thrift'. Yet the occupation of a small holding, the holding of an allotment, the keeping of a cow or a donkey, or the possession of poultry, is, in some Unions, a cause of disqualification. So is the possession of a cottage, a Post Office annuity, or a tiny investment of any sort. The only form of saving which the Boards of Guardians seem willing to recognize and encourage is that of subscription to a friendly society.

R.C. on the Poor Laws, Cd. 4499, *Minority Report*, pp. 739–44.

2

'Starvation Out-Relief'

The lowest scale [of Outdoor Relief] that we have come across is that of Hertford, which grants for each adult only 1s a week and 5 lbs of flour, or its equivalent in bread. More usual is it to find the scale allowing 2s 6d per week for an adult, or 3s, or 3s 6d, though in a very few Unions it is put at as much as 4s (as at Newport) and even 5s (as at Loughborough and Bradford).

For each child residing at home one Union still gives only 6d and 5 lbs of flour, others 1s and a loaf, occasionally 1s and two loaves, and in some cases 1s 6d or 2s – in most Unions, we understand, without anything additional being allowed for the mother, if she is an able-bodied widow – as compared with the 2s per week for each child which the Guardians of Bradford and Sheffield think necessary in addition to a sum for the mother herself.

One Union has a 'summer scale' and a 'winter scale', both very low, allowing a married couple with one child 5s a week in summer and 7s a week in winter, with 1s additional for each further child.

It will be evident that, even allowing for differences in the cost of living, the lowest of these widely divergent scales of relief can be described only – to quote the words of the Clerk of one of the most important Unions – as 'starvation out-relief'.

Cd. 4499, *Minority Report*, p. 746.

3

Promiscuity of the General Workhouse

We see no reason to differ from our predecessors, the Royal Commissioners of 1834, in their decisive condemnation of the General Mixed Workhouse. We do not wish to suggest or imply that the workhouses of today are places of cruelty; or that their 250,000 inmates are subjected to any deliberate ill-treatment. These institutions are, in nearly all cases, clean and sanitary; and the food, clothing and warmth are sufficient – sometimes more than sufficient – to maintain the inmates in physiological health. In some cases, indeed, the buildings recently erected in the Metropolis and elsewhere have been not incorrectly described, alike for the elaborateness of their architecture and the sumptuousness of the internal fittings, as 'palaces' for paupers. In many places, on the other hand, the old and straggling premises still in use . . . are hideous in their bareness and squalor. But whether new or old, urban or rural, large or small, sumptuous or squalid, these establishments exhibit the same inherent defects . . .

The dominant note of these institutions of today, as it was of those of 1834, is their promiscuity.

We have ourselves seen, in the larger Workhouses, the male and female inmates, not only habitually dining in the same room in each other's presence, but even working individually, men and women together, in laundries and kitchens; and enjoying in the open yards and long corridors innumerable opportunities to make each other's acquaintance. It is, we find, in these large establishments, a common occurrence for assignations to be made by the inmates of different sexes, as to spending together the 'day out', or as to simultaneously taking their temporary discharge, as 'Ins and Outs'. It has not surprised us to be informed that female inmates of these great establishments have been known to bear offspring to male inmates, and thus increase the burden on the Poor Rate.

No less distressing has it been to discover a continuous intercourse, which we think must be injurious, between young and old, innocent and hardened.

In the female dormitories and day-rooms women of all ages, and of the most varied characters and conditions, necessarily associate together, without any kind of restraint on their mutual intercourse. There are no separate bedrooms; there are not even separate cubicles. The young servant out of place, the prostitute recovering from disease, the feeble-minded woman of any age, the girl with her first baby, the unmarried mother coming in to be confined of her third or fourth bastard, the senile, the paralytic, the epileptic, the respectable deserted wife, the widow to whom Outdoor Relief has been refused, are all herded indiscriminately together.

We have found respectable old women annoyed, by day and by night, by the presence of noisy and dirty imbeciles. We have ourselves seen, in one large Workhouse, pregnant women who have come in to be confined, compelled to associate day and night, and to work side by side with half-witted imbeciles and women so physically deformed as to be positively repulsive to look upon.

In the smaller country Workhouses . . . the very smallness of the numbers makes any segregation of classes even more impracticable than in the larger Workhouses.

A large proportion of these Workhouses have, for instance, no separate sick ward for children, and, in spite of the ravages of measles, etc., not even a quarantine ward for the constant stream of newcomers. Accordingly, in the sick wards of the smaller Workhouses, with no restraint on mutual intercourse, we have more than once seen young children in bed with minor ailments, next to women of bad character under treatment for contagious disease, whilst other women, in the same ward, were in advanced stages of cancer and senile decay . . .

In many Workhouses we have found the children having their meals in the same room and at the same times as the adult inmates of both sexes, of all ages, and of the most different conditions and characters. Even the imbeciles are to be found in the same dining-halls as the children. In some Workhouses, at any rate, the boys over eight years of age have actually to spend the long hours of the night in the same dormitories as the adult men.

In all the small Workhouses, and in many of the larger ones, the infants are wholly attended by, and are actually in charge of, aged and often mentally defective paupers; the able-bodied mothers having, during the first year, daily access to their own babies for nursing, and, subsequently, such opportunities for visiting the common nursery as the Master may decide. . . . However desirable may be the intercourse between an infant and its own degraded mother, it is not to the advantage of the scores of infants in the nursery to be perpetually in close companionship for the first three or four years of their lives, with a stream of mothers of various types that we have mentioned . . .

Cd. 4499, *Minority Report*, pp. 727–9.

4

Children in the Workhouse

Notwithstanding all the efforts which have been made for the last seventy years, a very large number of children are still maintained in the workhouse. In many Unions the children are treated with the utmost kindness and care, and in all Unions the majority now go out to the public elementary schools. Elsewhere we have found children in surroundings so dreary that it seems strange that Guardians who have families of their own could acquiesce in them. The following are instances of places visited by us:

(1) The nursery was bad, very messy and the children looked miserable; some of the infants were being nursed by old women, some lay in cradles with wet bedding, and were provided with 'comforters'. The three-year-old children were in a bare and desolate room, sitting about on the floor and on wooden benches, and in dismal workhouse dress. The older ones had gone out to school . . . except a cripple, and a dreary little girl who sat in a cold room with bare legs and her feet in a pail of water as a 'cure' for chilblains. The washing arrangements are unsatisfactory; the children have no toothbrushes, and very few hairbrushes.

(2) The children (39 girls and 23 boys) are housed in the workhouse under the care of a male and a female industrial trainer, but they are not kept separate from the adult inmates. In appearance the children were dirty, ill-kept, and almost neglected. Their clothes might be described with very little exaggeration as ragged, and when the inspector told a group of children to take off their right boots large holes were displayed in six stockings out of thirteen.

(3) In the nursery we found the babies of one or two years of age preparing for their afternoon sleep. They were seated in rows on wooden benches in front of a wooden table. On the table was a long narrow cushion, and when the babies were sufficiently exhausted, they fell forward upon this to sleep. The position seemed most uncomfortable and likely to be injurious. We were told that the system was an invention of the matron's and had been in use for a long time.

(4) There were twenty children in the house. The babies were under the charge of the laundress, who also looks after the female tramps, and is responsible for the young women. This seemed a most unsatisfactory arrangement; the laundress was a much harassed young woman, and the

babies were inevitably neglected. One was in the heat and steam of the laundry, two were tumbling in the yard, two in a small room next to the laundry in charge of a disagreeable-looking pauper; and two could not be found until we hunted them down in the young women's dormitory. This was very untidy, with the beds not made . . .

Cd. 4499, pp. 39, 186–7.

5

Born in the Workhouse

The workhouses in the smaller rural Unions . . . have perhaps only half a dozen confinements each in a year. In the Town workhouses they are numbered in dozens, or by scores; and in such populous parishes or Unions as Liverpool, West Derby, Belfast, and Glasgow, a baby is born in the workhouse every day.

The women who thus resort to the workhouse in their hour of need are of all nationalities, all grades of character and conduct, and all degrees of intelligence. In the Metropolis especially there are many domestic servants, laundresses and the humbler members of such nomadic professions as that of the theatre and the music-hall. 'Poor girls refused the shelter of their own homes in time of trouble; syphilitic patients; women who have been knocked about, neglected and ill-treated up to the last minute; cases actually in labour when admitted; in fine, all sorts and conditions of poor women who have nowhere else to go, find their way to the Poor Law maternity wards where', optimistically observes an Inspector, 'they receive the most skilful and tender care for themselves and their little ones.' Some of these are 'Ins and Outs' of a peculiar type, recurring at something like twelve months' intervals.

Cd. 4499, *Minority Report*, pp. 777–9.

6

Putting the Imbeciles to Work

The total number of mentally defective persons now residing *in the ordinary wards* of the General Mixed Workhouses of the United Kingdom must amount to more than 60,000. These 60,000 persons, of all ages and conditions, exhibiting all grades of mental defectiveness, are receiving practically nothing in the way of ameliorative treatment . . . We do not suggest that all the 60,000 are suffering, either in body or mind, from the lack of special care or treatment. . . . But we have ourselves witnessed terrible sights.

We have seen feeble-minded boys growing up in the Workhouse year after year untaught and untrained, alternately neglected or tormented by the other inmates. . . . We have seen imbeciles annoying the sane, and the sane tormenting the imbeciles. We have seen half-witted women nursing the sick, feeble-minded women in charge of the babies, and imbecile old men put to look after the boys out of school hours. We have seen expectant mothers, who have come in for their confinements, by day and by night working, eating, and sleeping in close companionship with imbeciles of revolting habits and hideous appearance . . .

The evil consequences of this herding in the Workhouse of the mentally defective with the sane have been repeatedly pointed out. . . . We think we are not wrong in attributing the retention of these 60,000 defective persons in the Workhouses to the fact that their labour is useful – in the small rural Workhouses, indeed, actually indispensable. . . . We have ourselves been informed, in Workhouse after Workhouse, that they had to rely on the imbeciles for practically all the manual work of the establishment. . . . 'If you remove the feeble-minded women from the Workhouse, who will do the scrubbing?'

Cd. 3499, *Minority Report*, pp. 894–5.

7

'Spectacle of Human Demoralization'

Of all the spectacles of human demoralization now existing in these islands, there can scarcely be anything worse than the scene presented by the men's day ward of a large Union workhouse during the long hours of leisure on week-days, or the whole of Sundays.

Through the clouds of tobacco smoke that fill the long low room, the visitor gradually becomes aware of the presence of one or two hundred wholly unoccupied males of every age between fifteen and ninety – strong and vicious men; men in all stages of recovery from debauch; weedy youths of weak intellect; old men too dirty or disreputable to be given special privileges, and sometimes, when there are no such privileges, even worthy old men; men subject to fits; occasional monstrosities or dwarfs; the feeble-minded of every kind; the respectable labourer prematurely invalided; the hardened, sodden loafer, and the temporarily unemployed man who has found no better refuge. . . . *In such places there are aggregated, this winter, certainly more than 10,000 healthy, able-bodied men.*

Cd. 4499, *Minority Report*, p. 1058.

8

Prison-like Casual Wards

The Casual Ward in England and Wales is, in all but about a score of Unions, attached to the General Mixed Workhouse. . . . To these 638 Casual Wards, placed all over the country at intervals of a few miles, there resort nightly from 7,000 to 17,000 persons, according to the season, the weather, and the badness of trade. These represent an army 'on tramp' estimated to vary, according to the same influences, from 30,000 to as many as 80,000 separate individuals, who resort to the Casual Ward from time to time. Four-fifths of them are men, who are sometimes accompanied by women, and occasionally also by young children. The number of single women in the Casual Wards is infinitesimal.

We have visited Casual Wards having well-warmed and well-lit cubicles furnished with comfortable beds, and an ample supply of rugs, to which the 'occasional poor' are ushered after a really hot bath; and in which they are supplied with an ample meal of hot broth and bread – accommodation at least as eligible as that afforded by the better type of common lodging-house. These Casual Wards are very naturally appreciated by the professional tramp . . .

There is, however, another side to the picture. We have ourselves visited Casual Wards in which the premises, the sleeping accommodation, the food and the amount of work exacted, taken together, constitute a treatment more penal and more brutalizing than that of any gaol in England. . . . What has surprised us is to find rising up in the great midland and northern cities, great and costly cellular prisons, erected with the sanction of the Local Government Board, as the only refuge for the destitute wayfarer and houseless poor. Here the cells are dark and cold; the bare stone floor, with one rug, is the only sleeping-place. During the day the men are locked in solitary pens and kept for nine hours at stone-pounding, the hardest and most monotonous toil that has been devised.

The Superintendents of these Casual Wards pride themselves on having always vacant cells. Every man, in return for the shilling's worth of food and establishment charges, is detained for the full period of about thirty-six hours; and if he is rash enough to come twice in a month, he is detained for four days and five nights, which is nearly the equivalent of what the prison authorities construe as a sentence of a week's imprisonment. But the habitual inmate of a Casual Ward prefers a sentence of imprisonment to the severity of the more rigorous Casual Wards. The statistics prove, to use the words of the Departmental Committee [on Vagrancy, 1906], 'that certain men deliberately commit offences in order to be sent to prison. . . . To many of these men prison seems to afford a desirable change to the Casual Ward.'

Cd. 4499, *Minority Report*, pp. 1080–3.

9

Old People's Dread of 'the House'

The large majority of those who endure biting poverty without seeking relief from the Guardians are women. Old men go more readily into the Workhouse than old women. Families in poor circumstances find it is less possible to provide food and shelter for an old man who is a relative than for an old woman. He is more in the way, he expects not only a larger portion of the food but to share in the better portions. He does not fit into the household of a working family as an old woman does, and is not so useful in domestic matters. His welcome is colder, and he desires to get out of the way and goes to the workhouse. A decent old woman will cling to a home where she may be regarded as the drudge rather than as the grandmother or the aunt, and she will exist on the plainer portions of the meals, and will wedge in both day and night without encroaching much on the means of the family.

There are, in every Union, aged women of good character, who belong to no family into whose domestic life they can fit and on whom they can depend – women who have been domestic servants, assistants in shops, mill hands, nurses, seamstresses, women who have denied themselves in younger days to support parents and bring up younger brothers and sisters, widows of good repute who have outlived husbands and children, daughters of fathers who have failed in business, and women left with some provision which has been exhausted. If absolutely unable to earn small sums, they must, of course, apply for relief, but many of them do manage by sewing, knitting, washing, hawking of small articles, or minding children for mothers going to work, to eke out a very scanty living. Having been self-supporting up to old age, they have the most intense desire to keep from even Outdoor Relief, and an utter repugnance to entering the Workhouse. Yet they have the daily fear that the Workhouse must be the final refuge, and this fear is harder to bear than the pinch of hunger, the cold of insufficient clothing, or the poverty of their surroundings.

ALDERMAN MACDOUGALL, of Manchester, Cd. 4499, *Minority Report*, p. 909.

10

Pauperism in Scotland

In May 1908 the number of sane poor in Scotland was 111,205; that is to say, one person out of every fifty persons in the whole population was in receipt of poor relief.

Indoor Relief In Scotland, as regards the sane poor, the term 'indoor relief' is applied only to the maintenance of poor persons in a poorhouse – all relief in institutions other than a poorhouse being regarded as

'Women's War Work' (1917)

7. ROUGH WORK FOR WOMEN. These photographs were included in the War Office recruiting brochure of 1916, as indicative of the way in which jobs hitherto confined to men were now being tackled successfully by women and girls. But in fact females had been employed in such ways for many years before the War. Top: young women barrowing coke at a gas-works; and below, girls riddling cinders.

8. ‘WOMEN WHO FOLLOW THE HERRING.’ Right: a ‘healthy specimen’ of a herring-gutter; below, Scottish fisher-girls at Pittenweem, Fife, packing herring into barrels for export.

Scottish Fisheries Museum Trust Ltd, Anstruther, Fife

outdoor relief. In 1906 there were 70 poorhouses, possessing accommodation for 18,861 inmates . . .

The provision made for classifying the indoor poor is totally inadequate. Miss Haldane says that 'at present the lowest type of tramp or woman of bad character is associated with respectable persons who, for no fault of their own, have had to take refuge in the house'. Other witnesses say that the poorhouse almost of necessity lends itself to the herding together of the very bad, the vicious, and the weakly; and that 'it is not a place for the respectable poor; it has become a receptacle for the dregs and wastrels of humanity'.

At the same time it is pleasant to report that many of the poorhouses that we saw were excellently managed, their officials being active, intelligent, and full of zeal.

Outdoor Relief In the Scottish system of outdoor relief . . . the principle underlying the outdoor allowance is that it is merely an adequate subsidy in aid of earnings, assistance from relatives, or charity, and that full maintenance is given only when the poor person is 'totally and absolutely destitute' of all these resources. When compared with the standard of ten or fifteen years ago, the allowances are much more liberal. Allowances of from 10s to 18s per week are, we find, quite common. . . . In the course of our visits, we have repeatedly found, as in England, cases where the effect of the outdoor relief can only be to encourage dirt, disease, and immorality . . .

R.C. on the Poor Laws – Scotland, Cd. 4922, pp. 87–107.

II

'Land of Hope and Glory'

'Land of Hope and Glory' is a popular and patriotic lyric sung each year with rapture by thousands of voices. The enthusiasm is partly evoked by the beauty of the idea itself, but more by the belief that Great Britain does, above other countries, merit this eulogium, and that the conditions in existence here are such that the fulfilment of hope and the achievement of glory are more open to the individual than in other and less favoured lands.

To certain classes of the community into whose moral and material condition it has been our duty to enquire, these words are a mockery and a falsehood. To many of them, possibly from their own failure and faults, there is in this life but little hope, and to many more 'glory' or its realization is an unknown ideal.,

Our investigations prove the existence in our midst of a class whose condition and environment are a discredit, and a peril to the whole community. Each and every section of society has a common duty to perform in combating this evil and contracting its area, a duty which can only be performed by united and untiring effort to convert useless and costly inefficients into self-sustaining and respectable members of the community.

No country, however rich, can permanently hold its own in the race of international competition, if hampered by an increasing load of this dead weight; or can successfully perform the role of sovereignty beyond the seas, if a portion of its own folk at home are sinking below the civilization and aspirations of its subject races abroad.

Concluding paragraphs of the *Majority Report*, Cd. 4499, p. 634.

12

Challenging Conclusion of the Minority Report

At present, it is not too much to say that the average citizen of the middle or upper class takes for granted the constantly recurring destitution among wage-earning families due to Unemployment, as part of the natural order of things, and as no more to be combated than the east wind.

In the same way the eighteenth-century citizen acquiesced in the horrors of the contemporary prison administration, and in the slave trade; just as, for the first decades of the nineteenth century, our grandfathers accepted as inevitable the slavery of the little children of the wage-earners in mines and factories, and the incessant devastation of the slums by 'fever'.

Fifty years hence we shall be looking back with amazement at the helpless and ignorant acquiescence of the governing classes of the United Kingdom, at the opening of the twentieth century, in the constant debasement of character and *physique*, not to mention the perpetual draining away of the nation's wealth, that idleness combined with starvation plainly causes . . .

We have to report that, in our judgment, it is now administratively possible, if it is sincerely wished to do so, to remedy most of the evils of Unemployment; to the same extent, at least, as we have in the past century diminished the death rate from fever and lessened the industrial slavery of young children . . .

Less than a century ago the problem of dealing with the sewage of London seemed insoluble. Half a million separate private cesspools accumulated each its own putrefaction. To combine these festering heaps into a single main drainage system seemed, to the Statesmen and social reformers of 1820 or 1830, beyond the bounds of possibility. We now take for granted that only by such a concentration is it possible to get rid of the festering heaps and scientifically treat the ultimate residuum.

In the same way, a century ago, no one knew how to administer a fever hospital; the eighteenth century 'pesthouse' must, indeed, have killed more people than it cured. Yet it was only by establishing hospitals that we learnt how to make them instruments of recovery for the patients and of a beneficent protection to the rest of the community.

And, to take a more recent problem, less than half a century ago, when millions of children in the land were growing up untaught, undisciplined, and uncared for, it would have sounded wildly visionary to have suggested that the remedy was elaborate organization on a carefully thought-out plan. Could there have been anything more 'Utopian' in 1860 than a picture of what today we take as a matter of course, the 7,000,000 children emerging every morning, washed and brushed, from 5,000,000 or 6,000,000 homes in every part of the Kingdom, traversing street and road and lonely woodland, going o'er fell and moor, to present themselves at a given hour at their 30,000 schools, where each of the 7,000,000 finds his or her own individual place, with books and blackboard and teacher provided?

What has been effected in the organization of Public Health and Public Education can be effected, if we wish it, in the Public Organization of the Labour Market.

Cd. 4499, *Minority Report*, pp. 1214–15.

CHAPTER 5

LLOYD GEORGE'S AMBULANCE WAGON

On the whole, the 'documents' given in the preceding chapters cannot but make for rather depressing reading. A great multitude of poor people, leading hard and penurious lives; women working terribly long hours for a pittance, in occupations that were shockingly unsuitable and under the most demoralizing conditions; and a vast host of paupers, for whom there was nothing better at the end of life's road than the workhouse door.

All these things were true, and yet the picture we form in our mind's eye should not be one of unrelieved gloom. For on the horizon there were indications of a brighter tomorrow. As never before, the public conscience had been aroused to the shameful iniquity of the circumstances in which so many millions were condemned to live, and the Liberal government which had emerged so triumphantly from the general election of 1906 was committed to a vast programme of 'Social Reform'. Political activity was unprecedentedly intense and eager, and in this activity a most prominent part was played by Lloyd George, who, after a successful apprenticeship as President of the Board of Trade, in which capacity he had managed to get through Parliament a bill which was hailed as the 'Seaman's Charter', became Chancellor of the Exchequer in 1908 in succession to Asquith, who had taken Campbell-Bannerman's place as Prime Minister.

So active did Lloyd George show himself, indeed, that there were some who complained that he was in far too much of a hurry. That did not worry him in the least; so far from repudiating the charge, he made a boast of it. Speaking at Birmingham in 1911, when the controversy over his Insurance Bill was nearing its tumultuous climax, he brought his audience to their feet with the dramatic declaration that, yes, he *was* in a hurry; he had joined the Red Cross and was resolved to drive his 'wagon' to the rescue of the wounded wherever they might be lying.

The concept caught the popular imagination, and 'Lloyd George's ambulance wagon' became the synonym for dashing and daring efforts at social reform and human redemption.

By this time, indeed, a good beginning had already been made, what with the provision of school meals and the medical inspection of school-children, an eight-hours' day for miners, the setting up of Trade

Boards for the most notoriously 'sweated' industries, and the establishment of a network of Labour Exchanges. The most remarkable of the series of reforming measures, however, was the Old Age Pensions Act of 1908. Judged by present-day standards, the pension was paltry – 5s a week for persons of 70 and over, whose incomes did not exceed £21 per annum – but the scheme's importance lay in its being an entirely new departure in social provision. The pensions were payable entirely out of the National Exchequer, and were thus the first-fruits of the policy of 'taxing the rich for the benefit of the poor' – a point seized upon by *Punch* in its cartoon showing Lloyd George as 'The Philanthropic Highwayman'.

The first pensions became payable on January 1, 1909. At first, so Flora Thompson relates in *Lark Rise*, some of the old cottagers who came to the village post office to draw their pensions, wept tears of joy, and, as they reached to pick up their money, said fervently, 'God bless Lord George!', since they were not able to credit that one so obviously powerful and munificent could possibly be a mere 'Mr'.

Lloyd George's Budget in 1909 made history, as he had intended it should. His new taxes, especially those on land, aroused fierce opposition, and the speeches he made in their defence, notably the one at Limehouse, so infuriated the Peers that they took the unprecedented step of rejecting the Budget, and it was not passed until after a general election in 1910.

The great National Insurance scheme was launched in 1911. Framed on a compulsory and contributory basis, it covered all manual workers between the ages of 16 and 70, and also all other employed persons whose wages did not exceed £160 per annum. The contributions, paid weekly and attested by stamps affixed to individual insurance-cards, were 4d (3d for a woman), 3d, and 2d, made by employee, employer, and the State respectively. Lloyd George claimed that this meant that the worker was going to get '9d for 4d', but not everyone agreed with his arithmetic.

A tremendous agitation was worked up against the proposals, and Lord Northcliffe's newspapers in particular urged housewives to revolt against the 'indignity' of having to lick stamps to put on their domestics' cards. Only a week or so before the scheme was due to come into operation, *Punch* had a cartoon, 'The Coming Olympic Struggle', showing a mistress combining with her servant-girl to punch the head of a smiling-in-spite-of-everything Lloyd George. But on the appointed day the tongues did their duty . . .

The Insurance Act came into operation on July 15, 1912. Lloyd George had other schemes in the pipe-line, but the intensification of the

2. THE COMING OLYMPIC STRUGGLE

Active training for the Passive Resistance Event.

Punch (1912)

arms race with Germany left little cash available for further social advances. Then on a day towards the end of June 1914, the Austrian Archduke was slaughtered at Sarajevo and, as the world plunged madly into war, 'Lloyd George's ambulance wagon' was well and truly ditched.

1

What Unemployment Means

I do not think the better-off classes, whose comfort is assured, realize the sufferings of the unemployed workmen. What is poverty? Have you felt it yourselves? If not, you ought to thank God for having been spared its sufferings and its temptations. Have you ever seen others enduring it? Then pray God to forgive you, if you have not done your best to alleviate it.

By poverty, I mean *real* poverty – not the cutting down of your establishment, not the limitation of your luxuries. I mean the poverty of the man who does not know how long he can keep a roof over his head, and where he will turn to find a meal for the pinched and hungry little children who look to him for sustenance and protection. *That* is what unemployment means.

I have had some excruciating letters piled upon me, more especially during the last year or two, from people whose cases I have investigated – honest workmen thrown out of work, tramping the streets and from town to town, from one workshop to another, begging for work as they would for charity, and at the end of the day trudging home tired, disheartened, and empty-handed . . .

During years of prosperity the workman has helped to create those enormous resources of wealth which have been accumulated in this country since the last period of depression. Hundreds of millions have been added to the national wealth during the cycle of plenty. Surely, a few of those millions might be spared to preserve from hunger and torturing anxiety the workmen who have helped to make that great wealth . . .

D. LLOYD GEORGE at Swansea, October 1, 1908.

2

'This is a War Budget'

I have to thank the House for the very great indulgence which they have extended to me, and for the patience with which they have listened to me. The task has been an extraordinarily difficult one. It has been as disagreeable a task as could well have been allotted to any Minister of the Crown. But there is one element of supreme satisfaction in it. That is to be found in contemplating the objects for which these new imposts have been created. The money thus raised is to be expended, first of all, in ensuring the inviolability of our shores. It has also been raised in order not merely to relieve but to prevent unmerited distress within these shores. It is essential that we should make every necessary provision for the defence of our country. But surely it is equally imperative that we should make it a country better worth defending for all and by all. And it is that this expenditure is for both these purposes that alone could justify the Government . . .

I am told that no Chancellor of the Exchequer has ever been called upon to impose such heavy taxes in a time of peace.

This is a War Budget. It is for raising money to wage implacable warfare against poverty and squalidness. I cannot help hoping and believing that before this generation has passed away we shall have advanced a great step towards that good time when poverty and wretchedness and human degradation which always follow in its camp will be as remote to the people of this country as the wolves which once infested its forests.

D. LLOYD GEORGE, introducing the Budget in the House of Commons, April 29, 1909.

3

The Speech at Limehouse

The provision [in the Budget] for the aged and deserving poor – was it not time something was done? It is rather a shame for a rich country like ours – probably the richest in the world, if not the richest the world has ever seen – that it should allow those who have toiled all their days to end in penury and possibly starvation. It is rather hard that an old workman should have to find his way to the gates of the tomb, bleeding and footsore, through the brambles and thorns of poverty. We cut a new path for him – an easier one, a pleasanter one, through fields of waving corn.

We propose to do more by means of the Budget. We are raising money to provide against the evils and the sufferings that follow from unemployment. We are raising money for the purpose of assisting our great Friendly Societies to provide for the sick and the widows and orphans. We are providing money to enable us to develop the resources of our own land . . .

But there are some of our critics who say, 'The taxes themselves are unjust, unfair, unequal, oppressive – notably so the land taxes.' They are engaged in assailing these taxes with a concentrated and sustained ferocity which will not allow even a comma to escape with its life. Now, are these taxes really so wicked? Let us examine . . . the tax on undeveloped land and increment.

The Golden Swamp

Not far from here, not so many years ago, between the Lea and the Thames, you had hundreds of acres which were not useful even for agricultural purposes. In the main it was sodden marsh. The commerce and the trade of London increased under Free Trade, the tonnage of your shipping went up by hundreds of thousands of tons and by millions, labour was attracted from all parts of the country to cope with all this trade and business which was done here. What happened? There was no housing accommodation. This Port of London became overcrowded, and the population overflowed. That was the opportunity of the owners of the marsh. All that land became valuable building land, and land which used to be rented at £2 or £3 an acre has been selling within the last few years at £2,000 an acre, £3,000 an acre, £6,000 an acre, £8,000 an acre.

Who created that increment? Who made that golden swamp? Was it the landlord? Was it *his* energy? Was it *his* brains? – a very bad look out for the place if it were! – *his* forethought? It was purely the combined efforts of all the people engaged in the trade and commerce of the Port of London – trader, merchant, shipowner, dock labourer, workman, everybody *except* the landlord . . .

That is now coming to an end. In future those landlords will have to contribute to the taxation of the country on the basis of the real values – only one halfpenny in the pound! Only a halfpenny! And that is what all the howling is about . . .

Golder's Green

There is another little tax called the Increment Tax. We mean to value all the land in the kingdom, and if land goes up in the future by hundreds and thousands an acre through the efforts of the community the community will get 20 per cent of the increment . . .

Take cases like Golder's Green, where the value of land has gone up in the course, perhaps, of a couple of years, through a new tramway or a new railway being opened. A few years ago there was a plot of land at

Golder's Green which was sold at £160. Last year I went and opened a Tube railway there. What was the result? This year that very piece of land has been sold for £2,000. . . . My Budget demands 20 per cent of that . . .

Coal Royalties

I have just one other land tax to speak to you about. The landlords are receiving eight millions a year by way of royalities. What for? *They* never deposited the coal in the earth . . .

Have you been down a coal mine? I went down one the other day. We sank down into a pit half a mile deep. We then walked underneath the mountain, and we had about three-quarters of a mile of rock and shale above us. The earth seemed to be straining to crush us in. You could see the pit-props bent and twisted and sundered. Sometimes they give way, and then there is mutilation and death. Often a spark ignites, the whole pit is deluged in fire, and the breath of life is scorched out of hundreds of breasts by the consuming flame.

In the very next colliery to the one I descended, just a few years ago, 300 people lost their lives in that way. And yet when the Prime Minister and I knock at the doors of these great landlords and say to them: 'Here, you know these poor fellows who have been digging up royalties at the risk of their lives – some of them are old, they have survived the perils of their trade, they are broken, they can earn no more. Won't you give something towards keeping them out of the workhouse?' they scowl at us. We say, 'Only a ha-penny, just a copper.' They retort, 'You thieves!' and they turn their dogs on us, and you can hear them bark every morning.

If this is an indication of the view taken by these great landlords of their responsibilities to the people who at the risk of their lives create their wealth, then I say their day of reckoning is at hand.

We are placing burdens on the broadest shoulders. Why should *I* put burdens on the people? I am one of the children of the people. I was brought up amongst them. I know their trials; and God forbid that I should add one grain of trouble to the anxieties which they bear with such patience and fortitude. When the Prime Minister did me the honour of inviting me to take charge of the National Exchequer at a time of great difficulty, I made up my mind, in framing the Budget which was in front of me, that at any rate no cupboard should be barer, no lot harder. By *that* test I challenge you to judge the Budget.

D. LLOYD GEORGE at Limehouse, July 30, 1909.

4

'Rare and Refreshing Fruit'

Who ordained that a few should have the land of Britain as a perquisite? Who made ten thousand people owners of the soil, and the rest of us trespassers in the land of our birth? Who is it who is responsible for the scheme of things whereby one man is engaged through life in grinding labour to win a bare and precarious subsistence for himself, and when, at the end of his days, he claims at the hands of the community he served a poor pension of eightpence a day, he can get it only through a revolution; and another man who does not toil receives every hour of the day, every hour of the night, whilst he slumbers, more than his poor neighbour receives in a whole year of toil?

Where did the table of that law come from? Whose fingers inscribed it? These are the questions that will be asked. The answers are charged with peril for the order of things that the Peers represent; but they are fraught with rare and refreshing fruit for the parched lips of the multitude who have been treading the dusty road along which the people have marched through the dark ages which are now merging into the light.

D. LLOYD GEORGE at Newcastle, October 9, 1909.

5

'Blood' – or 'Bloom'

Amongst the many contrasts which a rich country like ours presents between the condition of the rich and the poor there is none more striking than the profligate extravagance with which land by the square mile is thrown away upon stags and pheasants and partridges, compared with the miserly greed with which it is doled out for the habitations of men, women, and children. You measure the former by the square mile; the latter is given out by the yard, and even by the foot.

The greatest asset of a country is a virile and contented population. This you will never get until the land in the neighbourhood of our great towns is measured out on a more generous scale for the homes of the people. They want, as a necessity of life, plenty of light, plenty of air, plenty of garden space, which provides the healthiest and most productive form of recreation any man can enjoy.

I am not against sport; I only want to extend the area of its enjoyment. A small number of people like to take their sport in the form of destroying something; the vast majority prefer cultivation to destruction. Some like blood; others prefer bloom. The former is considered a more high-class taste; but few of us can belong to that exalted order – they must be content with such humble pleasures as flower gardens and vegetable patches and fruit bushes can afford them.

In the old days there might have been some excuse for this congestion of housing space – the means of locomotion were so inadequate that men had to crowd together within the smallest compass; but now, with electric trams and the general development of our transport system, there is no excuse for it. A pernicious system which had its excuse in the exigencies of industrial life is now perpetuated through pure greed.

D. LLOYD GEORGE at London, October 17, 1910.

6

Here Comes the Ambulance!

The first thing we do in our [Insurance] Bill is to provide adequate medical treatment for every workman in the kingdom. What next? We have a provision for maternity – an allowance of 30s – money meant for the mother to help her in discharging the sacred function of motherhood by proper treatment and fair play, so as to put an end to this disgraceful infant mortality which we have got in this country.

What else have we got? It is no use sending men to sanatoria, it is no use even giving them free doctoring, unless you relieve them from anxiety about their household, so we are making provision for the maintenance of the family during the time a man is under the doctor's hands. When he is fighting the Angel of Death we look after his children for him. Let him have both hands free to fight with the help of a doctor, and we will pull through hundreds of thousands. The allowance we are making is not a sumptuous one to begin with, but it will grow. There is provision for 10s a week for the first 13 weeks, and it is also provided in the Bill that if they like to make provision for 26 weeks they can do so.

What happens to a man if he does not recover at the end of 26 weeks? Supposing he is broken altogether, what happens to him then? We make not a sumptuous allowance, but I will tell you what it is. Five shillings a week. I never said you could keep a family on that, but every man who has lived in workmen's homes, and I have done it, knows what it means to have a steady, dependable allowance, even though a small one, which you can always rely upon . . .

What else? One of the most terrible diseases in the land is consumption. Read its records: you cannot do so without a shudder; seventy or eighty thousand lives each year are carried away by it . . . worst of all, it kills people just in the period of life when they are attaining the height of efficiency – between fifteen and forty. What do we do under the Bill? We open a new prospect for the worker. We plant all over Britain cities of refuge to which he can flee from this avenger of life; we are setting a million and a half aside for the purpose of building sanatoria throughout the country. There will be a million for maintaining them. The worker will now be able to command medical attendance; he will discover the disease in time; he will be taken to these institutions; in a few months the bulk of the cases that are taken in time are cured; he will be restored to his hearth, restored to his workshop, a fit capable citizen instead of being a wreck . . .

This year, this Session, I have joined the Red Cross. I am in the ambulance corps. I am engaged to drive a wagon through the twistings and turnings and ruts of the Parliamentary road. There are men who tell me I have overloaded that wagon. I have taken three years to pack it carefully. I cannot spare a single parcel, for the suffering is great. There are those who say my wagon is half empty; I say it is as much as I can carry.

Now there are some who say I am in a great hurry. I *am* rather in a hurry, for I can hear the moanings of the wounded, and I want to carry relief to them in the alleys, the homes where they lie stricken . . .

D. LLOYD GEORGE at Birmingham, June 10, 1911.

7

'I See a Vision'

Here is this great National Insurance scheme which touches every household, every industry, every trade, and all our interests. If there are slips and little stumblings, remember it is the first time that the nation has been mobilized.

What for? Not to wage war upon their fellow-men, not to march into the territories of people who are flesh of our flesh and blood of our blood, to ravage and destroy, but for the purpose of securing health, for securing plenty, and for driving away the privation and hunger that have invaded millions of homes. That is the invader we are organizing this army of fourteen millions [of insured persons] to meet next Monday.

They [the Act's opponents] have assailed it bitterly with misrepresentations, with falsehoods, direct, unqualified, which they have refused to withdraw when their attention has been called to it. They have abused its author in a way, I believe, that no Minister of the Crown has been assailed in my time. My race, my origin – they are all the topics of their vituperation. I am proud of both.

There is one quality that my little race has that gives them peculiar offence, especially the dullest among them, and that is the gift of imagination. It has pulled me through many a fight, and it will pull me through this, because, when insults hurtle through the air, I can always see a vision on the horizon that sustains me. I can see now the humble homes of the people with the dark clouds of anxiety, disease, distress, privation hanging heavily over them. And I can see, again, another vision. I can see the Old Age Pension Act, the National Insurance Act, and many another Act in their trail descending, like breezes from the hills of my native land, sweeping into the mist-laden valleys, and clearing the gloom away until the rays of God's sun have pierced the narrowest window.

D. LLOYD GEORGE at Kennington, July 13, 1912.

CHAPTER 6
'ENGLAND IN TIME OF WAR'

From eleven o'clock on the night of August 4, 1914, Britain was at war with Germany. Since there was no 'wireless' in those days, most people did not learn of it until they opened their newspapers the next morning, and then they stared at the headlines with almost unbelieving eyes. But when the news had had time to sink in, they (to use a Biblical expression) 'girded up their loins' to face whatever might lie ahead.

How they went about it may be gathered from a remarkable series of articles published in *The Times* between December 1914 and February 1915. Selections from these articles constitute the 'documents' given in this chapter. Taken together, they present a picture, most vividly presented and intimately detailed, of an England reacting to the strains and stresses of newly experienced war.

I

Impressions of London

The streets are full of traffic. There seem to be (though we know there are not) as many motor-cars and omnibuses as usual; of commercial carts there are the usual thousands. The pavements are thronged with people, looking in the shop windows, apparently intent on buying. At luncheon-time the restaurants are full; at tea-time the theatres and music halls disgorge undiminished *matinée* crowds. The observer might be pardoned for thinking that all was as usual, but for khaki and the recruiting-bills . . .

On every omnibus and taxicab and van, on every shop window and on every hoarding, the recruiting bills call for men. Vast appeals for men shout from the walls of great shops and hotels, and the base of Nelson's Column is built in with them. Yet there is khaki everywhere. Long lines of whistling, singing khaki tramp down Oxford-street or Piccadilly. The parks are full of drilling khaki. Trench-making is practised behind Westminster Cathedral; there are horses tethered in the Green Park; and in the Inns of Court, in the big squares of Bloomsbury, in every large open space, the shout of the Sergeant-Instructor can be heard. The Underground stations are guarded by soldiers. Between one o' clock and two much khaki, with gold-lace on the cap-band and red tabs and every conceivable combination of medal ribbons, may be seen round Whitehall and Pall Mall . . .

By night the changes strike harder. In streets and shop windows the lights are few and thickly shaded, lest enemy aircraft should see their way to London. We must grope our own; and we must be saved from ourselves by the closing of the public-houses at ten o'clock. Since the rule applies, so far as wines and spirits are concerned, to clubs and restaurants, London has ceased to be a city of pleasure.

The theatres close as early as they can; there can be no more supper parties at the great hotels; the night clubs are shut. It is strange to observe, nevertheless, how full the streets are. The public seem never tired of walking to and fro, looking up to where, from the roofs of park gates and public buildings, the searchlights wheel across the ominous sky . . .

2

Jobs for All in the East End

East of Aldgate Pump the details of the picture are very much as they have always been. Beyond a strong recruiting rally and occasional visits from the newly enlisted youth of the district, there is little to bring home to these teeming millions the living realities of war. But by looking more closely at the picture one will find that the details are changing.

The substitution of 'Warsaw salami' for German sausage in the Delicatessen shops is just a sign of the times. The Jews, who are chiefly recruited from Russian Poland, have no German sympathies. The crisis has brought a new figure into the panorama of the Whitechapel-road, a Jew in khaki. Many a spectacled, round-shouldered youth has wrenched himself from the closely knit family life of the streets behind the London Hospital to join the New Army.

Trades and occupations are changing. In side streets off the Commercial-road one can see, through sealed windows, steaming workrooms in which a dozen men and women without pause stitch khaki into soldiers' uniforms. Over them stands their sweating employer, himself the victim of some invisible super-sweater. There is little romance in khaki when you reduce it to its lowest common denominator.

Another strange phenomenon – casual labour is at a premium. For once there are hardly enough men to feed the great maw of the docks. Sea-power means regular employment for the East End . . .

Ruin stared the pawnbrokers in the face at the beginning of the war – not because people had nothing to pawn, but because they had no money with which to redeem the articles already there. This queer phase has passed, and the old order has been resumed. Every Monday morning crowds of women pledge the Sunday clothes of the whole family. Every Saturday morning, with their wages and allowances in their purses, they take them out again.

The week-end is the danger time. The drinking evil is then at its worst. Unhappily there is no reason to doubt that drinking among the poorest classes of women has increased considerably since the outbreak of war. Still, no one could be prepared for the Bacchic welcome which Hoxton gave to the regulation that women shall not be served with drink before 11.30 a.m. The 11.30 queue of women is now a daily scene. Children coming home from morning school often find no dinner ready for them. [But] the slum children have gained at the other end of the scale. The 10 p.m. closing order for public-houses has had an almost magical effect in clearing the streets two hours earlier than before the war.

This tendency to keep better hours is general. An East End main road is terribly depressing in these days, with shaded street lamps and half-lighted tramcars and motor-omnibuses. The faded shop windows and frowsy housefronts look hopelessly uninviting. The darkening of this great wilderness of shabby streets has not led to any increase of violent crime, but it is more and more driving people to seek the sanctuary of their own homes. Every by-street has its link with the New Army, and a new consciousness of national rights and duties has come to thousands who have spent thier lives in the crowded isolation of East London . . .

3

No Time for Golf in the Suburbs Now

From the crowd which throngs the earlier trains to the City, between 7 o'clock and 9, only perhaps the station-master and the porters could tell you how many familiar faces of the younger men are missing. The regular traveller is at most aware that certain of his personal acquaintances have gone; and beyond that he has the impression that on the platforms now there are more women and fewer men than there used to be.

On the later trains not a few of the older men who have travelled first class now travel third, and the talk in the compartments has become curiously military and geographical. Almost every day some one of them has received a letter dropped out of the unknown in an unstamped envelope covered with strange postmarks and uncouth cancellations, which is shown on the station platform and passed round and discussed again in the railway carriage.

The letters are short and roughly scrawled, dated only from 'The Front', 'At Sea', or 'In Base Hospital on Active Service'. Some men there are, too, who, as everybody knows, will receive no more such letters. They are treated with a certain cheery and gentle deference by their fellow-passengers, and in their presence conversation about the war is carefully restrained . . .

Formal entertaining has almost ceased. There has not been, nor does there threaten to be, a dance this winter. The only festivities which the hall in which the public dances are generally held has seen this winter have been two or three war lectures and a patriotic concert in aid of various War Funds. And what place have dinner parties in the life of a man who, arriving home from his office at 6, must turn out again at 8 or at midnight for a four-hour vigil, as special constable at the local waterworks, or who takes his turn on two evenings of the week at the indoor rifle range? Moreover, there are the committee meetings, which have to be largely held after dinner – meetings in connection with the local work for the Belgian refugees, the Cottage Hospital, the new hospital for wounded soldiers now being organized, and above all in connection with the novel activities of the Golf Club.

From Saturday to Saturday, except a few stalwarts well beyond military age and an occasional pair of ladies, hardly anyone now uses the golf course for purposes of golf. Yet at certain of the holes the fairway is worn and trampled to a degree which no amount of honest playing could have achieved. At stated hours in the week these portions of the links become the scene of immense energy and enthusiasm, when the platoons form fours and wheel, extend and double . . .

While the men are away the women are busy, mostly in ways which are new to them. There is much less running up to Town for *matinées*, much less punctilious leaving of cards and dropping in to tea. And afternoon Bridge has almost disappeared. In place of these has come a great fervour of work and organization.

There is a great amount of British common sense in the suburbs. Before the doctor had given his first half-dozen lectures, everybody knew which of the younger women was likely to be of permanent use as a nurse, and which had taken it up merely for excitement or for the uniform. The managers of working parties soon learned which of the eager participants could really work or make a garment fit for a refugee, a hospital patient, or a man at the front to wear. The truth is, the War is doing the suburbs a world of good . . .

4

Where are the Youth of Oxbridge?

The generous youth of England has rushed to arms, and the effect upon Oxford and Cambridge is strange indeed. At 11 or noon the streets are not now a-flutter with gowns hurrying to lectures; at 1 o'clock the groups in the gateways are scanty or none. The motor-bicycles are at the front, carrying despatches. By night and by day there is a hush over the colleges, where set upon set of empty rooms seem to stare at the empty quadrangle in surprise. The parks and the playing-fields are given up to drill, and football is confined to scratch matches got up once a week 'to keep football going'.

On the river at Oxford the only boats are a few scratch fours or pairs; at Cambridge only the Belgian students may be seen. Perhaps Oxford makes more attempt than Cambridge to keep sport alive, partly because at Oxford the Officers' Training Corps is less able to be exacting in its demands. The Prince of Wales, of Magdalen, and others have sent funds to help the Drag do a weekly run in hard times, and the officers in and about Oxford are glad of the opportunity.

But by the end of November . . . all the oars of last year's Oxford eight, thirteen of the Rugby XV, nine of the cricket XI, eight of the Association XI, and all of the lawn tennis six had taken commissions. No wonder the university life languished . . .

5

'Busier *than usual*' *Birmingham*

Birmingham claims to have improved upon the war-time motto of industrial England – 'Business as usual'. 'Busier than usual' is its characteristic boast. There is the impression of a great community with its coat off and its sleeves rolled up.

There are not many articles required for the Army and equipment of the troops that cannot be made in Birmingham, and the War Office is availing itself to the full of the resources of its manufacturing industries. New factories are being built, new machines installed, new tools brought into use. Trades are changing, and workmen are adapting themselves to new occupations. Hundreds of skilled men eager to enlist have been forbidden to leave their jobs. Others, who were already undergoing their training, have been sent back to the ranks of the industrial army.

The pleasant garden suburbs to the south have lost much of their winter gaiety. There are vacant chairs at thousands of working-class tables. Still the routine life of the great city goes on very much as before. The public-houses keep their usual hours, and a man can get a drink in Corporation-street an hour later than in Piccadilly Circus. The lighting of the streets has been only slightly reduced, and the drawing of blinds and shading of lamps in public vehicles is perfunctorily carried out. The two great shopping streets. New-street and Corporation-street, are a blaze of light, and a scene of bustling animation in the late afternoon and early evening . . .

If you look more closely at the details you will find a new restraint in the demeanour of a notoriously proud and, in times past, almost assertive city. The new note of modesty is amusingly illustrated by the notice exhibited in a shop window. '*Ici on parle Francais un peu*', probably the corollary to a visit from one of the war Belgian refugees who are quartered in the hospitable homes on the outskirts . . .

For the workaday soul of Birmingham, one must leave the alluring shopping district and seek the neighbouring belt of two and three-storeyed workshops on which the prosperity of the city is based. There are to be found the small employer and the individualistic style of work which differentiates industrial Birmingham . . . working under novel conditions, adapting their labour to unaccustomed jobs without protest, framing no peddling trade union grievances, in short bending their energies to the prosecution of their share of the national task.

6

Bright and Lively Liverpool

Any Briton in search of a tonic in these anxious times could not do better than visit the home port of the Atlantic trade. His nerves will be braced as he passes from dock to dock and reads the majestic lesson of Britain's maritime power. He will see loading or unloading scores of ships, from small coasting steamers to the giants of the American passenger trade, warehouses piled to the roofs with barrels, boxes, baskets, sacks and crates, and an endless chain of wagons trundling over the cobbles of the long dock roads.

The highway is little changed. The steam ferries for the bedroom suburbs of Liverpool on the Cheshire side swing out in tune and time, and the thousands who cross in them are the eager, hurrying crowd one has always known.

It is the ocean passenger traffic which has changed the most. Sailings are not nearly so frequent. Many of the better-known liners have been taken into Government service and lie hidden behind the fog of war. With few exceptions the big vessels of the Atlantic trade have effaced their world-famous badges and assumed a uniform appearance with coats of black or slate-grey. Their movements are almost furtive. A liner now does not come up to the stage in a blaze of glory, the hour of her arrival known to the whole world, with crowds lining the gangways to greet the wanderer on her return. She creeps up to the stage like an uninvited guest. Nobody outside the military and the Dock-Board circle knows when she is coming . . .

As for the husk of the town, it seems as bright and lively as ever it was. London has long since lost its nightly blaze of sky-signs; they shine out with undiminished brilliance in Lime-street. The fine shops in Bold-street for the well-to-do and in Lord-street for the masses have never had more customers. The hotels are doing exceptionally good business. Labour at the docks has become so scarce that the authorities have had virtually to suspend the beneficent, strike-averting scheme by which casual employment was being stamped out. The port was actually becoming congested, so labourers from all parts were positively invited to enter the dock service . . .

4

Hard-hit Manchester

Manchester's material losses have been greater than those of any other city, with the exception of its small brothers, the cotton-producing towns.

'High Change' on Tuesdays and Fridays is the crowded and bustling picture it has always been. The majestic theatre of commerce and its many thousand actors are the same, but the parts they play are very different. Big men are thankful for small mercies. The severity of the blow which the war has struck at the staple trade may be judged from the fact that the banks are now clearing £2,000,000 a week less than a year ago. At the New Year 40 per cent of the weavers of North-East Lancashire and 20 per cent of the spinners in the districts adjoining Manchester were unemployed.

No trade has sustained such heavy casualties, but fortunately the situation steadily improves. The music of loom and spindle is giving out an increasingly cheerful note. The Government need more wool than cotton for the equipment of the troops. Still, several War Office contracts have gone out to the cotton districts for yarn for heavy overcoats and haversacks. . . . While cotton and shipping are depressed, the engineering works are at top pressure, chiefly for Government contracts. The city is sending the troops a great variety of necessary articles, from bedding and barbed wire to lime juice and 'tent duck'.

The sudden rush has led to a famine in skilled workers in certain trades, and it may be taken that the operative class is in clover. It is the middle class, the merchants and warehousemen, who have been the worst hit. This big middle class, which chiefly makes its home in the comfortable suburbs on the Cheshire side, is the embodiment of the Manchester spirit . . .

Your typical Manchester man is rather proud of the absence of change in his city's outward show. But behind the scenes, away from busy shops and crowded theatres, Manchester is vastly different. The dark and rather forbidding warehouse quarter is strangely subdued. If there seems to be as many people as ever walking with the quick step of the north along dripping pavements, there are far fewer trollies making day hideous, as their wheels jolt along the cobbled roads. Manchester is assuredly a less noisy and possibly a less smoky city for the war.

8

'Terrific' at Leeds

No English city, except London and Manchester, has a larger Jewish colony than Leeds. Its members are chiefly employed in the tailoring trade. The Jews are hard workers at normal times: it is as much as even they can do, with their inexhaustible industry, to keep abreast of Government demands in war-time.

Little but khaki is to be seen in the Jewish quarter now; it may be an undersized errand-boy staggering under the weight of a dozen half-finished overcoats, or a girl wheeling a perambulator crammed full of newly stitched and buttoned tunics. There is a good deal of homework in these narrow streets of back-to-back houses, where the family washing is hung across the road, every window is shut fast against the clean air that blows in somehow from the northern moorlands through the smoke-pall of a thousand chimneys.

Men and women are toiling all day and long into the night, and some of them are making small fortunes. Indeed, the whole city has probably never been so prosperous . . . The mills are working twenty-four hours a day and in some cases seven days a week. The main shift now begins at 6 a.m. and does not knock off until 8 p.m., with $1\frac{1}{2}$ hours for meals. It is a terrific working day in hot and noisy mills. . . . The dividing line between day and night is so obliterated that despair fills the heart of many a 'knocker-up', the man with the long pole who taps at the workers' windows with the cry, 'Three o'clock; all a-windy and a-blowing', like the night watchman of old.

9

Sheffield's Blood-Red Glare

Sheffield has been getting rather tired of the swaggering bluster of the panegyrists of Essen and Charlottenburg. Krupps have never been, and, as far as our information goes, can never hope to be, the equals of Sheffield in the craft of naval armour . . .

Since the outbreak of war wonderful things have been done in the secret labyrinths of the Atlas, Cyclops, and River Don Works. The thrilling machines of an armament factory, rolling mills which smooth out the raw steel into armour plate, hydraulic presses which squeeze 100-ton ingots into guns, 10-fathom oil tanks in which the ordnance is dipped for tempering, mammoth travelling-cranes, blast furnaces that throw a blood-red glare on the screen of night, are performing prodigies of well-ordered strength.

The war has caused some striking changes in the life and thought of the city. For a time the Army was badly in need of razors. Labour became so scarce that the razor-manufacturers had to appeal to Sheffield for help in their difficulty. The manufacturers met and patriotically resolved to inform the Cutlers' Company that they would be rendering a great national service by collecting razors from private donors and putting them into serviceable order for the troops . . .

There is no virtual prohibition of the enlistment of armament workers. The workmen remaining in the city are putting in very long hours every day, and they are earning more money than they have ever earned before. Indeed, the only complaint heard is that the men have too little time in which to spend their earnings.

'England in Time of War', *The Times*, London, December 1914–February 1915.

3. DELIVERING THE GOODS

Punch (1915)

CHAPTER 7

DELIVERING THE GOODS

For the first few months of the war the public at home were allowed to know very little of the real state of affairs at the front in France. A strict censorship was in operation, and the communiqués issued by G.H.Q. were blandly uninformative when they were not downright misleading. But in the spring of 1915 rumours began to spread, of shell-shortage so acute that the guns had to be rationed, while the Germans seemed to have abundant supplies of everything needful. Then Lord Northcliffe's newspapers, *The Times* and the *Daily Mail*, published their shocking exposures, of brave men deluged with German shells and unable to make any effective reply.

The resulting public outcry was such that Mr Asquith was obliged to reconstruct his government on a Coalition basis. In the Cabinet formed at the end of May there was found place for a Minister of Munitions, and the man chosen for the post was, inevitably, Lloyd George – inevitably, because for months past the Chancellor of the Exchequer had been well aware of what was going on and had urged again and again that the whole business of munitions supply should be taken out of the incompetent hands of the War Office and organized on a national scale.

The news of Lloyd George's appointment went a long way towards allaying the popular discontent. Already he had acquired the reputation of being a man of action, so that great things were expected of him. Even before his appointment as Minister of Munitions, indeed, *Punch* had published a cartoon, 'Delivering the Goods', showing Lloyd George driving, in place of the ambulance-wagon of earlier days, a shell-packed ammunition-wagon drawn by the twin steeds Capital and Labour.

The new Minister was quick off the mark. In the first week of June he toured the chief engineering centres, with a view to harnessing local experience and enthusiasm to munitions production. 'Capital' proved reasonably co-operative, but 'Labour' was in a suspicious mood, resentful of the high profits that the employers were said to be making, and complaining bitterly of the way in which wages lagged behind the ever-increasing cost of living. In speech after speech Lloyd George made his 'appeal to the workshops', but his proposals, which were interpreted in some quarters as an attempt to 'fasten forced labour on the working classes', went too far for public opinion. The Munitions of War Act

(July 1915) did not go as far as he wished, but all the same, it limited the right to strike on munitions work, suspended (for the duration of the war) a number of trade union restrictive practices, and severely limited the freedom of munition workers to change their jobs. These measures aroused stiff opposition among the more militant trade unionists, and the situation on the Clyde became so menacing that Lloyd George had to spend Christmas morning trying to persuade some thousands of workers to give of their best in the nation's war effort.

On the whole, Lloyd George was remarkably successful. One of his most important innovations was the appointment of prominent businessmen – hustlers, men of 'push and go' – to important executive posts. Even more important was the recruitment of female labour on an unprecedented scale. Yet another departure from accepted practice was the Ministry's assumption of responsibility for the health and welfare of all those employed in munitions and allied establishments. This combination of new ideas and new methods enabled him, as is stated in the *History of the Ministry of Munitions*, to lay 'the foundations of the Ministry's productive capacity on a scale so vast that it was almost sufficient . . . to carry the country to the end of the war'.

1

The Appeal to the Workshops

This great conflict . . . is a war of munitions. We are fighting against the best-organized community in the world, the best organized whether for war or peace, and we have been employing too much the haphazard, leisurely, go-as-you-please methods, which, believe me, would not have enabled us to maintain our place as a nation, even in peace, very much longer.

The nation now needs all the machinery that is capable of being used for turning out munitions or equipment, all the skill that is available for that purpose, all the industry, all the labour, and all the strength, power and resource of everyone to the utmost . . .

The regulations, the customs and practices, which may be, and probably are, of great service in times of peace are utterly inapplicable and out of place in this terrible urgency of war.

The enlisted workman cannot say, 'Well, I am prepared to fight at Neuve Chapelle, but I won't fight at Festubert, and I am not going near that place they call "Wipers".' He cannot say, 'Well, I have been in the trenches ten hours and a half, and my trade union won't allow me to work more than ten hours.' He cannot say, 'You have not enough men, and I have been doing the work of two men. My trade union won't allow me to do more than my own share.' The veteran who has been seven years at the job, seven years in the Army, cannot say, 'Who is this fellow by my side – this mere fledgling? He has only had just a few weeks' training, and it is against my union's regulations, and I am off . . .'

Everything must give place to duty, good fellowship, comradeship, and determination to put the whole of your strength into the victory for your native land and for the liberties of the world.

D. LLOYD GEORGE at Manchester, June 4, 1915.

2

Appeal to the Miners

I have seen the miner in many spheres and capacities. I have seen him as a worker, and there is no better. I have seen him as a politician, and

4. SELF OR COUNTRY?

Coventry Striker: 'If I was a soldier and they tried to shift me to another part of the line just as I was comfortable, I'd down tools.'
Fighting Man: 'No, you wouldn't. If you were a soldier you'd be out to down Huns.'

Punch (1918)

there is no sounder. I have heard him as a singer, and there is no sweeter. I have seen him as a footballer, and he is terrible to behold. I have seen him sometimes – you must forgive me for reminding you – as a striker, and he is very difficult. I have seen him as a soldier, and there is no better warrior in Europe. In all capacities he is always in deadly earnest, always courageous, always a loyal, steadfast friend but a dangerous foe.

The Government appeal to him today as a friend, as their friend, as the country's friend, as the friend of liberty in all lands and in every clime. We are short of coal to run the country in a great crisis. We are suffering from the patriotism of the miner. A quarter of a million of them have gone into the fighting line. The demand for coal is greater than ever; the supply of labour is less than ever.

In times of peace coal is the most important element in the industrial life of the country. The blood which courses through the veins of industry in this country is made of distilled coal. In peace and in war 'King Cole' is the paramount lord of industry. It enters into every article of consumption and of utility. It is our real international coinage. We buy goods abroad, food and raw material; we pay, not in gold but in coal.

In war it is life for us and death for our foes. It not merely fetches and carries for us; it makes the material and the machinery which it transports. It bends, it moulds, it fills the weapons of war. Steam means coal. Rifles mean coal. Machine-guns mean coal. Cannon mean coal. Shells are made with coal – the very explosive inside them. And then coal carries them on right into the battlefield to help our men . . .

D. LLOYD GEORGE at London Opera House, July 29, 1915

3

'Spare in money – spill in blood'

It is too early to talk about over-production. The most fatuous way of economizing is to produce an inadequate supply. A good margin is but a sensible insurance. Less than enough is a foolish piece of extravagance. £200,000,000 will produce an enormous quantity of ammunition. It is forty days' cost of the war. If you have it at the crucial moment your war might be won in the forty days. If you have *not* got it, it might run to four hundred days. What sort of economy is that?

But it is not merely that. It is this – *What you spare in money you spill in blood.*

I have a very remarkable photograph of the battlefield of Loos, taken immediately after the battle. There was barbed wire which had not been destroyed. There was one machine-gun emplacement intact – only one. The others had been destroyed. There, in front of the barbed wire, lay hundreds of gallant men . . .

These are the accidents you can obviate. How? Every soldier tells me there is only one way of doing it. You must have enough ammunition to crash in every trench wherein the enemy lurks, to destroy every concrete emplacement, to shatter every machine-gun, to rend and tear every yard of barbed wire, so that if the enemy want to resist they will have to do it in the open, face to face with men better than themselves. That is the secret – plenty of ammunition . . .

You must spend wisely. You must spend to the best purpose. You must not pay extravagant prices. But for Heaven's sake, if there are risks to be taken, let them be risks for the pocket of the taxpayer, and not for the lives of the soldiers!

D. LLOYD GEORGE, House of Commons, December 20, 1915.

4

Christmas Morning in Glasgow

On Saturday morning [December 15, 1915] St Andrew's Hall was fairly well filled. . . . The meeting began with a storm of hissing and booing, and the Chairman [Mr Arthur Henderson, M.P.] suffered a running fire of interruption. . . . On rising to speak Mr Lloyd George was received with loud and continued booing and hissing. There was some cheering, certainly, and about a score of hats were waved in the area, but the meeting was violently hostile. Two verses of *The Red Flag* were sung before the Minister could utter a word. Owing to the incessant interruption, and the numerous altercations going on throughout the hall, it was quite impossible to catch every word of Mr Lloyd George's speech.

'. . . Let me put this to you, friends: Whilst we are comfortable at home on a Christmas day – (interruption – "No sentiment; we're here for business") – there are hundreds of thousands of our fellow-countrymen, some of them our sons, some of them our brothers, in the trenches facing death. ("You're here to talk about the dilution of labour.") It's on their behalf, and at their written request, that I come here to put before the workmen of Glasgow their appeal for help.

'We need a very large number of heavy guns and projectiles, and I am going to put before you a business proposition. ("For the exploiters.") Do you think these men in the trenches are exploiters? ("Don't hedge.") ("The shipowners are doing their bit.") Do let me state the facts. ("We know them.") . . . What steps have we taken? We have started great National Factories, State-owned and State-controlled; every timber and nail in them belonging to the State. My friends, these are great Socialist factories. (Violent interruption.) Believe me, the whole of them owned by the State, erected by the State; no profit made by any Capitalist, because they don't belong to the Capitalist.

'What is the issue? Does anyone deny that these factories we are building are State factories? (A voice: "Yes.") If you deny that, you would deny anything . . .

'Is it too much to ask the British workman to help his comrades in the field? ("No; what about the Munititions Act?") . . . I want to talk to you in all sincerity as a man brought up in a worker's home. I know as much about the life of the worker as any man here. The responsibility of a Minister of the Crown in a great war is no enviable one. ("The money's good," and laughter.) I can assure you it is no laughing matter.

'There will be unheard-of changes in every country in Europe; changes that go to the root of our social system. You Socialists watch them. It is a convulsion of nature; not merely a cyclone that sweeps away the ornamental plants of modern society and wrecks the flimsy trestle-bridges of modern civilization – it is more. It is an earthquake that upheaves the very rocks of European life.

'And to go on chaffering about a regulation here, and the suspension of a custom there, under these conditions – why, it is just haggling with an earthquake. Workmen, may I make one appeal to you? (Interruption.) Lift up your eyes above the mist of suspicion and distrust. Rise to the heights of the great opportunity now before you. If you do, you will emerge after this War is over into a future which has been the dream of many a great leader.' (Cheers: loud hissing and booing.)

Forward (Glasgow Socialist weekly), January 1, 1916; quoted as Appendix XIX, *History of the Ministry of Munitions* (1921), vol. 4, pt 4, pp. 176–80.

5

Farewell to the Ministry

In his farewell to a department which he had entered with 'a great deal of anxiety', Mr Lloyd George reminded his hearers of his first day at the Ministry.

'There was a table. I forget whether there were one or two chairs, but there was no carpet allowed by the Board of Works. That was not in the Regulations. I believe I had a greater struggle over getting that carpet than I had over getting 50 millions for munitions. I said to Dr Addison: "Look at that table! Do you see those two chairs?" "Yes," he said, "what is the matter with them?" I said, "Those are the Ministry of Munitions."'

He showed how within a year the Ministry had grown by the exertions of 'a body of picked men from every sphere of life . . . every profession, the Civil Service, every trade and every industry in England and the Colonies', and by hard work throughout the office from those at the top down to the 'little girls bustling about the corridors carrying messages', into a department administering between 400 and 500 millions a year, a department which had quickened the industry of the country and inaugurated a new epoch in the productive economy of the British nation.

'I have never seen a department work like it. . . . There was a cheerful activity; it was like an ant-heap, each one carrying a bigger load than himself, and carrying it successfully until at last this great structure was built up which has made its mark on the history of the country and on the history of the world.'

History of the Ministry of Munitions, vol. 2, pt. 1, pp. 45–6.

CHAPTER 8

HEALTH AND WELFARE OF MUNITION WORKERS

As Minister of Munitions Lloyd George was primarily concerned with 'delivering the goods', but at the same time he saw in his appointment a golden opportunity for 'introducing into industry a great forward movement' for improving the condition of the workers, adult and juvenile, men and women. With this end in view he appointed in September 1915 the Health of Munition Workers Committee, charged 'to consider and advise on questions of industrial fatigue, hours of labour, and other matters affecting the personal health and efficiency of workers in munition factories and workshops'.

The Committee was a strong one, representing the concentrated experience of the Home Office Factory Department, employers and employed, and medical experts. Its chairman was Sir George Newman, MD, formerly chief medical officer to the Board of Education, and among its members were J. R. Clynes, prominent Trade Unionist and Labour MP, Mrs Tennant, who as Miss Abraham had been one of the first 'lady inspectors', and Miss Rose Squire, a serving member of the Factory inspectorate. In due course the Committee issued two Reports: an Interim (Cd. 8511) in 1917 and a Final (Cd. 9065) in 1918 plus seventeen Memoranda on a variety of subjects and a number of other publications intended for more general circulation.

Speaking in February 1916 Lloyd George paid a warm tribute to the Committee's work. 'It is a strange irony,' he said, 'but no small compensation, that the making of weapons of destruction should afford the occasion to humanize industry. Yet such has been the case.'

I

Looking After the Women and Girls

The fact that women and girls of all types and ages have pressed and are pressing into industry shows a spirit of patriotism which is as finely maintained as it was quickly shown. Conditions of work are accepted without question and without complaint which would, if continued, be ultimately disastrous to health. It is for the nation to safeguard the devotion of its workers by its foresight and watchfulness lest irreparable harm be done to body and mind both in this generation and the next.

Night Work

The imperative necessity of war has revived, after almost a century of disuse, the night employment of women in factories. Prohibited for the textile trades by the factory legislation of 1844, it disappeared gradually in Great Britain, and also in other countries, until it was banished by international agreement from the twelve European countries which signed the Convention drawn up by the International Conference held at Berne in 1906.

The agreement was based upon the results of enquiries into the effects, economical, physical, and moral, of night work upon women. The reports showed deterioration in health caused by the difficulty of securing sufficient rest by day; disturbance of home life with its injurious effects upon the children; and diminished value of the work done – the common experience being that night work was inferior to day work. Now once more all the half-forgotten facts are in evidence in Munition Factories.

Evidence is highly conflicting as to the merits of continuous night work as against those of a weekly, fortnightly or monthly change of shift. . . . It has been stated by some managers and foremen that the last few hours of a twelve-hour shift yield little output . . .

In one factory visited at night the manager stated that fatigue prevented many women from making the effort to go from their work to the mess-room, though in itself the room was attractive. In another, visited also at night, several women were lying, during the meal hour, beside their piles of heaped-up work; while others, later, were asleep beside their machines. . . . The Committee are satisfied, therefore, that the employment of women at night calls for particular care and supervision, and that adequate pauses for rest and meals are indispensable.

House Accommodation and Transit

While the mother's time, and the time of the elder girls, is largely given to the making of munitions, the home and the younger children must inevitably suffer. Where home conditions are bad, as they frequently are, where a long working day is aggravated by long hours of travelling, and where, in addition, housing accommodation is inadequate, family life is defaced beyond recognition.

If the home is to be preserved from such processes of destruction, greatly improved conditions of transit and housing must be secured, as well as the best possible hours of work by night and day. It is far from uncommon now to find some two or three hours spent on the journey each way, generally under the fatiguing conditions of an overcrowded train or tram, often with long waits, and a severe struggle before even standing room is obtained.

The superintendent of a factory situated in a congested district stated that the women constantly arrive with their clothes torn in the struggle for a tram, the satchel in which they bring their tea being sometimes torn away. The workers were of an exceptionally refined type, to whom such rough handling would be altogether unfamiliar, but they bore these conditions with cheerful resolution.

Tribute is continually paid by foremen and managers to a similar spirit; they tell of workers readily working overtime in the knowledge that their action means the loss of the last tram and a four- or five-mile walk at midnight.

Often far from offering rest from the fatigue of the day, the home conditions offer but fresh aggravation. A day begun at 4 or even 3.30 a.m. for work at 6 a.m., followed by 14 hours in the factory, and another two or two and a half hours on the journey back, may end at 10 or 10.30 p.m. in a home or lodging where the prevailing degree of overcrowding precludes all possibility of comfortable rest. Beds are never empty and rooms are never aired, for in a badly-crowded district, the beds, like the occupants, are organized in day and night shifts. In such conditions of confusion, pressure and overcrowding, home can have no existence.

Hours of Labour

Long hours, particularly when they are worked during the night, are perhaps the chief factor in fatigue. . . . The importance to women of a wise limitation of their hours of work and an appropriate distribution of the pauses in those hours can hardly be overstated. . . . The three systems of employment most commonly adopted for women in munition works are: One shift of 13–14 hours; two shifts of 12 hours; three shifts of 8 hours. Of these the system of 8-hour shifts appears to yield the best results in the long run . . .

Where women are employed on eight-hour shifts an interval of half an hour for a meal may be regarded as normally sufficient, but where longer hours are worked it is important that they should be allowed an hour for dinner and for the principal meal during the night. Half an hour provides but scant time for the eating of the meal. Ten minutes are easily spent in reaching the mess-room and returning to work, certainly another five are occupied in the washing of hands and in the service of the dinner. And so but fifteen remain for the meal.

Sanitary Condition of the Factory

The effect upon the health and energy of women and girls which results from clean, bright and airy workrooms, well warmed in winter, can hardly be exaggerated. . . . The refreshing effect of washing and its influence on self-respect, especially where the workers are heated by their work, have been dwelt upon by many witnesses.

The lavatories . . . should be provided with a good supply of hot and cold water, soap and nailbrushes. Clean towels should be supplied before every meal, and the lavatories should be kept scrupulously clean. Cloakrooms should provide facilities for changing clothes and boots and for drying clothes in bad weather.

The provision of adequate and suitable sanitary accommodation is a matter of special importance. The necessity for proper equipment and the maintenance of cleanliness, privacy and convenience of access should be borne in mind. It is the more necessary to call attention to this matter since in many instances women are now employed in factories where, until quite recently, there have been male workers only . . .

Physical Condition of Women Workers

It is obvious that many women now entering upon employment in the factory system are quite unaccustomed to its conditions. In considering the physical capacity of such a woman to withstand the fatigue consequent upon continued work of this kind it should be remembered that her body is physiologically different from, and less strongly built, than that of a man; that her muscular system is less developed; and that she may have lived a sedentary or domestic life and is not in the habit of taking active and regular exercise . . .

The lifting and carrying of heavy weights and all sudden, violent, or physically unsuitable movements in the operating of machines should, as far as possible, be avoided. . . . Prolonged standing has been found a highly provocative cause of trouble to women and girls. When standing is absolutely unavoidable, the hours and spells of employment should be proportionately short, and seats should be available for use during the brief pauses which occasionally occur while waiting for material, or for the adjustment of a tool.

Management and Supervision

Briefly, the Committee recommend that in all cases where women are employed, consideration should be given to the appointment of Forewomen, Nurses and Welfare Supervisors.

The Committee have watched, in several factories, a steady stream of workers bringing to the nurse troubles of many kinds; sometimes a girl who has just fainted, or a girl whose feet are badly swollen by long standing; or hands have been injured, or eyes struck by a splinter of steel; or there is a burn from some boiling splashing liquid or from some explosion in the danger area.

Health of Munition Workers Committee, *Memorandum No. 4: Employment of Women*, Cd. 8185, pp. 3–9.

2

Cases of Pregnancy

A pregnant woman in this [National Ordnance] factory is expected to see me that I may assure myself that her work is not harmful to her in any way. Provided that the work is not injurious to her, she is retained as long as possible. . . . When the child is three months old the mother is reinstated at her old work . . .

The case of the unmarried mother presents greater difficulties. It is a great anxiety to me to obtain the necessary knowledge early enough to be able to assure the girl that care will be taken of her during her pregnancy and help given her in her trouble. I have found that once her confidence is gained and the girl understands that for her child's sake she is entitled to every care, a much happier and healthier state of mind and body exists. Should there be no home care available for the girl during her confinement . . . we generally manage to keep her at quiet work until very close to her confinement, and she is admitted to the [Workhouse] Infirmary immediately on application.

I have never deviated from my rule regarding the three months' absence from the factory, even in the case of the homeless girl, but some arrangement has always been made for her care and well-being. Friends have been found for her and she has had a weekly grant from the Hospital and Benevolent Fund, also advice and help as to putting her in the way of receiving maintenance from the father of the child.

I have, at different times, brought in a girl, whose case has been difficult to deal with, to work as cleaner in the Canteen on days only. The baby comes with its mother and lies (in summer) in a cot on the verandah. The baby thrives, and is a source of interest and joy to the factory girls . . .

A Woman Welfare Supervisor, Cd. 9065, p. 24.

3

Female Ailments

The ailments most frequently observed are all frequently met with among women workers, and cannot be attributed specially to munition work.

Indigestion in many forms was noted. Pain after food was fairly common, but was often explained by an unsuitable choice of food. The amount of tea consumed is large, but the tea seemed practically always to be freshly made, and was drunk at once, so that ill-effects were probably not produced as a rule.

Constipation Most workers seemed to take aperients fairly regularly. In one factory nearly all the workers, and especially the younger ones, took salts, usually with their morning tea, two or three times a week, before beginning work. *Lack of appetite* was most frequent on the night shift, a considerable number stating that they could not eat substantial meals in the night. Many had no desire for a proper breakfast.

Headache was often an accompaniment of anaemia or constipation, and in other cases was undoubtedly due to eye strain. *Anaemia* was particularly common where arrangements for meals were not satisfactory, and difficulties of transit existed. *Muscular pains, foot-ache*, etc., often due to prolonged standing, were common. Few cases of flat-foot were noted, and the foot-ache usually disappeared to a great extent, though the feet and ankles of girls obliged to stand during the whole shift were apt to become swollen towards the end of the day or on the night shift.

Disorders of menstruation occurred in a certain proportion of workers, and in some cases had increased with factory life usually either in young workers unaccustomed to standing or in older women with climacteric symptoms. . . . The medical findings are on the whole satisfactory . . . Most of the inspectors had expected to find far more fatigue directly attributable to the conditions of work, and were agreeably surprised at the general physical condition of the workers.

JANET M. CAMPBELL, MD, and LILIAN E. WILSON, MD, Cd. 8511 (1917), pp. 115–16.

4

Rules for 'Exporting' Female Labour

Only normally healthy, clean and wholesome women and girls should be exported [i.e. recruited and sent to work in a munitions factory away from home]. In some cases women and girls received in lodgings and hostels have been found to be in such a condition of person and clothing that the assistance of the sanitary authority had to be invoked for cleansing or disinfection. In other cases women and girls have been imported who suffer from physical disabilities, or are in an unsuitable physical condition. In some instances women of bad character have been associated in lodgings or hostels with respectable women and girls.

Such instances, even if not numerous, exert far-reaching effect, and rumours spread quickly through a neighbourhood, losing nothing by repetition, and cause many housewives to close their doors against munition workers as lodgers.

The Committee accordingly suggest that all women and girls, before being exported, should be examined by a doctor or by a nurse working under his supervision.

Mothers of infants or of families of young children should not be exported. The arrival of mothers in a town accompanied by quite young infants, or three or four young children, having travelled long distances, is by no means uncommon – the mother is attracted, in the absence of the father on active service, by the prospects of high wages in munition works, and brings her baby or children with her. To find lodgings where these are not unwelcome, and where someone will undertake the care of the children while the mother is out at the factory, is no easy task. The Committee consider that this practice of taking children across country by train to some distant munition area, and leaving them to strangers all day or all night, should be discouraged.

No woman or girl should be exported without a sufficiency of clothing or of money. Women and girls frequently arrive at munition centres without luggage or any clothing except what they are wearing, and without any money; they are often hungry and thirsty, having had no food on a long journey. In some cases poverty is the cause, in many others the reason given has been that they had heard that everything necessary was provided free. As the first wages are not due for a week, and frequently are not paid until after ten days or a fortnight, the plight of these women and girls in a strange town is not only uncomfortable, but a serious danger . . .

Travellers across country should be seen off and met at the station. The need for this protection of those unaccustomed to travel, especially if the distance is great, is well recognized. Where such services have not been organized, serious inconvenience and evil has arisen in many instances. To meet these difficulties, arrangements are generally made to meet them at the station on arrival, and direct them to the Employment Exchange or lodgings.

A reception or clearing-house should be provided for any women and girls arriving without having secured lodgings, and for whom such cannot be found before nightfall. . . . The house should be under the charge of a lady superintendent with considerable experience in dealing with women under any emergency; she should preferably have had some nursing training, and be a person of kindly, tactful character. The inmates should have separate cubicles, adequate washing and bathroom accommodation, and facilities for washing clothing should also be provided. Good plain appetizing food and a cheerful warm sitting-room are necessary.

A homeless woman or girl, full of vague fears at taking up unaccustomed work, especially in an explosives factory, may spread uneasiness and even alarm among her associates. Depression and fear are contagious, and have been known to cause many to return home the day after arrival. But cheerfulness and courage are also contagious, and the influence of a lady superintendent or voluntary helpers among new arrivals at a reception hostel is of great value. The stay is generally only for a night or two – a week, unless the case be exceptional, should be the maximum – the inmates being found suitable lodging [or hostel accommodation] at the earliest moment.

CD. 9065 (1918), pp. 113–14.

5

Living in a Hostel

Hostels have not always been popular. The objections most commonly put forward by women and girls and by their trades unions have included the following: (a) Girls dislike the idea of living in large communities or of spending their leisure hours with the persons with whom they work and with whom they may have no sympathy or social affinity. (b) However well organized a hostel may be, some restrictions on personal liberty are inevitable. (c) When a hostel is provided by a private firm the girls are subject to the control of the firm during the whole 24 hours. If they lose their job they are likely at the same time to lose their place of board and residence. (d) Hostels are not always self-supporting, and girls object to being 'beholden' to anyone, most of all to the firm by whom they are employed . . .

Much depends upon the personality of the Superintendent and upon the character of her assistants and servants. As much freedom as is compatible with good order should be allowed; the inmates are independent workers not living under any community rule. The bedrooms should be self-contained cubicles. The dining- and recreation-rooms should be bright, airy, and well warmed. The need should be recognized for rest and the companionship of a few friends, and should be met by the provision of a sufficient number of small sitting-rooms. The absence of these has doomed some otherwise satisfactory hostels to failure, since many women and girls soon tire of organized recreation night after night, and having worked hard in a factory for many hours crave the quiet rest of a room more nearly resembling home.

Cd. 9065, pp. 114–15.

6

Recreational Facilities

Emphasis has been laid on the importance and the necessity of providing the relief from monotony and the change of environment which are essential aids to recovery from fatigue.

The question is one of special importance in areas where large numbers of workers have been congregated, and are thus deprived of the means of recreation to which they are accustomed. Especially should the leisure of the week-end be provided for. This important matter cannot be left to chance. If opportunities for wholesome amusement, refreshment and recreation are not provided, the public-houses and less desirable places of entertainment may benefit, but everybody else suffers.

Until recently there has not been in any munition area a systematic attempt to cope with the problems of industrial recreation, or even to co-ordinate the activities of such organizations as exist. The Committee are, however, glad to recognize the increased attention now being paid to the subject.

The clubs established are very varied in character and provide for men and women, as well as for boys and girls. In addition to the usual games, indoor recreation includes concerts, dances, theatricals, lectures, cinemas, classes of various kinds, including physical exercises, dancing, and dressmaking. Open-air provision includes games, swimming, and open-air camps. Mixed clubs for men and women are increasingly popular. . . . The need should not be overlooked for providing small clubs easily accessible to tired workers, who desire quiet occupation, and may not wish to journey to more central institutions.

In more than one instance, it has been found practicable to arrange for well-to-do residents to offer hospitality in their own houses during Saturday and Sunday to parties of women and girls, and to allow the use of their gardens in summer. Such facilities are greatly appreciated, and may do much to remove class prejudices and misunderstandings.

Cd. 9065, p. 117.

7

'A Day of My Life as a Welfare Supervisor'

At 9 a.m. I clock on (we all do this from the manager downwards) and start dealing with letters. These are of all kinds: postcards returned by absentees explaining why they are away from work, letters from other factories asking for the characters of women who have left us, letters from solicitors and the Finance Department of the Ministry of Munitions about compensation cases, letters from women and girls asking for work.

I read the report left by the assistant supervisor on night duty. Perhaps the shop has been too hot or too cold, there has been a theft in the cloakroom, an operator and a viewer have had a quarrel, a pipe has burst in the lavatory; there are also several complaints that the train from W— arrives so late that the women have to run from the station to be at the factory before the gates close, and reach their work in an exhausted condition . . .

The next business is to deal with absentees. After three days' absence each case is either visited or written to. In many cases we decide to ask for help from the Welfare Committee, a kind of benevolent society to which all workers subscribe and which gives grants in cases of necessity, hospital notes where special medical attention is needed, convalescent changes, etc.

Choosing labour can be a very skilled work when there is an ample supply to choose from, and no great hurry in filling vacancies. Each worker should be just the right type for the work she is put to; she should be examined medically and her references taken up, or, in the case of young workers, her character from school enquired into. One rejects the old, the infirm, the undersized, the short-sighted, the dirty, the flashy, the anaemic and the corpulent.

Ever since I came in at 9 o'clock there has been a constant stream of women from the shops with questions and complaints. Mrs A – wants a job on days as her husband is ill and cannot be left at nights; Elsie B – complains that the charge hand is always 'shouting' at her; three viewers state that their rises are due but have not been given; two operators are not satisfied that their wages are correct, and the matter has to be thrashed out.

Although I have not been in the shop, my assistant has been there off and on all the morning, either in the little works office or walking about the shop. The women go to her with difficulties and complaints, and the forewomen, too, for advice, and she is in close touch with superintendents and foremen, helping them to smooth over the many difficulties arising out of the employment of large numbers of both sexes. When she is not in the office she is walking round the shop seeing that the girls are behaving well, wearing their caps, and are not loitering about the cloakrooms and lavatories, also that the latter are well supplied with towels, soap, etc.

I take with me into the shop notes of the matters I have to discuss with the superintendents and works manager, and when I have seen them I walk round and note new developments, the drinking fountains for which I have agitated are being put up, a new pattern of seat is being fixed to the machines, a big draught from an opening which might be closed up. . . . On my way back to the office I call at the ambulance-room and see that all is well there. The sister in charge tells me of a woman who has been in with bad varicose veins who should not be standing at her work; she tells me that one of the nurses wants to leave, and warns me that an old woman has been in with an old wound which has broken out again, but which she is claiming to be a fresh injury for which she requires compensation.

My assistant comes back before 1.30 so as to be free during the last half of the dinner hour. Sometimes she has arranged a concert and sometimes the members of the military or the orchestra bolt their own meal so as to entertain the others, but none of these things happen as often as we would like, as unfortunately our canteen does not lend itself to entertainment. Occasionally we have a War Saving or other meeting, but here again we are hampered by the unsuitability of the building. A little before 6 o'clock the matron comes down and speaks to me about towels and soap and overalls and other domestic details.

At 6.15 p.m. there is a meeting of the Sports and Recreation Committee. Having had a most successful dance the night before (which, by the way, kept me up until after 11 o'clock though I was only a wall-flower) we decide to organize a series of whist drives for the various sections of the works, followed in each case by a few dances. The football section sends a report on the first half-season's play, and we get a satisfactory account from the Choral Society of their performance of the concert version of *Merry England*. A discussion on finance follows, and it is after 7.30 when we get away.

If this imaginary day is a Tuesday, Wednesday or Thursday, I am now free to go home, but two nights a week I go back to the factory after a hasty dinner and stay until 9 o'clock seeing the new people who are turning in for the night shift and making a final tour of the shop before the night supervisor takes over.

Cd. 9065, pp. 103–4.

8

What Miss Barker Accomplished at the Arsenal

About 18 months ago, bearing in mind that many of the women and girls employed in the Royal Arsenal were living in hostels and lodgings away from home, I drew up and inaugurated a scheme to provide for them social and educational facilities out of Arsenal hours. The result has more than passed my expectations, as some hundreds of women have availed themselves of the opportunities offered.

As many of the workers are engaged in processes necessitating a sitting position while at work, it seemed to me that provision should be made to counteract any ill-effects that might accrue from long hours of sedentary work: therefore I arranged that gymnastics, physical exercises, Morris and country dancing be included in the scheme. During the summer months, swimming is also included. I am sure that it is far better for women and girls to perform health-giving exercises under wise and trained supervision, than for them to walk about the darkened streets of the neighbourhood, aimlessly. Many of the workers are engaged in purely mechanical processes, and for these I felt that opportunity should be given for them to use their reasoning powers and to develop their intelligence. Therefore, I arranged for classes in dramatic literature, and elocution, thus giving students a taste for good reading.

A large proportion of the women being engaged on more or less dangerous work, I felt it would be wise for them to have some knowledge of first-aid, home nursing, etc. These classes are most popular, and have attracted large numbers, many of whom presented themselves for special examination and were granted certificates of proficiency by the London County Council.

[An application] to the London County Council for the loan of a neighbouring school met with a ready response; and on guaranteeing a sufficient number of students, the Council offered to provide and remunerate instructors and instructoresses. A charge of 1s per subject is made for each session. The curriculum includes gymnastics, physical exercises, Morris and country dancing, singing, dress and blouse making, etc. I may add that the men employed in the Arsenal are permitted to join in the singing, and the addition of their voices enables the class to enjoy the rehearsal of four-part glees, choruses, etc. This class has rehearsed Elgar's *Banner of St George* and assisted in the chorus of the mystery play, *Eager Heart*.

At varying times the students arrange social gatherings on Saturday evenings; each member of the class is allowed to invite a non-member, and the girls are specially encouraged to introduce their male friends. Twice at least during the season members of the gymnastic classes give displays in the Town Hall. The literature class also contributes a public performance, producing scenes from standard plays and authors. But though a large number can, and do, attend these classes, there is a far larger number who have no time for recreation except on Sundays. I therefore organized Sunday concerts at Woolwich Town Hall, for which we obtain the best talent possible, and at which we endeavour to reach a very high standard and tone . . .

Several hockey and football clubs have been organized throughout the winter. The members of the various classes and clubs have given performances for the entertainment of wounded soldiers. Another outcome of the scheme has been the inauguration during the winter season of a series of dances, under welfare supervision.

MISS LILIAN BARKER, Lady Superintendent, Woolwich Arsenal, Cd. 9065, pp. 118–19.

9

Working Conditions of Men and Boys

The enquiry extended over a period of six months, from the middle of February to the middle of August, 1916. Eight factories were selected for the examination, the works being situated in four of the principal industrial areas of England.

In the *very heavy trades* nearly all the men complained of feeling thoroughly tired and weary at the end of their day's work when the shift was more than 8 hours. The rarity of the 8-hour shift in these trades struck me as remarkable. . . . At one factory . . . the shop manager said that in his opinion the men had worked magnificently, but would not be able to continue at the same pressure . . .

This class of work causes the men to become very thirsty. For an onlooker, unaccustomed to industrial conditions such as these, the greatest sympathy for the workers is excited, because the effort called for is tremendous and the way these men perspire as a result of their heavy work and exposure to the furnace is astonishing. Beer is the usual refreshment. A few of the workers are abstainers from alcohol in any form. These latter are usually the most reliable men. When the supply of drink was restricted by the closing of the public-houses in the district, a great improvement in the health and the timekeeping of the workmen was noticed and was admitted by the men. No satisfactory substitute for beer, so far as is at present known, has been introduced. The use of such substitutes as oatmeal water and barley water is stated to cause skin eruptions and boils.

In the *heavy trades*, almost with one consent the men tell you that at the end of the day they have had as much as they can possibly stand. In many instances these men, in order to do their work satisfactorily, absent themselves for a couple of days for rest purposes. I am assured by the firms that so long as the departmental managers know that these men are absent justifiably, no notice is taken . . .

The physical fatigue of the *medium and light* occupations is not such that it produces a feeling of weariness and overwork of itself. Monotony and long hours added to weight of work are the chief causes. Several of the men I examined complained of the continuous work without a break. In these trades, both for men and boys, the effect of work and long hours is shown by the weariness and generally 'fed-up' conditions of the workers.

LLOYD GEORGE'S MUNITION GIRLS

Imperial War Museum

9. RIFLING A NAVAL GUN AT THE ROYAL ARSENAL, WOOLWICH.

Ministry of Munitions

10. Assembling fuses (top), and (below) turning the copper band of a 9·2-inch high-explosive shell.

Hours of Labour

The hours of labour were found to vary considerably. In some cases for boys under 14 years of age they were limited to 48, but in others boys of 18 were found to be working an average of over 80 hours per week, and it was ascertained that they had worked 90 and even 100 hours per week. In the case of men, the net average has ranged from 53 to 108 hours per week.

Hours of labour must be considered in relation to the distance many of the workers have to travel to and from their work. While engaged for 12 hours per day in the factory, they spend in a large number of cases from two and half to four hours travelling to and from their homes. . . . My general impression is that hours tend to be too long for the proper preservation of health and efficiency . . .

Works Canteens

Only four of the factories I visited had made this valuable addition to their establishment.

All the arrangements at the first factory were perfect. The space allocated was ample, and a large number of the workers, both male and female, took their meals at the canteen. The kitchen equipment was model in every detail, and the cleanliness of the whole place delightful. The service was most expeditious, 300 dinners being served in seven minutes. Any food brought by the workers was heated or cooked free of cost, and boiling water was also supplied free. Trolleys containing food such as Bovril, soup, sandwiches, pork pies, mineral waters and coffee were taken round all the shops at 11 a.m., 4 p.m., and 3 a.m. The canteen was open for both day and night shifts.

In the second works, canteens were numerous, but could in no way compare with the above. At the third a dining-room is provided but there is no provision for serving dinners. In the fourth the arrangements were fairly good. At one large steel works employing more than 10,000 men no canteen was then provided . . .

Washing Accommodation

In most of these factories, where men are engaged on very dirty work, and even where basins with hot water laid on were installed, towels were not provided. Soft soap is given to men engaged upon dirty, oily work, since it is difficult to clean thoroughly the hands without hot water and soap. . . . The boy workers are much keener about washing, and it is unfortunate that they should be brought up in industrial surroundings which prevent them from following closely their present taste for cleanliness . . .

CAPT. T. H. AGNEW, RAMC, *Report on the Health and Physical Condition of Male Munition Workers*, Cd. 8511, pp. 100–6.

10

How to Run a Factory Canteen

In order to ensure effective results of the establishment of Industrial Canteens, certain conditions seem to be essential. It is useless to establish a canteen which is inconvenient or unattractive. It should be situated near the works. The premises should include an ample dining-room, with a buffet bar attached, with separate accommodation for men and women. The food supplied should be varied, fresh, and good; suitable in quality and sufficient in quantity, well cooked, appetizing, and obtainable at low prices. For example:

Dinner – meat or fish, 2 veg.	4d – 8d
Hot-pot, cottage pie, meat puddings	2d – 4d
Meat pies and other prepared meat or egg dishes	2d – 4d
Soup, bovril, oxo, etc. (with bread)	1d – 2d
Puddings and stewed fruits	1d – 2d
Suet, bread, currant, jam and fruit puddings	1d – 2d
Bread and cheese	1d – 2d
Cakes, buns, jam tarts, bread and butter, sandwiches	1d – 2d
Tea, coffee, cocoa, milk, lemon, barley, aerated and mineral waters, etc., per cup or glass	½d – 1½d
All kinds of fresh fruit in season, oranges, lemons, bananas, prunes, plums, apples, pears, tomatoes, etc.	

In certain districts there may be a case for the establishment of 'wet' canteens, where alcoholic beverages may be obtainable. The quick service of meals is important . . . probably the best method is long serving counters from which workers fetch their own food.

SIR GEORGE NEWMAN, MD, Health of Munition Workers Committee, *Memorandum No. 3: Industrial Canteens*, Cd. 8133, pp. 4–6.

CHAPTER 9

'THE LURE OF THE DRINK'

Long before 1914 the British working-man had the reputation of being a boozer, and the vested interests of the Drink Trade were well content that he should remain so. But the outbreak of war created a new situation. The consumption of intoxicating liquors went up by leaps and bounds as a condition of full employment and good wages developed. Men who before had drunk nothing but beer now were able to indulge in spirits. Never had there been such boozing (if reports were to be believed) as was now going on in shipyards and industrial areas, and it was rumoured that large numbers of women and girls, most of whom had never tasted liquor before, were now joining the men in their spirituous spree.

Early in 1915 reports of failure to 'deliver the goods' because of bad time-keeping, absenteeism, and slack working came pouring in, and in a speech at Bangor Lloyd George denounced 'the lure of the drink' as a bigger enemy than all the German submarines. A month later he received at the Treasury a deputation from the Shipbuilders' Federation, and at his suggestion the Home Office arranged for a number of special investigations to be made of working conditions in the principal shipbuilding centres, the results of which were published in a White Paper, *Shipbuilding, Munitions, and Transport Areas.*

Some Government action was considered imperative to control and reduce an evil which was now seen to be assuming the most menacing proportions. The Shipbuilders' deputation had urged total prohibition during the period of the war of all excisable liquors, but it was speedily recognized that this went far beyond what public opinion would be prepared to sanction. Then it was proposed that the State should buy out all the private interests in the sale of drink, and this in turn was ruled out because of the immense cost and also because the Temperance party were firmly opposed to the State becoming directly involved in the supply of strong drink. In the event a compromise plan was worked out, providing for the establishment of a Liquor Control Board to exercise, by way of 'Orders', complete control over the sale of intoxicating liquor in areas to be specified (which by April 1917 covered nearly the whole of Great Britain), and this was speedily enacted.

I

'The Lure of the Drink'

Most of our workmen are putting every ounce of strength into this urgent work for their country, loyally and patriotically. But that is not true of all. There are some, I am sorry to say, who shirk their duty in this great emergency. I hear of workmen in armament works who refuse to work a full week's work for the nation's need. They are a minority. But, you must remember, a small minority of workmen can throw a whole works out of gear. What is the reason? Sometimes it is one thing, sometimes it is another, but let us be perfectly candid. It is mostly the lure of the drink. They refuse to work full time, and, when they return, their strength and efficiency are impaired by the way in which they have spent their leisure. Drink is doing us more damage in the War than all the German submarines put together.

D. LLOYD GEORGE at Bangor, February 28, 1915.

2

Drink and Shipbuilding

Shipbuilding is the main industry of the districts visited, but there are also many engineering works and other factories engaged on Government contracts. Owing to the demands made by the war . . . the pressure of work in these districts is unprecedented. The demand for labour is greater than the supply, especially as large numbers of the regular workmen have enlisted in the naval and military forces. Wages are uniformly high, which means a large increase in the spending power of the working classes. Wages of £5 or £6 a week are common, and it is possible for a skilled mechanic to earn as much as £10 or £15 a week.

The hours of work are about fifty-four a week, excluding overtime. The day is divided into two shifts of eleven or twelve hours with intervals for meals, but many of the men work overtime. There is also a certain amount of Sunday labour with the attraction of double pay, but this has not proved altogether a success. Steady workmen feel the strain of working seven a days a week, while others are disposed to work on Sundays and lose time on other days.

An important feature of shipbuilding is the system of working in gangs consisting of two riveters, one holder-up and one or two boys. While many of the men are working regularly and steadily beyond the normal hours, there is a considerable number, especially among the 'black squad' in the shipbuilding yards who are not working up to the maximum of their capacity.

The reasons given for irregularities of attendance are mainly statements of fatigue due to long hours over an extended period; unusually high wages leading to idleness; and habits of drinking. The reports are unanimous in the conclusion that drink is by far the most important factor.

Many of the workmen engaged in these industries are, in normal times, heavy drinkers, partly, no doubt, owing to the nature of the work. Much of it is hard manual labour in severe heat, which creates a desire for stimulant. It is not suggested that all the workmen drink heavily. Many of them are abstemious, and in Scotland especially there is a considerable proportion of teetotallers. To those who are heavy drinkers, the facilities for drinking are unfortunately very great. An instance is given in one street where there were no less than thirty public-houses within a distance of half a mile. The yards and works are surrounded by public-houses and drinking bars, where every possible facility is offered for obtaining drink for consumption both on and off the premises.

The drinking habits of the workmen on the Clyde differ somewhat from those of the English workmen. The popular drink there is half a gill of whisky, quickly followed by a schooner of beer (about ¾ pint), and the beer is of a heavier quality than English beer. This particular combination of liquor, though it does not apparently produce much effect on the hardened drinkers at the moment, is not calculated to improve the capacity of the men for sustained work. Heavy drinking on Saturday in the public-houses, and on Sundays in clubs, is described as a feature of the life of the workmen on the Clyde, which frequently results in unfitness or loss of time at the beginning of the week. There is also a prevalent custom in Scotland of taking whisky in bottles home in the evening, especially on Saturday night for consumption on Sunday when the public-houses are closed.

On the Tyne, and in Barrow, spirit drinking is not so common, as the popular drink is beer, and the English workman's drinking appears to be more evenly distributed over the week, though the effect is very much the same in all the districts referred to.

Apart from the public-house great facilities for drinking are offered by clubs, which are open to members and to which visitors can be readily introduced. These places are freely resorted to on Sundays when the public-houses are closed.

Attention is drawn in the reports to the fact that many of the workmen take insufficient food, which not only increases the temptation to drink, but makes the effect of the liquor taken more injurious, so that the result is to incapacitate the workmen for the strain of heavy work. The men whose homes are near the works are able to obtain meals without difficulty, but owing to the lack of housing accommodation many workmen are obliged to travel long distances to get to their work. This is especially the case at Barrow-in-Furness. The usual practice is for the workmen to take cold food with them, which is generally consumed in the public-houses with their liquor. Reference is made in some of the reports to cases where food could not be obtained at the public-houses, and it is evident that the sale of drink is out of all proportion to that of food. The reports emphasize the need for mess-rooms and canteens in the yards where the men could get good meals in comfort without having to resort to the public-houses. Such accommodation is very rarely provided.

The practice of paying the whole wages of a black squad to the leader is also said to be productive of drinking as the men go to the public-house to divide the money, and the custom is for each member of the squad to stand drinks all round.

Much absenteeism is caused by the 'black squad' system. If one of the members is absent from idleness, or drinking, the rest of the squad is held up, and where several squads are affected the cumulative result is very marked.

The evils of excessive drinking are readily admitted by some of the better workmen, who considered that the action of a minority was bringing unmerited discredit on the workmen as a whole. Others considered that the part played by drinking had been exaggerated, that the workmen had been subjected to too great a pressure and were suffering from the strain, and that the deficiency of output was largely due, especially on the Clyde, to the withdrawal of skilled men who should be recalled from the colours.

Shipbuilding, Munitions, and Transport Areas, No. 220 (1915), pp. 10–11.

3

'A Most Remarkable Letter'

I have had a most remarkable letter from a man who had read a speech made by an Hon. Friend of mine, in which it was said that the workers were not drinking. It was so remarkable that I said it could not be true, and that a man who was really doing these things would not write at all about them. So I made special investigation. I think it is really worth reading. This is from a man on the Clyde who says he was amazed at the speech of the Hon. Member and that the Hon. Member knows nothing about it . . . (*Reading the letter.*)

'As late as Friday the 2nd April I got my pay, as thousands of others. I, as the rest, got pretty full up – went to work the next day at 7.30, the 3rd I did not do any work, nor was able to do so, owing to my condition, not even able to clean my machine either. At 12 we stop work. I went again, got pretty well royal. At 6.30, I went on purpose for a country walk, met a friend, got his company, went for a three-mile walk. But three miles from home we got hopelessly drunk, never knew when we parted, but on Sunday I had a skinned cheek bone and eyebrow. My friend had his bottle of whiskey broken and a discoloured nose. None of us knew how we came by it, owing to our intoxicated state. On Sunday I could not leave my bed. I was so bad under its influence, and my sores which I got on Saturday night. On the Monday the 5th I was so bad I could not do any work at all.'

If anybody will look at the time-sheet, he will see blue marks, and little red marks against the men coming on after the first quarter. But I will tell you something that is not on the sheets, and that is the kind of work they do when they are in that condition. The letter continues: 'I tried to get my mates to stop at 12 noon, but they did not. At 12 I had two glasses of whiskey and one pint of beer, went back to work not caring how things went. At 5.30 I had three glasses of whiskey, one pint of beer before home – after that a good deal. Tuesday was so bad after effects did not go to work at all, drinking all the time. Wednesday, the 7th, was so weak and helpless was an agony to put in nine hours. Thursday the 8th and a few drinks to soothe the stress; but Friday . . . I was not myself, or able to do my bit.'

I am not going to say that the man is a type of many men, but there are too many of that type of man, as anyone must see who will look at the time-sheet . . .

D. LLOYD GEORGE, House of Commons, April 29, 1915.

4

'Not Proven'

The middle-class press was not slow to emphasize the indictment against the workmen of the North. This caused a feeling of bitter resentment, and contributed in no small degree to produce the suspicious and irritable temper which distorted the judgment and stained the good name of the men on the Clyde in the months that followed.

For the indictment was not proven. The figures indeed showed a very serious loss of time. But no attempt was made to determine how far that loss was due to unavoidable causes. The weather had been unusually severe during the weeks to which the statistics referred. Bad weather impeded work on the hulls of ships, and the exposure greatly increased absence through sickness. Work day and night and seven days a week wrought its inevitable nemesis. Moreover, many of the strongest men had joined the Colours; and their places were taken by men who had retired or men on the fringe of the trade who in normal times were rarely in good employment. No allowance was made for men who were sent home because slips or staging material were not ready for them. And as Mr Bonar Law pertinently asked [in the House of Commons]: 'How can anyone know that the heroes of one week are not the slackers of another week? How can we know without evidence that the same men who wrought 85 hours one week are not taking it easier the following week?'

Drink, no doubt, was a source of grave evil among a large number of the Clyde workmen, as it had been for many years. But the remedy was not simple and obvious. One cause was the lack of facilities for obtaining wholesome food or drink in or near the works. The numerous public-houses at their gates were drinking bars without even a seat on which a man could rest after a long spell of exacting toil.

But the root of the trouble was the housing of the people. Nearly half the population in Glasgow in 1911 lived in houses of two rooms. More than one-eighth lived in single rooms. And the housing conditions of the neighbouring towns were no better. Only sordid experience or a strong imagination can realize the significance of these appalling figures . . . And the evil has been aggravated during the war by the influx of munition workers and the stoppage of building.

If the Clyde workman has not always done all that he might have done to bring this War to a victorious issue, if he has followed the lure of drink, if he has shown a sullen and suspicious temper and embraced too readily revolutionary ideas and the gospel of class hatred, his Country, which has failed to provide for him the first condition of making a home for his family and himself, cannot with justice or a good conscience cast the first stone.

History of the Ministry of Munitions, vol. 4, pt 2, pp. 43–4.

5

'Enormous Reduction in Drunkenness'

It is to the stringent restrictions placed upon drinking in licensed premises and clubs, and particularly in the restriction of hours (which, under the ordinary law, varied from 16 to 19½ out of the 24), that the enormous reduction in public drunkenness is regarded as mainly attributable. . . . The extent of the fall which has taken place may be judged broadly from the fact that in 1914 the total number of convictions in Greater London and the cities and boroughs in Great Britain with a population of over a hundred thousand, was approximately 156,000, and in 1916 was reduced to 77,000, the corresponding figures for women being 41,000 and 24,000 respectively . . .

But the figures of conviction for drunkenness relate principally to the habitual or occasional drunkards, who form but a small proportion of the total population. The extent of the restriction of hours and of the comparatively short and broken periods during which intoxicating liquors can be obtained, is far more widespread. The habit of 'soaking' has been practically suppressed, and a vast amount of drinking, falling short of drunkenness, but nevertheless unnecessary or excessive, has been prevented. Increased efficiency and improved time-keeping have resulted, with a consequent material increase in the industrial output.

Allegations of increased home-drinking have frequently been made since the outbreak of the war. The Board have carefully investigated many of the most specific of these allegations, and they are satisfied that in the great majority of cases they were unsupported by substantial evidence. They rest for the most part on the impressions of individuals who are not trained observers, and many of whom have only lately been brought into contact with the conditions under which the poorer classes live.

Central Control Board (Liquor Traffic), *3rd Report*, Cd. 8558 (1917), pp. 7–8.

6

Soldiers' Wives and the Public-House

Newspapers are discussing the melancholy increase of drinking among the wives of soldiers and sailors. As soon as we think for a moment of the circumstances of these women we see that the force that drives them to this habit is almost irresistible.

An excitement and interest has gone out of their lives. There is no longer the business of preparing for the return of the husband. The husband may be good or bad, cruel or kind, drunken or sober, but he is, in all cases, an immensely important part of the life of the home. When he is gone, the 'lonesomeness' is intensified. And if an interest has gone out of life, making the home routine lonely and monotonous, another interest has entered, making the public-house almost indispensable. What would life be at the moment to people of other classes if they could not get the war news constantly and regularly, if they could not discuss it with others sharing their public and private anxieties and griefs, if they could not explore and pursue all the emotions that belong to the most terrible and extraordinary experience of their lives?

The public-house draws the soldier's wife as his club draws the officer's father, and the chief difference between the two is that if a woman spends some hours in a public-house, it is almost impossible for her not to drink to excess, whereas a man can spend the whole day in his club without drinking at all.

The Nation, November 7, 1914.

7

Girls Who Take 'a drop too much'

Quite respectable lower-middle-class women nowadays will enter a bar and ask for a drink, or stand outside with their friends guarding their babies while chatting over a glass. That is, doubtless, a new phenomenon, but it must be remembered that the entire character of licensed premises has changed within recent years. People can enter them, especially at certain hours, without fear of insult or annoyance; and in regions where A.B.C.s and Lyons' establishments do not exist they form the only places where women can shelter from the rain, procure refreshment, and entertain an acquaintance.

Still, after every allowance has been made for exaggerations and misconceptions, it is only too true that there exists a woeful legion of women who have succumbed to the temptation of excessive drinking. It therefore remains to be seen whether any fresh light can be thrown on the origin and development of the female inebriate by calling on the experience of her friends and neighbours.

In the first place, their testimony shows that, though most employers do their best to check the consumption of alcohol on their premises, many a woman's subsequent downfall can be traced back to factory or workshop days. 'I've been a hand in most places round here,' said Mrs D, 'and in each of them there were some girls who drank and who led others astray. If a girl earns eleven shillings, she'll give her mother eight, put a shilling in a clothing club, and out of the balance she'll stand threepence or fourpence on a Saturday night in a pub with her friends. They don't really care for the drink; they do it for a bit of pleasuring.'

'There's a lot of drinking among factory hands,' confirmed Mrs R. 'If one is going to be married she'll smuggle in a bottle of whiskey to drink on the sly, or her mates will make a collection and buy a bottle between them. If a girl won't join, they sneer at her and call her "miserable". Sometimes they get up little "ding-dongs" at one of their homes and get in a bottle. They finish it before they leave, and are then so excited that they go into a pub. for more. I've known quite respectable girls – girls you wouldn't be ashamed to go about with – come back drunk after a party.'

Questioned as to the phenomenon of the smartly-dressed and well-got-up young women whom it is such a shock to the novice to see appear in a police court on charges of 'being drunk and disorderly', one woman explained, 'It's mostly along of their chaps. The girls go out with them, get a drop too much, and start quarrelling; or the men get "a bit on" and begin to fight. Then the girls try to separate them and start using language, so they all get arrested together. The men often get off, though; they carry their drink steadier, and so the police don't interfere. Sometimes even one glass of spirits will make a girl lie down and kick.'

'Working Women and Drink', *The Nineteenth Century*, December 1915.

8

Drinking Among Women in Birmingham

The evidence the Committee have had shows that *there are a large number of women who frequent public-houses*, but they have *no evidence that any great number of these women are drinking to excess*, or that munition work is being materially delayed or interfered with on this account . . .

Again, they have not found it possible to ascertain definitely whether the percentage of women using public-houses is greater than before the war, but they think there is a strong presumption that the number is greater, not only actually but relatively to the population. They believe that this is due to various causes, but chiefly to the gradual alteration of public opinion with regard to greater freedom of manners and customs among women, and the increased wage now being earned by women and girls. They believe that the employment of women in the same industrial work as men has led to the gradual adoption by women of some habits and customs hitherto particular to men, and that the prevailing opinion among young people of both sexes no longer acts as a restraint and does not condemn a young woman for having a glass of beer or stout in a public-house with or without her men friends. They think that this tendency to a greater freedom of manner is likely to continue . . .

The witnesses were almost unanimous in desiring that some measure should be taken to prevent young women frequenting public-houses, but in view of the fact that this habit does not appear at present to involve either excessive drinking on the one hand or interference with munitions work on the other, the Committee have no alternative but to advise the Board that, within the terms of their reference, there is no immediate call for restrictions in this regard . . .

Report of Committee appointed to inquire into Drinking among Women in Birmingham, Cd. 8558 (1917), Appendix 2, p. 25.

CHAPTER 10

WOMEN WAR WORKERS

When the appeal was made to the country's womanhood to 'come and help win the war' the response was immediate. At first, indeed, more women applied for jobs than there were jobs going, what with the general muddle, the fact that many of the new factories were hardly off the drawing-board, and the opposition (in which there was an element of sexual jealousy) of some male trade unionists who feared that women might be used as a form of cheap labour. By the middle of 1915, however, all these obstacles had been largely overcome, and women and girls were entering industrial employment in ever-growing numbers.

Still there were not sufficient, however. The War Office was insatiable in its demands for more men, to repair the terrible losses incurred in the Somme offensives, and in September 1916 it embarked on a recruiting campaign on its own account. Under its auspices there was published a well-illustrated volume, entitled *Women's War Work, in Maintaining the Industries and Export Trade of the United Kingdom*, in the hope that, as was stated in the prefatory note, 'a more widespread knowledge of the success which has been attained by Women in all branches of men's work . . . will lead to the release of large numbers of men to the Colours who have hitherto been considered indispensable'. Certainly the photographs must have made it clear that there were precious few jobs, even those of a notoriously hard and dirty character hitherto regarded as falling exclusively within the male domain, which women were not only willing to do but were already doing.

I

How Women Met 'the fiery trial of war'

The great test of war, which tried the whole fibre of our national life, fell with not least severity on women's capacity for work. From 1914 onwards the demand for certain articles became enormous; at the same time male workers were enlisting in hundreds of thousands, and were allowed to do so without regard to the dislocation of industry.

Consequently when about the beginning of 1915 it became possible roughly to gauge our national requirements and the labour power available to meet them, it was at once plain that unless new sources of supplies were tapped we could not continue to take so large a part in the war as the military situation demanded.

The only unused supply of labour was women. The need was extensive, immediate and long continued: the response of women was wide, enthusiastic and sustained. No better test than the fiery trial of war could be devised for ascertaining Woman's possibilities.

* * *

Over 1,500,000 women have entered industry and commerce since the war of whom 1,200,000 are new entrants who before August 1914 did not work outside their homes. The occupations are multifarious, ranging from carrying on of a solicitor's business to the work of a bricklayer's labourer. . . . The barriers which excluded women in the past, traditional or social as they were, have largely vanished . . .

Report of Women's Employment Committee, Cd. 9239 (1918), pp. 9, 16.

2

Where Did the Women Come From?

Who are the thousands of munition workers, the girls undertaking men's jobs, and all the army of a million women who were not at work in July 1914?

The increase during the first months of war in the industries equipping the troops was met for the most part by a transference of workers from slack to busy lines. . . . In retail trade also there was often a transference from slack to busy shops, as from dressmaking and millinery to the grocery trade. Middle-aged professional women whose ordinary occupations were unfavourably affected by the war frequently took the positions in banks, insurance offices, and other business offices which had for the first time been opened to women.

Very early in the war, also, married women who had worked before marriage returned to industry. A large proportion of the expanding needs of the woollen trades was filled in that way. In 'drapery' shops, many of these 'dug-out' married women also appeared. Municipalities, when substituting women for men on tram-cars and in other services, frequently gave preference to the wives of men who had enlisted. Soldiers' wives likewise entered munitions work in large numbers. While probably the reason for their re-entering work was largely economic – rising food prices and 'separation allowances' insufficient to maintain a skilled worker's standard of living, particularly if the family was large – yet their choice of occupations appears to have been at least partly dictated by patriotic motives.

As the war went on, the transference of women from 'normal' women's occupations, such as domestic service, dressmaking, textiles, the clothing trades, and laundry work to the more highly paid lines, especially munitions work, became more and more noticeable. For example, skilled women left laundry work, and their places were filled by charwomen, or young girls fresh from school. Not infrequently the skilled women went to almost unskilled work, as from textiles to munitions.

On the other hand, war conditions have occasionally kept women at home who were previously employed. In districts where large numbers of soldiers were billeted women were kept busy at home attending to their needs. Especially in colliery districts where married women were thrown out of work at the beginning of the war the rise in men's wages caused them to become indifferent to obtaining new positions. In some cases, notably in the Dundee jute mills, separation allowances placed the wives of casual workers who had enlisted in a state of comparative prosperity, and they ceased to go out to work. But on the whole the war doubtlessly increased the employment of married women.

* * *

In spite of impressions to the contrary, the proportion of previously unoccupied upper and middle class women entering 'war work' was by no means large. Some young girls from school who would not normally have gone to work and some older women who had never worked before entered clerical employment. A limited number of well-to-do women took up such temporary farm work as fruit picking from patriotic motives. Many of the women working behind the lines in France and as military nurses were from the 'upper classes'. And an appreciable number of munition workers were drawn from the ranks of educated women. The 'week-end munition relief workers', or 'W.M.R.W.', who worked Sundays in order to give the regular staff a rest day, were rumoured to include among their members 'dukes' daughters and generals' ladies, artists and authors, students and teachers, ministers' and lawyers' wives', but this class of workers was, after all, small and was not increasing.

Mainly, however, the new needs of industry have been filled by working women or the wives of working men. Former factory hands, charwomen, and domestic servants are found on the heavier work, and shopgirls, dressmakers, and milliners on the lighter work. A fairly large proportion of the increase may, moreover, be accounted for without the recruiting of new workers. Hundreds of home workers, of half-employed charwomen, and of small shopkeepers and other employers have voluntarily become regular employees. Fewer women have married and fewer seem to have left industry on marriage since the war.

IRENE OSGOOD ANDREWS, *Economic Effects of the War upon Women and Children in Great Britain* (Carnegie Endowment for International Peace, New York, 1917), pp. 68–71.

3

'If Women stick this . . .'

It appears that the one absolute limit to the replacement of men by women lies in those heavy occupations and processes where adaptation of plant and appliances cannot be effected so as to bring them within the compass even of selected women, of physical capacity above the normal. Very surprising, however, is the outcome of careful selection, even in fairly heavy work, in rubber manufacture, paper mills, oil-cake and seed-crushing mills, shale oil works, shipyards, iron and tube works, chemical works, gas works and stacking of coal, tan yards, coarse ware and brick making, flour milling and other trades.

'If they stick this, they will stick anything,' a manager is reported as saying of the grit and pluck of the women in a gas works in the recent severe weather.

Ministry of Munitions

11. Inside one of the great new National Projectile Factories established under the Lloyd George regime at the Ministry of Munitions: women, with the minimum of skilled male oversight, engaged in turning the outside and forming the nose of 9·2-inch high-explosive shell.

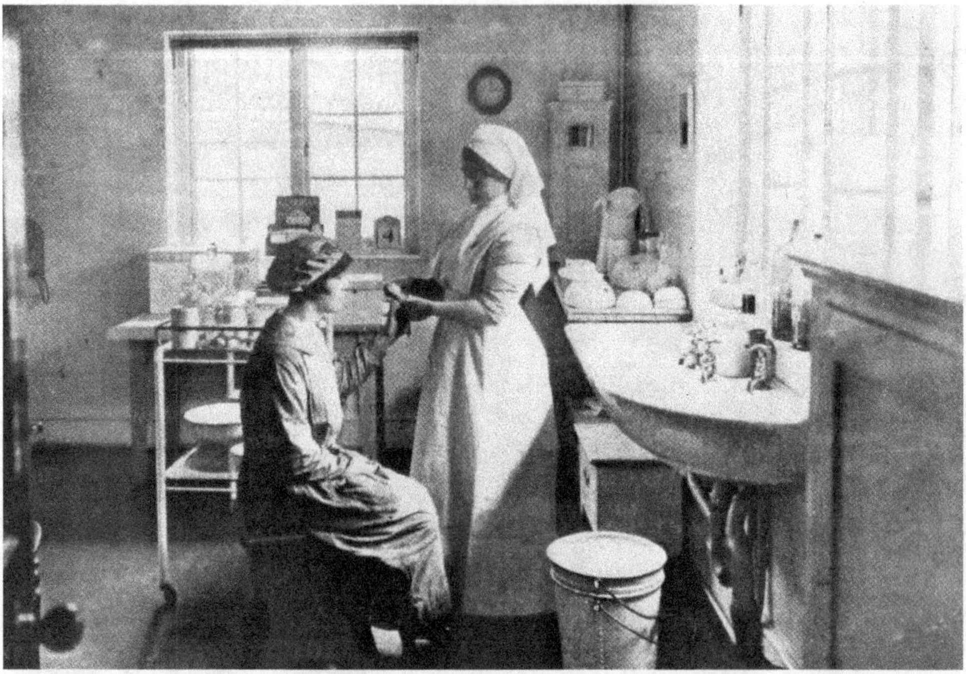

Ministry of Munitions

12. A minor casualty being treated in the first-aid room attached to a munitions establishment; and (below) a cup of tea after dinner in the works canteen.

WOMEN WAR WORKERS

It is permissible to wonder whether some of the surprise and admiration freely expressed in many quarters over new proofs of women's physical capacity and endurance is not in part attributable to lack of knowledge or appreciation of the very heavy and strenuous nature of much of normal pre-war work for women, domestic and industrial.

MISS ANDERSON, H.M. Principal Lady Inspector of Factories, *Factories & Workshops Report for 1916*, Cd. 8570 (1917), p. 5.

(*a*) LLOYD GEORGE'S MUNITION GIRLS

With much the same pride as the young men who rushed to join the colours in the early months of the war were proud to be designated 'Kitchener's Army', the women and girls who hurried to take their places at the workbenches in the new munition factories were proud to be called, and call themselves, 'Lloyd George's munition girls'.

Lloyd George, for his part, was never tired of extolling their patriotism, the quality and greatness of their work, and the courage and hardihood they showed in doing it.

In particular his sympathies went out to those who were employed in the factories in which shells were filled with the dangerous and potentially deadly TNT. They had to adopt such repellent precautions as wearing oppressive respirators and greasing their faces with a special grease, and even when every precaution had been taken their faces were often turned a repulsive yellow by toxic jaundice, whence they were nicknamed 'canaries'. For girls and women whose natural instinct it was to take a pride in their good looks and complexion the blotching ugliness of TNT poisoning was a peril which tested their courage even more, perhaps, than the risk of mutilation or death by explosion. His admiration was deepend when he learnt that the victims were often proud of their nickname, as something they had earned in the performance of their duty.

I

'Bits of Fluff'

One sees rows of girls sitting in wire-caged compartments piling up the little gleaming brass discs that form one of the fifteen parts of a fuse, and they look like a kindergarten class playing with counters, or like customers examining toys at some Christmas show in a West End toy-shop. Or over the oily blackness of a heavy machine a girl appears to be scattering gold dust – cloud after cloud of it – as she carves off small rounds from a long block of brass and bores holes in them. Or in a room filled with steaming vats an ethereal-looking creature – for one can be a 'bit of fluff' in a factory as well as in Kensington if one happens to have the taste for it – moves from one to another with a big bunch of tiny, silvery-looking hemispheres dangling from a hook and washes them in one vat and then dips them into a copper-plating one till, against the black cleanliness of the walls, they look as bright and decorative as a bouquet of Cape gooseberries on a coster's barrow.

One may be deceived by the cheerful appearance of these women, by the ease and swiftness with which they seem to do their work. One hears them singing on their way to a meal in the canteen towards the end of a long shift, one hears them laughing uproariously as they eat, one sees them dancing and rioting in the recreation-room, one hears them singing and laughing again as they go back to their work. They seem so gay and happy that one may almost forget the problems that underlie their employment.

Yet there are two things about them which drag one back to a wholesome cynicism. First, beneath the charming fitness of the mob-caps and overalls one frequently has glimpses of a complete unsuitability of boots. Second, a large majority of them – even girls who look scarcely more than sixteen – wear wedding-rings.

The first fact reminds one that, although last winter the papers were full of advertisements of the expensive footwear which was said to be the only kind suitable for the adventurous Society woman who worked in munitions factories for exhausting week-ends, there appears to be no kind of boot, stout and enduring and comfortable, which is easily attainable by the woman who works in a factory for a weekly wage of from twenty to twenty-five shillings, and is dependent upon it.

The second fact compels one to bear in mind that most of these women are the wives of soldiers, and that, although they may have begun their work in the belief that it would be temporary, the future of many of them is likely to be one in which they must continue indefinitely in the labour market, because their husbands have been killed or have returned from the war maimed or shell-shocked or otherwise shattered and permanently incapable of working.

W. M., *The New Statesman*, January 13, 1917.

2

Meet the 'Khaki Girls'

We got out of the tram and walked up the short, muddy path, past the sentry, who with fixed bayonet guards the entrance to A3, the 'shop' in which we work. It was twenty minutes past two – ten minutes before the hour for the shift to begin – so there were plenty of our fellow-workers passing through the door. Among the three hundred girls employed on this shift there are not more than four or five lady-workers, so the crowd was made up of 'khaki girls', the colloquial name given to the industrial hands, originating from the fact that when women were admitted last July to the munition shops they wore khaki overalls, which since have been replaced for economical reasons by those made of black material.

We had grown accustomed to the sight of the endless procession of girls pouring into the factory . . . all of the same type, rather wild, yet in their quieter moods giving an impression of sullen defiance, ready to answer you back if you should happen to tread on their very tender corns. So long, though, as you keep off those corns, and do not let these wayward creatures feel you are intruding nor provide yourself with anything which they have not, even though it be merely a newspaper to sit upon in preference to a dusty board, they will show their good nature to you – and they have plenty. Then there is their good humour and their gay spirits. No matter how strenuous the work, nor how wearing the hardships, they will always give out from this wonderful gaiety of spirits, and keep the ball rolling with their sense of humour – obvious and childlike – running as it does mostly to nicknaming, pelting the mechanics with orange peel, or skipping with a rope of steel shavings cut from the shell on the lathe.

Every one of them carries a brown or green despatch-case. Most of them are flashily dressed: a cherry-coloured coat, a black-and-white check skirt, a satin blouse trimmed with swansdown, a hat, small in shape but too large to fit, so it drops over one eye, and down-trodden boots, is typical of what they wear. Some of them are exceedingly pretty; they are all heavily powdered, and in some cases rouged. Their hair is dressed with great care, and even if it does fall about their eyes it is not untidiness, but an effect purposely arranged by the aid of the small mirror – often a beautiful thing to look upon, either encrusted with shells or mounted on scarlet plush – carried in that despatch-case which is the essential part of a khaki girl's equipment, since it contains the food with which she is obliged to provide herself.

We stood in the doorway a moment looking at the sun shining down upon the river. 'Do you think the Zeppelins will come tonight?' one of us said to the other. 'It will be a good night for them.' 'There's no moon.' 'Nor wind – and they were at Paris last night.'

Then we went to our work, and the absorption of screwing plugs into shells, turning them on the lathe, taking them out and gauging them, working to exceed the standard number, swallowed up every other thought.

BRENDA GIRVIN and MONICA COSENS, *The Englishwoman,* June 1917.

3

'Theirs is the highest courage'

The greatest honour seems to be due to those women who, knowing the risks, voluntarily undertake work in the danger houses of factories where high explosives (such as TNT) are handled . . .

TNT poison is absorbed through the skin. The mouth, the face and the hands are therefore the parts to be guarded, and the girls are supplied with respirators, veils, and gloves. In neglecting to wear the veils there seems to be no excuse; the girls leave off wearing them simply because they grow careless. But the respirators irritate the skin round the mouth and frequently rub it raw; the refusal to wear them all day long seems rational enough. As for the gloves, they are never worn by good workers. Overlookers and welfare supervisors agree that they cannot be worn, for example, in processes in which knots and loops have to be tied. But it is precisely through the hands, constantly in contact with the explosive, that the poison is most commonly absorbed.

And having been absorbed, it may have several results. Cases of death are very rare. More often, the result is a skin eruption, short-lived but unpleasant; a worker who develops it is supposed to be removed from the work immediately, and should not be allowed to return. Most frequently the vulnerable part is the liver. Occasionally there are effects which make some supervisors believe that young women who handle TNT are sometimes permanently sterilized by it. But undoubtedly all that can be done – if young women must necessarily be employed in this work – is done, in Government-owned factories at least. The girls are medically examined before they are engaged, and are not allowed to undertake this kind of munition work unless they are passed by the doctor. They remain under medical supervision all the time. They are removed from work immediately, if they are discovered to have so much as a headache. They are not allowed to remain in the danger-houses for more than a fortnight at a time, and are transferred at the end of it to some other department for at least a fortnight and in some cases a month. Their caps and overalls are washed at frequent intervals in the factory. They are supplied daily with half a pint of milk (this, apparently, is an insufficient allowance, for the welfare supervisors urge the girls to buy more milk for themselves at the canteen). They have meals provided in the canteen at wonderfully low rates. They are reminded to wash their hands and faces before eating. And in most cases the welfare supervisors surround them with a care and solicitude which is like that of a close personal friend.

It seems unfortunate that the work is light and easy. Otherwise it might be given to men and boys, who seem to be comparatively insusceptible to the poison. It also seems regrettable that it is given to young women, whose health is so much more valuable to the nation than that of elderly women. But at least there can be no question that the young women who undertake it are doing a very gallant service.

Theirs is the highest courage, for many of them are nervous. After a time the simplicity of the work and the fact that so many are immune from ill-effects makes most of them indifferent to the danger. But the writer has seen a little group of new workers – young, fresh-skinned, healthy-looking girls – in tears because, although they had undertaken to work in the danger houses, they were scared when the moment came to go there. It is all the more to their honour that they were insisting through their tears that they 'would be perfectly safe if they were careful'.

W.M., 'Women's Greater Sacrifice', *New Statesman*, February 3, 1917.

4

When the Munition Girls Wept

I am in every sense proud of the women in my factory, and am not afraid to say so. They seldom, if ever, give me any worries or anxieties beyond commonplace ones which would in any case obtain. They are willing and cheerful; they sing at their work, and are immensely keen to get as big an output as possible. Many a time have I noticed chalked on a machine a message from the girl who has been operating that machine during the day to the girl coming on to it on the night shift, a challenge-like message somewhat as follows: '120, Lizzie! Beat that if you can, and let me hear from you!'

I have actually known of girls, who, because their machine may have broken down for a short time, or perhaps because a batch of hard steel has come through, shed tears because their output has fallen short of that of the girls at adjacent machines.

General Manager of a National Shell Factory, *Ministry of Munitions Journal*, July 1917.

5

The Bogey-Man

Before the war Old Rabbit [our foreman] had only men under him. Because he is not used to girls he is diffident in his treatment of us, and is more like an indulgent mother with her children than the strict foreman. He scolds us gently, and gives us sweets to make up. On principle he will never let us have everything we want, and when we ask for too much he conjures up a Bogey-Man with which to frighten us.

'Will you make out an order for a new file, please? This is as smooth as a piece of satin.' The old file is passed to Rabbit for his inspection. 'What's the matter with that file?' says Rabbit. 'It's a very good file indeed.'

The hand in desperation invites Old Rabbit to come and file with it, and if he has a spare moment or two he will, for he is a good filer and he likes to teach the girls to file 'pretty', as he expresses it. If it is beyond all use he will own it is not as good as it was and gives an order for a new one. But if there is any life in it yet, he will stand holding it while he shakes his head and tells how the 'Meenister of Munitions' is wishful that his girls should economize by not using too many files. So we are threatened with the Bogey-Man – the Minister of Munitions.

Once upon a time we were allowed to leave the workshop during the seven minutes' break and take our food and rest outside, but this was changed and we were told to take it beside our machines. When we objected on the plea that there was nowhere to sit down, up rose the

Bogey-Man again. 'The Meenister of Munitions wishes you to have it in the shop to save time.'

It is an unwritten law that you must leave your machine at the end of the shift swept of its swarf [metal filings, etc.], and as clean as though it had never been used. Occasionally a girl is slack about this. If Old Rabbit finds her out he uses the chance to conjure the Bogey-Man. 'What would the Meenister of Munitions be saying if he saw your machine unbrushed?'

Shell-turning is dirty work, and no matter how much care you take you get your hands and wrists black with grease. Dotted about the factory are small tanks filled with oil. It is a great temptation to wash in them, for the oil removes the grease in a second, whilst it is difficult to get it off with soap and water. There is no rule against it, but there is a risk of catching what is known as 'oil-rash', which is caused from the fact that the oil is not pure, and if it gets into a cut on the hand it sets up an irritation. To see a girl bending over an oil-tank gives Old Rabbit another chance of threatening her with the Bogey-Man.

'I do not like to see you do that. It is very bad for you, and I will tell you why. You will get pimples on your wrists, and they'll worry you and make you scratch, scratch, scratch. That would be awkward, you know, if you were in company. And what would the Meenister of Munitions say if you came out with oil-rash? He would be displeased . . .'

MONICA COSENS, *Lloyd George's Munition Girls* (Hutchinson, 1916), ch. 13.

6

'A Lady' in Shop Sixty

It was great news that Cragside's (as I shall call it), one of the largest engineering firms in the country, had consented to employ a certain number of educated women on munition work. The scheme did not take long to organize, and volunteers came flocking. We were to spend two afternoons in preliminary training, and after that were to work at the week-ends during the hours that the regular women have holiday and the machines would otherwise be idle . . .

Judging the feelings of the others by my own, it was rather a nervous little party that set out for Shop Sixty for the first time. All our lives we had heard stories of the Shops; many of us had husbands and brothers working there, all had friends; but I do not think any of us had set foot in one of them. But we had a better reason for nervousness than mere strangeness – almost all our engineer friends had tried to dissuade us from the adventure. The girls at Cragside's, they said, were ordinary factory girls, a class not celebrated for refinement; 'we little knew what we were laying ourselves open to' – a threat frightful in its vagueness.

In the cloakroom we were somewhat reassured. It was the dinner hour, and a number of girls were about, some making tea at the great boiler, some gossiping, and some sound asleep on a bench. Our arrival caused no excitement; a few greeted us with smiles, most continued their pursuits with polite indifference . . .

More cheerfully, then, we put on our long blue overalls and tied our blue handkerchiefs round our heads. In single file we made our way down a muddy railway line and at last entered Shop Sixty.

The whole place was full of women of all ages, from grey-haired matrons to little giggling girls fresh from school; but the great majority were young, in the prime of their health and strength. Some were pale, as seems natural in young things condemned to spend half their lives in that great, gloomy, echoing place, where there never seems enough daylight to work by; but others again had so fresh a colour that it would not have shamed a milkmaid; and the whole impression left on the mind by these hundreds of girls was a very pleasant one of comeliness and friendly smiles.

Presently I was given into the care of one of the machine-girls, a slight little thing with soft blue eyes like a kitten's, pretty white arms and long taper fingers, which managed so easily the stubborn wheel that I could hardly move with both hands. She taught me how to run her machine, as I sat beside her on her narrow form, and also something about the life of the girls at Cragside's.

To all who know freedom it seems terribly hard to have scant three or four hours in the twenty-four to call your own, [but] the girls at Cragside's seem to be as happy as other mortals. They are full of talk and fun; all sorts of silly little schoolgirl jokes run up and down the crowded benches. The work they do is not unpleasant, and they are not kept too closely at it – incessant work for such long hours would probably end in breakdown. Then they earn good wages, many as much as thirty-five shillings a week. How do they spend it? One, the chief breadwinner of the family, gives it all to her mother. Another says, with a laugh, that with sweets and cinemas and new clothes it soon disappears.

Of ourselves, the week-enders, I have little to say. We are paid, of course, for all we do, and some of us earn 'good money'. At Cragside's our one ambition is to 'get our doggie'. This cryptic phrase is equivalent to 'earning your bonus money', 'doggie' being the average or correct number of parts turned out in a given time at any operation – the 'Bogey' as it were. It is regularly turned out by experienced girls, except when they are delayed by break-downs; but of course it takes some time for beginners to work up to it. When you do get your doggie, the satisfaction is intense; you count up the probable rise in your wages, you boast of it to your fitter.

One frosty night, the first that I made my doggie, I was under the care of a fatherly old foreman; he gave me a tray to keep my feet from the cold floor and showed me all the dodges for getting through the work quickly. 'I ought to know them,' he said, 'I've been here seventeen year. I saw the first girls come – that's sixteen year ago come Easter; there's only two of those girls still here, and me; then I was here when they were all sent off – that was after the South African War. And now there's a thousand girls in this shop alone. I've had some experience of women; you may say I've made a study of them.' 'And what was the result?' I asked eagerly. 'The result was – I got married,' said the foreman with satisfaction. Now was not that a pretty compliment to us all?

R. D., 'Shop Sixty – England', *The Englishwoman*, March 1916.

7

'We felt we must come and help kill Germans'

First of all we visit the 'danger buildings' in the Fuse Factory, where mostly women are employed. The girls all wear, for protection, green muslin veils and gloves. It gives them a curious, ghastly look, that fits the occupation. For they are making small pellets for the charging of shells, out of a high-explosive powder. Each girl uses a small copper ladle to take the powder out of a box before her and puts it into a press which stamps it into a tiny block, looking like ivory. She holds her hand over a little tray of water lest any of the powder should escape.

In another room a fresh group of girls are handling a black powder for another part of the detonator, and because of the irritant nature of the powder, are wearing white bandages round the nose and mouth.

There is great competition for these rooms, the Superintendent says! The girls in them work on two shifts of 10½ hours each, and would resent a change to a shorter shift. . . . After the Fuse Factory we pass through the High Explosives Factory, where 250 girls are at work in a number of isolated wooden sheds filling 18-pounder shell with high explosive . . .

But here are the women and girls trooping out to dinner. A sweet-faced Superintendent comes to talk to me. 'They are not so strong as the men,' she says, pointing to the long lines of girls, 'but what they lack in strength, they make up in patriotic spirit.' I speak to two educated women, who turn out to be High School mistresses from a town that has been several times visited by Zeppelins. 'We just felt we must come and help kill Germans,' they say quietly. 'All we mind is getting up at 5.30 every morning . . .'

MRS HUMPHRY WARD, *England's Effort* (1916), pp. 79–81.

8

Break-time in the Canteen

The YWCA canteen is a long, low building filled with narrow tables and chairs. At the far end are two counters, one piled with buns, oranges, sweets, lemonade; the other given up to urns of boiling water, mugs of tea, glasses of milk, whilst above it swings a large blackboard on which is written the day's list of hot dishes prepared in the kitchen close at hand – Sausage and Mash 2½d, Mince and Mash 2d, Gravy and Mash 1d, Patties 1d, Stewed fruit 1d, Beans 1d, Milk pudding 1d – and the announcement that 'workers' own food will be cooked at a charge of one penny'.

Our mealtimes are, on the afternoon shift from 5.30 to 6, and on the night shift from 1 to 1.30, and on the early morning shift from 9 to 9.30.

In spite of the threat that anyone who leaves her machine until the hooter sounds will be fined half a crown, two or three minutes before break-time will find a long stream of girls lined up before the small door leading from the cloakroom into the canteen, which is kept bolted until the precise moment for mealtime arrives. Oh! the joy of the moment when the bolts are drawn from the inside and the little door swings back! Oily fingers flash through it. They dart from this table to that to pick up a teapot or a mug, and rush with them to the enormous urns in which water is ready boiling for them.

''Ere, 'oo yer pushin . . .'
'Get out of that, young Gert!'
''Ere, leave some of it in the urn!'

The last remark is hurled at someone who comes with a 'company' teapot containing a spoonful of tea from each girl at her table. And those teapots! Brown, green, khaki, green and gold, white with pink roses, blue with pictures of the King and Queen, without lids, without spouts, with rubber spouts, chipped, broken, cracked, even leaking, but each one descriptive of its owner, loved by her, and bringing with it into the factory the atmosphere of home.

The pictures of mealtime change quickly. First, the hubbub outside the door, the excited crowd, noisy and clamorous. Next the darting figures of the girls as they run to the far end of the Canteen, where they swarm and push round the counters, the gradual dispersing of it as each takes her place, which is rigorously kept from shift to shift. The sudden descent of a cloud of silence, broken only by the clatter of knives, forks and spoons upon plates and dishes as every one eats with a fear the half-hour will be over before she has had sufficient.

Twenty minutes have gone already. Teapots, mugs, knives and forks are being replaced in the brown and green cases. Pudding basins are being passed round to collect the dèbris. Everyone is talking again. Gradually the Canteen empties. Miss Tommy Atkins, with an arm round one girl and an arm round another, saunters back to her machine.

It is two minutes to the half-hour. The machinery is idle, for it has been stopped during the break. If it is the meal in the night, the lights have been turned low. Now the factory is the most peaceful spot imaginable.

We stand before our machines, ready. The whirring sound recommences and passes like a wave throughout the workshop. Our straps begin to revolve. The machinery is on again. We reach up and push the control levers and continue turning the shells which have been left often half-finished when the break-time came. So we go back to our work.

MONICA COSENS, *Lloyd George's Munition Girls*, pp. 58–65.

(b) THE FIRST WOMEN POLICE

Within a few weeks of the outbreak of war in 1914 members of two women's organizations were carrying out police duties. The first were the Women Police Volunteers, formed under Miss Nina Boyle, an author and militant Suffragette, and commanded by Miss Damer Dawson (1875–1920), a 'lady' of pre-1914 vintage. Mostly professional women, they joined for full-time, were paid a weekly wage, and wore uniform – dark blue, with W.P.V. on the shoulder.

The first uniformed policewomen to appear on the London streets were members of the W.P.V.; this was in September 1914, and in November Miss Damer Dawson was invited to send two policewomen to the great new military camp established on the outskirts of Grantham. Early in 1915 the force was reorganized under Miss Damer Dawson's sole control as the Women Police Service, and its work came to be so highly thought of that in 1916 the Ministry of Munitions entered into contract with Miss Damer Dawson for her to supply and control a disciplined body of women police for service in munition works. Nearly a thousand women were employed in this way in the next two years, and at the end of 1918 members of the W.P.S. were on duty in 28 munition factories and 48 towns, including London, Glasgow, Edinburgh, and Dublin.

The second body of women police consisted of Women's Patrols, formed in October 1914 as a voluntary, part-time organization for welfare work in areas where there were military camps and centres. Their only distinguishing mark was an armlet with the letters W.P., but they worked in close co-operation with the Police. In December 1918 a hundred members of this body were incorporated in the Metropolitan Police as full-time, paid, and uniformed policewomen.

I

Early Days at Grantham

The condition of Grantham at that time [November 1914] was causing great anxiety. There was a camp of 25,000 men outside a small town of 20,000 inhabitants unaccustomed to military occupation. . . . The Chief Constable gave his permission to two policewomen to work there, provided they did not get in his way. . . . On November 27, 1914, the two first uniformed policewomen went up [to Grantham]. Miss Mary Allen was one, and Miss Harburn was the other. I also went up and worked with them on the streets.

There we got our very first experience of police and street work. We were asked to deal with the women and children and to help keep the girls in their houses. Just as we went there the General had issued an unhappy order, by which women were to be kept in their houses from 8 o'clock in the evening until 7 o'clock the next morning in certain districts. This caused a great deal of feeling amongst the women's organizations, and we were very much censured because we allowed our policewomen to work in a town where there was this restriction against women. My answer was that if we found it a mistake we could easily point it out and the restriction could be removed . . .

A Defence of the Realm regulation gave us power to go into the women's houses and to see if the girls were in bed, and to see who was in the house. We found that the women were getting large quantities of drink and were entertaining the men in their houses instead of being out in the streets, and, as we pointed out to the military authority, that was doing more harm than if the women had actually been in the public-houses and in the streets where people could see them. We turned hundreds of soldiers and girls out of these houses, and reported it to the military authority and to the Chief Constable, with the result that the order restricting women was taken off.

Then began the usual work of clearing lanes and dealing with drunken crowds, and the Chief Constable found that the moral influence of women in uniform was very extraordinary. We were able quite by ourselves to deal with lanes and places which no military picket ever thought of attempting to clear. There was a lane from the camp to the town where stalls of fruit and cakes were kept every night, and there were quantities of children there. There were several cases of assault upon these children. We were able to stop that and look after the children and to insist that their parents should keep them at home.

If there were cases of apoplexy in the streets or fits from drunkenness we were able to keep men from setting on the fallen men and to get them back to camp. We simply got together amongst them and called for a non-commissioned officer to take them home. We used to get large quantities of them home every night quite easily. . . . By day we visited the people whose girls we had come across at night and dealt with those cases which had to be removed from the town . . .

We started at Hull in May 1915. Then began the Zeppelin raids. We were out in the first raid on Hull, and I had the first opportunity of testing the grit of the policewomen. Although the bombs were falling they were out in the streets and at their posts within seven minutes of the call. They were given charge of the women and children and were told to keep them quiet as much as possible and get them home. They all migrated out of the town, and were in charge of them during all those Zeppelin raid nights.

MISS DAMER DAWSON, OBE, *Committee on Employment of Women on Police Duties*, Cmd. 1133 (1921), pp. 54–5.

2

Guardians of Decorum

Just as in University towns there are proctors, and in military centres there are military police, so where large numbers of women and girls are assembled for munition work Women Police and Patrols are required.

Special dangers beset young women away from home and friends; the impossibility of excluding altogether from those who now flock into munition areas some women of bad character, the necessity for subduing the lighting of streets and courts and open spaces, and the change of shifts at the factory early and late – all contribute to conditions of difficulty for which trained women are well adapted.

A large number of Women Police are employed by the Ministry of Munitions inside factories. In many towns Women Police are working successfully under the Chief Constable; they wear uniforms and are trained as recognized members of the Force, and in some towns they are 'sworn in'. Women Patrols have been found very useful working in co-operation with the Police. They are more especially helpful in dealing with young girls whose thoughtlessness may be placing them in the way of temptation.

In the report of H.M. Inspector of Constabulary, Home Office, for 1918 it is stated that seven counties and 24 cities show women as part of the actual strength of the Police Force. The Inspector mentions the duties allotted to the Women Police. Among them is 'the maintenance of public decorum among women and girls upon whom the presence and advice of women in authority has a more restraining influence than those of a man'.

Health of Munition Workers Committee, Cd. 9065 (1918), p. 119.

3

Among the Munition Girls

March 14, 1917. Arrived at —— where I am to be for a short time. All seems awfully strange and much to my surprise we are all living in wooden huts. This really gives it a war-time feeling. Everything is very rough.

Had breakfast at 6 a.m. to get up to the factory in time. I went to see the girls clock in and after to the search-room, where most of the girls were searched before going into the factory. The girls all look upon this as a huge joke. They are all very careful not to bring things into the factory, but as no metal of any kind is allowed in we have to even cut off the buttons from their clothing, etc. My stay at this factory was only a short one, and I was transferred to —— on April 2nd.

You can't think what a shock the factory gave us. There was no order, and everything was in a most neglected state. Nothing was done for the comfort of these poor girls who have to work long hours. They were a much rougher class than those at ——. It was hard work at first, but I soon got to know the women and to like many of them. We got many things done to improve the place, and put a stop to the awful thieving which was going on among the workers.

I remember an occasion when I was going on duty, when a policeman who was often round about the factory, saying that he would not like to change with me that night. Well, as there was a thunderstorm raging I thought the man meant on account of the storm and the danger to the factory, and laughed at him, saying, I did not mind. I had not gone far when I heard a terrible noise of angry voices. I then knew what the constable had in mind; my heart gave a little leap, for no one knows the munition girls until they work amongst them.

On my arrival at the factory the shouts went up, 'the little constable has arrived' (the name the girls had given me). Imagine me with four to five hundred angry women! It seemed they wanted to go home. I think it only right to mention that these poor women had faced four nights of air raids, and the fifth brought this awful storm. It was not to be wondered at that the poor things were unnerved. Still, I told them that if they would go to the canteen I would come and hear what it was all about. They went after a time, and I told them that if they were the women I had always thought they were they would understand that if they did not do as they were told it would be a great disgrace on me, as I was there to keep order. It was my duty, but if they were not with me I could not carry out my duty. This I knew would strike home and it did. They all remained in the canteen singing until the storm was over . . .

From a Policewoman's diary, *Police Chronicle*, November 1, 1918.

4

The Blue Armlet

Women in uniform are so frequent nowadays that the passer-by scarcely spares a glance for a hard 'bowler' kind of hat, plain blue clothes, and a blue armlet with white letters on it . . .

Women police are very carefully chosen and trained. Recruits must be well-educated, physically sound, and provided with unquestionable references. The curriculum includes drill, first aid, and the procedure and rules of evidence in police courts; civil and criminal law, especially the Acts relating to women and children; patrol, domiciliary visiting, etc. Examinations must be passed. When the recruit is trained, she finds more than enough work of a kind specially suited to women. Take, for example, the visitation of common lodging-houses. In this class of dwelling live girls so poor that many of them have but one set of under-clothes, which have to be washed, partially dried and put on again before the owner can go out. Women alone ought to have the *entrée* to the rooms inhabited by such as these.

A child, again, turns instinctively to a woman. Every police court is familiar with the spectacle of a child so frightened that it cannot tell the truth, much less give a clear and detailed statement. The policewoman – very likely herself a mother – knows how to approach the child, allay its fears, calm its mind; and in time, as if by accident, win from it what the Court wants to know.

There is another field in which the policewoman has a special task – the streets at night. Without any authority to control the women and girls who, for their own ends or for fear of some threatening brute in the background, prey upon the sons of English mothers and of mothers overseas, the policewomen have already done much to cleanse the public thoroughfares. The method employed is the exertion of an unobtrusive vigilance, a steady pressure of observation. 'Here I am!' says the blue armlet, passing quietly by at the very moment when secrecy is most desired. When it appears, groups disperse, loiterers discover urgent business elsewhere, time is given for that second thought which is often the salvation of the tempted; the consciousness that decent well-bred women are out in all weathers taking thought for his welfare may well check a young man's reckless impulses.

There remains, of course, the drunkard; and the drunkard, if he is not too far gone for persuasion, is delivered by the blue armlet – for once exerting physical force – at the nearest YMCA hut, to be properly ashamed of himself, it may be hoped, when he learns who brought him there.

A Correspondent, *The Times*, April 17, 1917.

5

'Don't you carry a truncheon?'

Our street is one of the worst streets in London. So I am informed and certainly I hope that there are not many that could be called worse. True, since the 'Women Police' have worked there a big difference has been noted and commented on by such varied authorities as the sergeant of the men police, a lady of the street with whom we have had one or two 'scraps' but who is now one of our firm allies, and a ragamuffin of about 15 years, too early initiated with the evils of the world, yet of a sunny, unspoiled disposition. He is the great champion of the Women Police Service.

'Don't you carry a truncheon?' he asked me one day; 'I bet yer does.' 'What should I do with a truncheon?' I temporized. "it 'im on the 'ead" was the reply given with great relish.

Naturally, we were received with some surprise and aversion in 'our street' at first, and many were the discussions among the inhabitants in which we were fiercely attacked and hotly defended, with a wealth of language at least as forcible and unconventional on the part of our defenders as of the adversaries. 'I tell yer,' we overheard one day, 'the d——d b——ds are only doing their b——y duty, and I respects them.'

Police Chronicle, April 26, 1918.

6

Good Work in a London Vice-spot

Between Victoria station and Westminster, the Horseferry-road and the streets adjacent are a hot-bed of immorality, undisguised and unchecked. Prostitutes of all types and ages, but noticeably in most cases young and rather showily dressed, parade the streets, loiter at the corners, and solicit the soldiers who are about. Dark back streets and courts and out-of-the-way places serve the purpose of the more degraded of them, and conventional 'lodgings' abound in every direction.

Public-houses which once were tolerably 'respectable' have gone down the scale as they have been used more and more by depraved women and the men who consort with them, and reports of thefts from soldiers who have been encouraged to drink – occasionally drugging is alleged – are constantly being received.

The most distressing feature is the number of quite young girls, between the ages of 15 and 18, who haunt the streets near the Australian Military Headquarters, and thrust themselves on men who, it must be confessed, are not always displeased by their attentions. Hundreds of these girls are to be seen about the district every night, and the arrival of a thousand men or more from time to time invariably brings them flocking towards the Horseferry-road in even greater numbers.

The work of the women patrols who have voluntarily undertaken the thankless task of protecting these girls from themselves, only touches the fringe of the evil. They have no real police powers, and if a girl with whom they have remonstrated in a kind and friendly way chooses to ignore their advice, they must stand aside. Their efforts, however, even in this limited way have been valuable . . . and the experiment justifies the demand for a recognized force of women police to assist in the moral cleansing of the streets.

The Times, February 24, 1917.

7

Police Women on Patrol

Report of work done by Police Women in a District near London.

Patrols. We have devoted special attention to park, station enclosures, etc.

Activities. With women. We have warned them for soliciting, protected them from undesirable attention from men, and have advised and helped them when they have appealed to us. *With men.* Warned them off certain areas when they have been annoying women. Assisted and protected from undesirable women, soldiers under the influence of alcohol. Cautioned them when breaking the law for minor offences. *With children.* Warned them off allotments. Cautioned them when found climbing trees, damaging property, fighting, running on the road when leaving school, running behind buses, cabs, etc. Prevented them from picking unripe blackberries, warned them when misbehaving themselves. Prevented them from committing a nuisance in public places, sent them home at dusk, prevented them trespassing on railways. *With girls.* Cautioned for behaving in an unseemly manner with male companions. Warned them of evil consequences. Sent them home when found loitering about late at night and in undesirable localities. *With youths.* Cautioned them when found loitering in undesirable localities with girls. Reasoned with them for discourtesy. Warned them when found breaking the law for minor offences.

Conditions in certain areas. Park. Conditions here when we first began our work left much to be desired with regard to the behaviour of men and women, youths and irresponsible young girls. We cautioned several couples found lying about in the pavilions at night, and young people for misbehaving in the grounds, i.e. noisy and unruly, climbing park fences, damaging property, etc. Conditions after dark on the verandah of pavilions will doubtless continue until the park is closed at night, for couples make a point of going to these places after leaving the public-houses at 9.30 p.m.

Locality of railway station. We received complaints from women that they had been accosted by strange men while waiting to meet relatives; also, the same complaint from young men with reference to their sisters, etc. We visited this spot, and found that it was frequented nightly by undesirable men and women, also by numbers of irresponsible young girls and young men. We cautioned the young people, who have not visited the locality since. We have warned off men and women of undesirable character. We have been able to protect soldiers the worse for drink, protect women from annoyance, and have taken home lost children.

Public-Houses. We have hastened the departure of women from the public-houses, especially when they have had children waiting for them. We have prevented children from lingering in the vicinity of public-houses, and in one instance we fetched a little girl of 10 years of age out of a public-house. She had been standing inside for 25 minutes. The bar was full of people drinking, and the language we heard was most undesirable for a child to hear. Two soldiers and one civilian (male), the worse for drink, tried to interfere with us in the course of our duty. When we invited them to come to the Police Station with us they withdrew.

Police Chronicle, October 11, 1918.

(c) THE STORY OF THE LAND GIRLS

Women have always worked on Britain's farms, but mostly they have been the wives and daughters of farmers and smallholders, engaging in such things as dairying, milking, and poultry-keeping. During the Great War, however, the demand for female labour was greater than ever before. Women and girls of all classes were urged to undertake work on the land, and it was made clear that they would be expected to make themselves generally useful, doing jobs which hitherto had been reserved to men. As the President of the Board of Agriculture expressed it in a recruiting speech, there would be no occasion for 'lilac sunbonnets'.

The warning was soon shown up as an impertinence. First in the field were such voluntary organizations as the Women's National Land Service Corps (formed in January 1916), and then in the spring of 1917 the Women's Land Army was started under the auspices of the Ministry of Agriculture. In the next two years some 23,000 women and girls passed through the Land Army's training centres, and the highest number of 'Land Girls' at work at any one time was 16,000 in September 1918.

Land Girls received a month's free training, free railway passes to and from their homes, and a free outfit, consisting of two overalls, a hat, a pair of breeches, boots and leggings, a jersey, clogs, and a mackintosh. A second issue was made later in the year. Their wages started at 18s a week (which may be compared with the male farm worker's average wage of 14s a week before the war), rising to 25s or 30s.

'Breeched, booted and cropped', wrote Lloyd George, the Land Girl 'broke with startling effect upon the sleepy traditionalism of the English countryside. . . . She was certainly the most picturesque figure, and perhaps in some ways the most valuable,' of the various labour resources that were applied to agriculture during the war.

The Women's Land Army were 'demobbed' in November 1919, and at a meeting in London Princess Mary presented awards to some sixty members who had shown special courage and devotion to duty. Thus one woman had had charge for more than a year of a flock of sheep in Cornwall. Another had rescued a cow from a rapidly rising river. A third, when a cow went mad with pain after calving and was killing her calf, and no man would dare to go near her, went into the box, pacified the maddened creature, and saved the calf. And yet another was a girl who, when a man entering the box of a bull to put on its chain was knocked down and the bull was beginning to gore him, climbed the barrier and kicked the bull so violently on the nose that the beast backed, thus giving the man a chance to make his escape. This incident, it was reported, had a romantic ending . . .

I

What a Woman Should Know about Work on the Land

Last year it was pioneer work. We [members of the Women's Defence Relief Corps] were feeling our way, learning what we could, gaining experience. Many of us were Cockneys who didn't know wheat from barley and we were of all sorts – housemaids, schoolmistresses, singers, painters, writers, women of leisure, factory packers, sick-nurses, and shop assistants. These in the main are our discoveries.

In the first place, it is a healthy occupation. Singers talked of their delicate throats, painters showed their fine hands, ordinary women spoke of nerves and muscles. They all admitted in the end that their health and physique were greatly benefited, that the experience had proved invigorating, and they had no longer any nerves.

Harvesting was soon found to be within a woman's powers. The labour proved hard, almost too hard for the first three days, but no longer. The women found they were equal to any work the farmer wishes them to undertake. They had splendid appetites, could sleep anywhere and at any time, and they gave satisfaction.

Three days on the farm 'put them wise'. They were shown how to handle hoes, rakes, and pitchforks, and they took to it as if farm work was in their blood – and perhaps it is.

Another thing we learnt was that before sending girls to a farmer it was wise to inspect the accommodation offered, and necessary to have a contract drawn up. The pay is not good. A well-paid labourer makes £1 a week, and we have to make sure of that. Women working on the

5. THE FAVOURED UNIFORM

Indignant Lady: 'I suppose *I'd* have had a chance if I'd had breeches on.'

Punch (1919)

6. *Farmer*: 'Now let me see if you can milk that cow.'
Girl (*by vocation barmaid – regarding the horns*): 'Which handle's for the milk and which for the cream?'

Punch (1916)

land must remember that they have to be careful not to lower the wages for the men who have gone to fight. They must insist on that £1 a week.

With regard to clothes, we found the most convenient garb was shirt, knickers, gaiters, stout boots, shady linen hat, and a long loose white calico painter's coat. This served instead of skirt and came to the knee. It can be bought at any colour shop for 2s 6d.

The early part of last year's harvest was rainy. The girls got wet through, sometimes once a day, sometimes more often. They needed change of underclothes, and two, if possible three, pairs of boots and gaiters. The latter being of leather, when soaked were difficult to dry and remained wet for days. Not one girl, however, caught cold because of her soakings. If they did not have the stoutest possible gloves (housemaids') their hands were cut and torn. They needed several pairs.

The accommodation offered varied. Twice it was a barn with a stone floor. Once a big attic at the top of the farmhouse. Several times it was an empty cottage. The farmer provided a trestle table, benches, and was usually kind enough to lend saucepan, kettle, frying-pan, some enamelled ware, and a zinc bath. The beds were simple. Each helper took a large and a small calico bag, which the farmer filled with chaff, and they thus became mattress and pillow. She also took what rugs and blankets she needed, and a knife, fork, spoon, mug, plate and camp-stool. A party would club together for a few other necessaries, such as a dish for the roast, a big milk-jug, and enamelled washing-basins.

C.A.D.S., *The Lady*, March 16, 1916.

2

Flax-pulling in Somerset

'How about flax-pulling for aeroplanes in Somerset?' said the business-like lady I interviewed. 'The Government has commandeered all the flax grown in the district, and we are sending down a hundred workers. I *might* manage to squeeze you in. . . . It's hard work, you know . . .'

My pride was touched. 'Oh, I don't mind that,' I said airily, and left the office a few minutes later, plus a khaki armlet with the inscription, 'Women's National Land Service Corps' and a large paper which announced that, being a war worker, I was entitled to a return ticket, Waterloo–Yeovil, for a single and a quarter fare . . .

This happened on a Friday. The following Monday I left for Somerset and reached Yeovil Junction at half-past five in the afternoon. Apparently nobody had come to meet me, and I set out in torrents of rain along a very muddy lane to get to Barwick House, where the War Office had seen fit to billet us. After half an hour's brisk walking I arrived, and walked through an open door into a small hall, full of tin cans and cups and trestle tables. Someone in a blue overall emerged and said, 'Are you Miss ——?' and then led me up some very noisy stairs to a wide landing.

'All the rooms are called by different names,' said Blue Overall. 'This landing is called "Pandemonium",' and I quite believed it. We passed 'The Sardine Tin', 'Olympus', 'Valhalla', 'Arcadia', and finally arrived at 'The Hotel Cecil'. 'You can go in here,' I was told, 'I don't think there are more than eleven in it at present.' ('Eleven! Great heavens above! Where did they all fit?' I wondered.)

At this moment the raucous hoots of a motor sounded outside, and we went down into the hall in time to see a flock of extremely muddy and noisy girls crowd in and seize cups of hot tea, and then grab for the letters arranged alphabetically along the piano-lid. About half an hour afterwards the supper-bell rang. We sat at bare tables, and some half-dozen girls who were 'orderlies' came round and dumped plates of food and glasses of water before us. They were kept busy, as most people returned from work ravenously hungry. After supper we went to a messy little room called the 'Dug-out', where we washed up our own plate, spoon, knife, etc. Two small buckets of greasy water looked far from inviting, but after a day or two I peacefully washed my plate in the same water that had been used by some fifty others! We left the orderlies to sweep the room and lay the tables for breakfast, and trooped upstairs.

Every window, every landing, every flight of steps was occupied by a bunch of girls – talking, writing, smoking; while a dozen gay creatures crowded round the piano and sang all the newest musical-comedy hits. I was very glad to undress under cover of the friendly darkness and slip into my smelly but warm grey army blankets . . .

After hurried dressing, I got down to breakfast. People worked in 'gangs', each under a 'gang-leader', and I was told that I was to be in 'A' gang. Soon after breakfast, some small cars, two large motor-lorries, and a shut-up affair known as the Black Maria, rolled up, and we packed in, each taking with her a tin can half full of milk and water. By eight I found myself in a flax-field, pulling for dear life.

The flax has to be pulled up by the roots. This naturally involves much stooping, and results in backache of the most fiendish description. My gang-leader hovered near me for a while, showing me how to pull the flax by a series of small jerks, instead of the herculean efforts I first expended on it. We each had a strip of some two yards' width, and never will I forget my despair that first day. . . . At 11 a.m. we stopped, and thankfully flung ourselves down under a shady tree, and ate our lunch – an enormous sandwich. At 11.30 we were back at work. At 1.30 we were given half an hour's rest. At 3.15 one or two of the girls went off to the nearest farm to fetch tea for the gang. It generally arrived in a bucket.

After tea, we worked again till 6.30 p.m., when the motors came to fetch us home. Once in the lorries all woes were forgotten, and everyone sang vigorously, and waved cheerfully to each and every passer-by. All the villagers flocked out to smile at the 'flax-ladies', and the children cheered madly. Supper was a rowdy meal, and frequently friendly sparring took place . . .

Occasionally we had a pouring wet day, when no work was possible. On such days we trooped into Yeovil and ate ices smothered in Devonshire cream, and bought pumice-stone, soap, and Keating's powder in large quantities. These were, unhappily, very necessary . . .

Some of our days were miserable – cold and wet and misty. Not wet enough to knock off work completely, and yet wet enough to make us seek the shelter of very damp and drippy hedges every hour or so. The very worst remembrance of flax-work I have is that of laboriously 'turning' acres of mouldy, wet flax, festooned with true-lover's knots of worms – fat, pink things – throughout an entire day. Our aches were a hundred times worse that night . . .

R. GOSS, *The Englishwoman*, December 1917.

3

A Cockney's Harvesting

With a party from the Women's Defence Relief Corps I went to a farm in Suffolk. . . . The first day we were given reaping-hooks, and were told to cut down all the thistles we saw in a certain meadow, about half a mile long, with a ditch all the way round. It took two of us nearly all day; some of the thistles were like trees.

Next day, and for the best part of a whole month, it rained. The farmer had no indoor work to give us, but, as we said we must earn something to pay our way, he remembered he wanted some logs carried. We all put on lots of clothes, and started out in the rain to walk to a wood, one and a half miles away. The logs which I thought in my ignorance would be small pieces of wood turned out to be trees, or what I called trees. At the end of an hour we were soaked to the skin, but we went on for about three hours, when the farmer came and said, 'Well, you've stuck it better than I thought you would.'

The following day we cleared ditches with the reaping-hooks, very wet work, but rather nice, and then we went dock-pulling. When it was wet we got soaked to the skin, and the docks were easier to pull; but dry days – well, sometimes I thought I should pull myself right through the ground. Very often in pulling we only got the head off. This did not count, for we were only paid 1d for a hundred roots. I remember whenever I ate a 1d bar of chocolate, I used to think 'Bang go a hundred roots!'

Then came hoeing – hoeing thistles from hemp just growing up. We worked from 9 to 7 each day, bar one hour for our meal. Most days the rain came down and made the earth stick to our boots, so that we seemed to be carrying the field along with us, and collect on our hoes till they weighed tons. That field, too, seemed endless. It took us on wet days four hours to get from one end to the other, hoeing two lines on either side. Our trouble was what I call the 'line bother'. We started with two lines on either side, that is four between each of us, and there were continual quarrels as to who had stepped out. 'You're hoeing my line.' 'No, I'm not. I've never moved off my original.' 'Neither have I.' Then, after much counting and worrying, the mistake was found and we would start again. Then somehow we always saw thistles in other's lines, and never would believe we had left one in our own.

I used to comfort myself when hoeing that at any rate our next job must be nicer, because nothing, nothing in this world could be more monotonous than hoeing; but then I knew nothing of bean-gleaning.

My present idea of hell would be a bean-field, where I had perpetually to glean.

The first day we shocked the beans which had already been cut by the binder. Shocking is carrying four, six, or eight sheaves, and making them into one shock by leaning them against one another. Beans are nice to shock, as they are rather stiff and stand up easily. But gleaning, which is going up and down the lines, picking up loose beans and breaking off any that the binder had not cut (owing to the rain having beaten the crop down) was hateful. Beans are nasty dirty things when wet and smell horribly – in fact, there is nothing nice about them.

Gleaning sounds all very well in the Bible; but going up and down the field all day, bent double like the letter 'U' reversed, is hard, wearisome work . . .

Our next job was to turn tares with pitchforks – 'pickels' the farmer called them – a delightful job after the gleaning, for we stood upright once more. After tares we shocked oats in shocks of six and eight. Oats were not so easy to shock as beans. The work is done by two together and the sheaf had to be lifted in the air and brought down rather hard on the ground and placed opposite your partner's. The first day of harvest we three shocked an eighteen-acre field, the farmer, his wife, and everyone worked. We did not finish till night. That was a day! Hot sun and the unaccustomed work made us long for drinks, and I never shall forget how delicious the tea was, which was brought out to the field. At the end of the day the farmer shook hands with us, and thanked us all, and said we had done splendidly.

After that all the fine days we did harvest work. First the oat-field, then the barley-field. Barley is nice and light, and quite easy to shock, but of course I have some complaint to make. Barley gets through all one's clothes and pricks, and bound up with it were a heap of thistles, which made our hands very sore.

After that we shocked another oat-field, then a wheat-field. This wheat was naturally very heavy, and its weight was increased by the rain. Most sheaves were about six to seven feet high. At first we could scarcely lift them, and I never thought I should be able to do a whole day of it; but I did, and so did two or three of the others, not nearly so strong as I am. One or two days I stood on the stack and received the sheaf from the man unloading the cart and pitched it on to the man building the stack . . . I enjoyed shocking and pitching, but the job I really liked best was leading the horses and shouting 'hold tight!'

AMY J. DRUCKER, *The Englishwoman*, April 1916.

4

Winter and the Land Girl

When summer is over, and chilly rains give us a taste (in lanes and tracks) of what the famous Flanders mud must be like, the fine-weather farmeress hies back to town, fearing the lonely monotony and cold of our long rural nights. But this season we are getting very few of these deserters. The fact is we are getting more used to life on the land and farmers are getting more used to us.

'Why, there never was a woman shepherd,' I heard one of them say, 'but little Bo-Peep. And look what a mess *she* made of her job!' Well, I play Bo-Peep to a biggish flock. I'm often up at 4.30 a.m. to milk fifteen or twenty cows, and feed eighty pigs after that. I have three pals with me – and here is the secret of content. We are never lonely. Our health and appetites are great. We have big log fires, and get a weekly box of the latest books from London.

I feel sure the farmer everywhere is now converted, and views his new aid in smock and breeks as a really valuable worker, often far more reliable and punctual than the man she's replaced. Of course, it took time to convince the farmer in this way. He was at first a sad, inconsolable satirist. 'On which side do you milk a cow?' a trustful greenhorn asked him. And his curt reply was, 'On the *out*side!'

'How much does Buddy give?' another novice put to her unhappy boss about a pedigree beast. 'She don't give a drop,' he returned, 'you got to strip it away be main force!'

I hope we've cured the farmer of all these vapours – especially now he sees us sticking it all the winter through. Dairy work goes on all the year round – milking, cleaning utensils, and keeping the cow stalls in order. Rearing calves, the care and feeding of stock, tending the sheep – these are winter as well as summer duties. Cutting thistles and digging docks is an autumn work. So is the clearing and burning of couch, and the occasional spreading of 'muck'. Pulling and stacking roots is another job of this time. On hop farms we pick in September and clear the bines in October and November. Market garden work is pretty heavy in autumn, keeping accounts is an all-the-year labour; and during the winter months we clean and oil machines or mend sacks, and attend to all the gear – the oil engines and fixed machines that grind or crush the corn, cut chaff, and mix the food.

It is this late autumn and winter work that sifts out the land girls, and leaves the farmer with helpers who are worth while – women who can milk their ten cows an hour, or take entire charge of 120 sheep and a few colts. After all, as Mr F. D. Acland of the Board of Agriculture told a farmers' meeting at Stafford, 'When women tackle the job they generally carry it through – whether it's managing a husband or milking a cow!'

'All-the-year-Rounder', *The Lady*, November 7, 1918.

7. A STRAIN ON THE AFFECTIONS

Norwegian (to Swede): 'What, you here, too? I thought you were a friend of Germany?'
Swede: 'I was.'

Punch (1916)

CHAPTER 11

THE MEN WHO BEAT THE U-BOATS

Before the outbreak of war in 1914 the British Mercantile Marine, with its nearly nine thousand steamships of an aggregate gross tonnage of not far short of twenty millions, manned by getting on for three hundred thousand men and boys, was by far the largest in the world. But behind the imposing statistics lay a sorry tale. Labour relations were about as bad as they had ever been of recent years: the National Sailors' and Firemen's Union, in which ninety per cent of the men of the lower deck were organized, and the Shipping Confederation, comprising most of the ship-owners, were at daggers drawn.

The great seamen's strike of 1911 had been successful in getting a rise of 10s a month for able bodied seamen and firemen, and there was a further rise of 10s in 1913; but even so, the monthly wage of trained seafarers was only £5 to £6; the regular hours of duty were inordinately long; and living conditions on board ship were generally deplorable and often foul. In the circumstances, it was hardly surprising that ships often left Liverpool and the other ports seriously undermanned.

Such was the situation when on August 1, 1914, Winston Churchill, as 1st Lord of the Admiralty, called up the Naval reservists, and in under 48 hours over 8,000 of the best men in the Mercantile Marine had donned the 'blue' and joined the fleet. As soon as war was declared, most of the crack liners were requisitioned for transports, and numbers of cargo vessels were taken over for military purposes. Thus a much reduced merchant fleet was left to carry the food and raw materials without which the British war effort – and indeed that of her Allies – would have foundered.

For a year or so things seemed to be going fairly well, but in 1916 the Germans produced submarines (U-boats) that were capable of spending weeks at sea and could cover long distances without having to return to port for refuelling. Now the British merchant seamen were in the front line of the battle, far more dangerously exposed than most of the men in the Royal Navy, and their situation was worsened by far when towards the end of 1916 the German Government embarked on what it called, rightly enough, a ruthless submarine campaign, in which every ship, Allied or neutral-owned, found in a war zone, was liable to be sunk at sight with a complete disregard for the long-established and generally observed rules of the sea.

By the spring of 1917 a million tons of shipping were being sunk a month, and the authorities at the Admiralty were at their wits' end to halt these frightful ravages until Lloyd George, as Prime Minister, insisted that the Convoy system should be given a fair trial. Almost at once there was a marked improvement in the situation, and by the summer of 1918 the German submarine offensive which, at one time, had threatened to bring Britain to her knees, and with Britain all her allies, had been decisively mastered. Such was the achievement of the 'men who beat the U-boats'.

I

War-time Grievances of British Seamen

By December 1916 the wages of seamen had risen to 160s or 180s a month, representing an increase of from 40 to 60 per cent on the rates current in August 1914. Even at these rates, however . . . the merchant service was thoroughly discontented . . .

What the men complained of most bitterly was that no adequate provision was made to redress the hardships suffered by the survivors of torpedoed ships. Nothing rankled more than the fact that the old rule, by which wages ceased with the loss of a ship, was applied to war casualties. . . . Another very genuine grievance was the expense to which men were put in travelling to their home ports from the ports to which their ships had been diverted to avoid submarine danger areas, to discharge Government cargo, or to facilitate convoy arrangements. A man who had been engaged at his home port of London might find himself discharged at Hull or Liverpool, with a heavy railway fare to pay before he could see his family.

During the summer of 1917 some attempt was made to remedy outstanding grievances. The War Risks Compensation Scheme was revised to bring it into accord with the increased cost of living, and in August the Board of Trade announced that arrangements had been made for the universal payment, to the survivors of ships sunk by enemy action, of one month's wages. . . . In September it was announced that free railway passes would be granted to the crews of diverted ships. These concessions were well received . . but the truth is that the spirit of unrest had become too deep and widespread to be removed by any concessions which did not go to the root of the trouble – the question of the standard wage and the control of engagements.

It was not that there was any sign of war-weariness or lack of determination. How little the 'unrestricted' submarine campaign acted as a deterrent may be illustrated by the singular defence successfully set up by a man who was prosecuted for failure to join a transport. He was able to prove that his failure was due to the refusal of his shipmates to sail with him, on the ground that he had already been in six torpedoed ships and was evidently a 'Jonah' of the worst description. This man was quite ready to take the risk of a seventh torpedo, and there are instances of men who escaped from a still greater number of casualties. The increased ruthlessness of the attack served only to stiffen their backs . . .

Apart from occasional atrocities, such as firing on boats, the whole methods of submarine warfare constituted a violation of the accepted canons of war at sea that could not but be bitterly resented by men who clung with peculiar tenacity to the traditions of their calling. . . . But if the British seamen were wholehearted in the prosecution of the war, they were no less wholehearted in the determination to secure what they deemed to be their rights; and [in October 1917] the principle of a national standard wage, for which the seamen had so long been fighting, was definitely conceded . . .

C. E. FAYLE, *The War and the Shipping Industry* (Carnegie Endowment for International Peace, New York, 1927), chap. 16.

2

Living Conditions that Shocked the Royal Navy

The Ninth Cruiser Squadron was composed of armed merchant cruisers and naval cruisers. . . . The Admiralty somewhat naturally assumed that the armed merchant cruisers, as they stood, were the ideal vessels for the Atlantic Blockade job. With those great holds was there not capacity for carrying coal, water, stores, and provisions by the thousand tons? Could they not comfortably keep at sea for months? . . . Appalling, nay, impossible as at first it seemed . . . in many of these enormous ships no proper accommodation for civilized seamen and firemen had been provided.

The first, and worst, and rudest shock reached us on the first Sunday on which we went 'rounds' of the living quarters allotted to the deck hands and firemen of the ship's original crew. . . . The quarters allotted to the crew of a man-of-war are assuredly not laid out in over-luxurious fashion. There is, for each twenty men or so of the crew, a long well-scrubbed table, with 'stools' (plain strong benches) on each side of it. There is a locker, or its equivalent space, for holding each man's clothing or kit bag; there are 'mess-shelves' for holding crockery, knives, forks, etc., and there is tinned ware for the table. It is not comfortable furniture, but it is adequate, and, above all, it is clean. There is air, anyway, and usually quite a fair amount of space. As to beds, each man has his hammock. Then there is ample washing accommodation for everybody, and, for the stokers, large bathrooms, so that there is every possibility for cleanliness and refreshment after a long watch amidst oil, coal dust, boilers, and engines. . . . In our ignorance, we supposed such to be the sealed pattern accommodation for *all* seamen, merchant as well as naval. So, when we stepped jauntily on that first bright 'Sunday rounds', into our men's quarters, for inspection thereof, the amazement, and gradually, the horror, at sight of what we then encountered, remain fresh at the end of five years of experience sufficiently overwhelming to blot out most other things.

We were conducted into the very 'eyes' of the ship – the forecastle, and the narrow depths beneath it, to the part which in the great Atlantic liners dips, shuddering, into the monstrous head seas. . . . No place this, at any time, for men; but especially for men tired out in long watches below, among the boilers, or on deck, in the fierce wind, and rain, and cold spray. Yet this was the region allotted to the crew, squeezed away here into the least possible area by the greedy owners of the ship, so as to permit of more space for cabins in the comfortable parts, farther aft, for those who *paid* for their accommodation.

There were three decks, one above the other, each divided into steel-walled compartments. The decks, also steel, were thickly bedded with cement. Each compartment was illuminated by two tiny and hermetically screwed-up glass scuttles, and was 'ventilated' by a pipe leading from the 'ceiling' to the upper air – but now tightly stuffed up with a black and dripping rag, in order to exclude the salt sea that poured down it (at every dip of the labouring ship) from its opening in the forecastle.

The deck hands occupied the upper compartments, which, as they opened more or less on the upper air, were much the best; the firemen inhabited the deeper depths beneath, and with a horrified interest we descended. Round the filthy sides of each den there were riveted as many bed-frames, one above the other, as spaces could be found for them, to the number of about fourteen. Regardless of the solemn hour of 'Captain's Sunday rounds', each bedplace contained its proper human occupant, dirty and sweaty, just as he had come from the stokehold. . . . Each man was crouched on a 'donkey's breakfast'. This consists of a coarse brown sack, tightly stuffed with old hard straw. As for the rest of the furniture or fittings, there was none: no table, no chair, no bench; and as a receptacle for clothes, a little shelf that scarce would hold a cup.

The long-sanctioned custom was that each man, as he came off watch, whatever the day or hour, threw himself on the bunk, just as he was, and there remained until it was time for him to go to his next turn of watch in the stokehold. As for meals, when the time for them came round, the members of each den took it in rotation to go up to the cook's galley and bring down thence, in a large tin dish, the mess of meat and gravy, or whatever was provided. On its arrival, each man reached forth

8. Poster issued by the Ministry of Food

from his bed, took with his hand, out of the dish as it went by, his gruesome portion, and lying there, devoured it.

This interesting interval of refreshment was, in fact, in process at the time of rounds, so that we had the advantage of actually seeing the animals fed without extra charge. It was, indeed, a much more degrading spectacle than any that the Zoo, at its most carnivorous, has to offer. There were no plates, knives, or forks, no table on which to lay them, nor even a bench on which to sit down to eat.

The arrangements for personal washing were outside the dens, and consisted of a row of minute enamel basins, each holding a proportionate supply of water. An enquiry as to the position of the 'stokers' bathroom' was met with a smile of pitying amazement. . . . We must forbear from any description of the bestially primitive 'conveniences' of these terrible abodes. They had instantly to be closed . . .

Inspection completed, the order went forth on the spot, and the ship's carpenters were set to work without delay to convert one of the big empty decks into a proper living place . . with tables, 'stools', bed-places, bedding, clothes lockers, and baths . . .

REAR-ADMIRAL BOYLE SOMERVILLE, 'The Ninth Cruiser Squadron', *Blackwood's Magazine*, February 1920.

3

Pay in the British Merchant Service

Foreign-going Cargo Steamers, Monthly Rates. Exclusive of Food.

	1914	1919
	£ s £ s	£ s £ s
First mates	12 5 – 14 5	23 0 – 32 0
Second mates	9 5 – 12 5	21 10 – 25 10
Third mates	7 10 – 10 10	19 0 – 20 10
Chief engineers	16 15 – 24 0	27 0 – 41 0
Second engineers	12 5 – 14 15	23 0 – 32 0
Third engineers	8 15 – 11 15	21 10 – 25 10
Carpenters	7 0 – 7 10	17 0 – 21 0
Boatswains	6 5 – 6 10	16 0 – 18 0
A.Bs.	5 0 – 5 10	£14 10s
Firemen	5 10 – 6 0	£15 0s

C. E. FAYLE, *The War and the Shipping Industry*, Table No. 24, p. 436.

4

'These heroic men!'

At the peril of their lives the Merchant Seamen have fed our workers, our wives and children! . . carried the armies of Democracy over the sea! . . . supplied our armies with munitions of war! . . . dared the challenge of the despot! They have met the Unseen Death unmoved. They have endured martyrdom at the hands of the pirates. In the open boats they have been scorched with heat, withered by cold, tortured by hunger and consumed by thirst. They have perished in thousands from mine, shell, and torpedo. The grand traditions of British seamanship have carried them through four years of Hell in the deep sea. Every man, woman and child owes individually his or her freedom to these heroic men, who have done their duty by their God, their Country and their king.

SIR MARK SYKES, in a letter to the President of the National Union of Sailors and Firemen, July 11, 1918; quoted in FATHER HOPKINS' *'National Service' of British Seamen* (1918), p. 77.

CHAPTER 12

THE DAWN OF SUMMER TIME

('Daylight saving' in the shape of 'Summer Time', first proposed by William Willett, a Chelsea builder, in 1907, was enacted in Britain as a war economy measure in May, 1916.)

It is almost universally stated that the extra hour of daylight was generally used for outdoor recreation and pursuits, in particular the cultivation of gardens and allotments, and will have proved beneficial to the health of those who enjoyed it . . . The closing of the public-houses before dark during several weeks materially assisted the greatly reduced police force in the execution of their duty. A marked decrease was noticed in some districts in juvenile offences.

The Women's Co-Operative Guild remarked on the tendency on the part of workers and their families to stay up late, and on the difficulty experienced by many mothers in getting their children to bed . . . The general view of employers was that their employees had taken full advantage of the extra hour's daylight, and a number had noticed increased vitality in their workers, and in some cases an improvement in their standard of work. We have received some letters stating that Summer Time involves hardship on those who have to get up very early in the morning. Taking the whole of our evidence, we are satisfied that the great bulk of the working classes are favourable to Summer Time.

Agriculture

It seems clear that on many farms and in some entire districts (as far as the agricultural community was concerned) the Act was not observed at all – the farmers and others refusing to alter their clocks. [This] resulted in two different times being kept in the same neighbourhood – old time on farms, and Summer Time in schools, post offices, railway stations, and similar places. This naturally caused confusion and friction, particularly in the homes of the agricultural labourer, who had to work according to old time, while his children went to school by Summer Time, with the result that the meal hours did not coincide.

Alteration of the Clocks

The transit from Normal to Summer Time and vice versa seems to have been accomplished without any public inconvenience of any kind, though we believe that summary methods of putting back the time on 30th September led to a number of casualties among striking clocks . . .

Report of the Committee . . . to enquire into the Social and Economic Results of the Summer Time Act 1916: Cd 8487 (1917), pp. 3–19.

9. A BAD DREAM

Spectre: 'Well, if you don't like the look of me, eat less bread.'

Punch (1917)

CHAPTER 13

FAIR RATIONS

For quite a time after the war started Britain's food supply seemed to give small cause for alarm. But about the middle of 1916 the existence of a food problem – urgent, grave, and increasingly alarming – forced itself upon public attention. Lloyd George was one of the first to appreciate it. In the Cabinet he pointed to the ever-lengthening list of sinkings by the German U-boats, and urged that immediate steps should be taken to make Britain as far as possible self-supporting in food. As the months passed, the situation got steadily worse, and one of Lloyd George's first actions when he became Prime Minister was to establish a Ministry of Food and appoint a Food Controller in the person of Lord Devonport, head of a flourishing provision business.

Under Lord Devonport the emphasis was on 'voluntary rationing'. Early in 1917 he appealed to the nation to ration itself to the extent of bread 4 lb, meat $2\frac{1}{2}$ lb, and sugar $\frac{3}{4}$ lb per head per week. This proved disappointing, however. The proposed scale bore no relation to the facts of life as the working classes knew them. *They* could not afford anything like $2\frac{1}{2}$ lb of meat per head per week, and on the other hand the bread ration was absurdly small. In May a compulsory meatless day in all public eating-places was enacted, but after a month the regulation was withdrawn as it was found that when people could not eat meat they ate more bread instead. Then a Food Economy campaign was launched with a great blare of publicity, but this, too, had not the effect desired. It became increasingly apparent that voluntaryism was played out. Lord Devonport resigned, and Lord Rhondda (D. A. Thomas), a big industrialist from South Wales who had been one of Lloyd George's most useful assistants at the Ministry of Munitions and was now President of the Local Government Board, reigned in his stead.

The year of Lord Rhondda's administration (June 1917 to his death in July 1918) witnessed (as Sir William Beveridge put it in his history of British Food Control during the War) the establishment of complete control over nearly everything eaten and drunk by 40,000,000 persons. The civilian population was catered for like an army; nothing was left to chance or private enterprise. The whole of the essential supplies imported or home-grown were bought or requisitioned by the Food Controller at fixed prices; the manufacturers, importers, and distributors became in various ways his agents on commission; they handled and distributed the supplies at fixed prices or fixed margins of profit under his directions.

Throughout the country a network of local Food Committees was set up, responsible for carrying out the Food Controller's decrees. Ration books were prepared and issued for every man, woman and child. Sugar rationing was introduced on January 1, 1918, and by the beginning of April meat, butter, and margarine were also 'on the ration'. On Sunday, July 14, 1918, when the country had been at war for nearly four years, the British people came for the first time under a general system of food rationing, and this continued, in gradually modified form, until the end of November 1920 – just over two years after the Armistice – when sugar, the first food to be rationed was the last to be derationed.

I

Beveridge on Rationing

Two fundamental characteristics of British Food Control during the Great War [were] the equal treatment of rich and poor and the thoroughness with which control was enforced.

Of the first point rationing was the great general example. The king was on rations like all his subjects and on exactly the same rations; his meat cards, duly registered with his butcher, were reproduced in all the papers. Rationing, indeed, in so far as it equalized conditions for all in respect of all rationed foods was felt most by the rich. To great masses of the people it meant no deprivation at all; to many it brought unwonted luxuries.

This was the case most strikingly with meat. To the rationers in the Ministry meat was meat, and all meat irrespective of quality went for the same price. No individual could get more than his rationed quantity, and none, by payment, could secure a preference in quality. The Ministry allotted different classes of meat to districts and butchers on the principle of giving each, as far as possible, a fair share both of the better and of the worse qualities; sometimes this meant requiring each butcher to take partly imported and partly British meat; sometimes the plan was tried of supplying districts with nothing but British meat for one fortnight and nothing but imported meat for the next fortnight. Whatever the precise plan, the result was that West End butchers whose customers had hitherto eaten nothing but British meat of the finest quality, had to take and sell their share of frozen meat, sometimes good, sometimes indifferent, while East End butchers were serving better meat than their customers had ever tasted before . . .

Meticulous pursuit of justice between places, classes and persons was one of the main factors in the success of food control and the condition on which Lord Rhondda secured so large a measure of public support and acceptance of all that he proposed. Indirectly it was the best method of enforcing his orders. Direct methods of enforcement were not unnecessary or lacking.

Thousands of Prosecutions

For enforcement, in the narrow sense of discovering and punishing contraventions of its orders, the Ministry relied mainly on the Food Control Committees. . . . In the two years 1918 and 1919 more than

50,000 prosecutions for offences against food orders were instituted in Great Britain; of these 46,600 or more than 92 per cent were successful. During the ten months of most stringent control, from February to November 1918, a hundred persons on an average were prosecuted every working day and ninety-two were convicted . . .

In Britain trivial fines were not the order of the day. On one farmer in September 1917 a fine of £5,500 with £250 costs was inflicted, and on another a fine of £3,700 in addition to two months' imprisonment. In both these cases the offence was that of selling large quantities of potatoes above the maximum price, and the fine did little more than take away the illicit profits made . . .

Apart from such special cases, the penalties imposed, though varying from place to place, were as a rule sufficient. The hotel-keeper who paid £25 for selling 3 ounces of chocolate at more than 3d an ounce, the grocer fined £100 for selling a bottle of whisky for 12s 6d, and the butcher fined £50 for selling 17 oz of shin beef at 1s 8d a lb – none of them did good business. Imprisonment without the option of a fine, though never common, happened often enough to be a real possibility and a deterrent.

One of the regular features of the *National Food Journal* was a summary of the most notable food prosecutions during the preceding fortnight or three weeks.

Amid a great variety of offences, the largest single heading is that of selling above a statutory maximum price. In Stepney a grocer charged with selling margarine above the maximum was reported as saying: 'It is my shop, my margarine and I shall do what I like with it'; the magistrate, however, holding that traders were now in effect trustees for the public, fined him £50 and sent him to prison for six weeks. . . . In the alien quarters of London prosecutions abounded and retailers of food were sometimes found to be wholesalers in crime. 'For selling new bread, selling it otherwise than by weight, selling less than an even weight, selling above the maximum, selling flour above the maximum and selling sugar without being registered,' J. R. of Bethnal Green was fined £194 with six guineas costs. . . . When it is realized that a grocer might be fined for selling a quarter-pound of corned beef at 6d instead of 5¾d because he had no odd farthings, and that a commercial traveller might be punished for wasting foodstuffs because he used real potatoes to show the working of a new potato-peeler, the narrowness of the way of innocence becomes clear . . .

Waste and Hoarding

Two orders directly touching the private citizen in his home were those prohibiting waste of foodstuffs and food hoarding respectively. Under the first of these orders it became a crime for a workman to leave a loaf behind on the kitchen shelf of the cottage from which he was moving (£2 fine), for a maiden lady at Dover to keep fourteen dogs and give them bread and milk to eat (£5), for another lady in Wales to give meat to a St Bernard (£20), for a furnaceman dissatisfied with his dinner to throw chip potatoes on the fire (£10), and for a lady displeased with her husband to burn stale bread upon her lawn (£5).

While many of the normal activities of peace were thus proscribed, war brought its own temptations to offend. A Justice of the Peace was led to feed pigs with barley on principle, because as a teetotaller he objected to the higher price allowed for barley if it were sold to brewers (£25). A woman in Lambeth on trial for bigamy was found to have drunk her double life out to the lees by obtaining two sets of ration cards. A Lincolnshire farmer finding himself able to buy seven stone of rock cakes cheaply from an Army canteen used them to feed pigs; as the food executive officer and a police sergeant were able to pick some of the cakes out of a swill-tub and taste them without bad consequences, the farmer was fined £10 for wasting human food.

Another farmer in Yorkshire made up for shortage of cattle-cake by feeding his stock on bread; his exclamation, 'Well, I'll tell you straight, my cattle is going to have something', put a point of view deserving of sympathy, but he suffered three months' imprisonment. Failure to thatch a stack of wheat (£20) or to protect it from damage by rats (£50) was another form of waste less deserving of sympathy in the spring of 1918. A farmer near Wycombe who had been compelled by a War Agricultural Committee unwillingly to plough up a meadow and sow it with oats, turned cattle in to graze on the resulting crop; he was then caught and punished by the Food Controller for damage to grain. Another farmer near Shap who said to a police officer, 'I am going to fill in no more forms; I put the thing on the fire,' was fined £20 and costs for neglecting to make a return of livestock.

The Food Hoarding Order forbade any person to 'acquire any article of food so that the quantity of such article in his possession or under his control at any one time exceeds the quantity required for ordinary use or consumption in his household or establishment'. A penalty was imposed also on the seller and a power of entry was given, to any premises whatever in which the inspector had reason to believe that food was being hoarded. There were exceptions for traders and for producers of food.

The order caused a great deal of apprehension when first it was promulgated in March 1917, but no systematic effort was made to enforce it till the beginning of 1918, when the Food Committees came into action. They flew at high game. In the first two months they secured convictions and fines against a best-selling novelist (£50), an earl's daughter (£80), a member of the House of Commons (£400 and confiscation of hundreds of pounds of food), a Parish Council (£20), and a retired civil servant who had devoted his leisure to standing in queues (£200 and confiscation), while a baronet wriggled out on the ground that tea was not a food . . .

The order added a fresh terror to automobilism (a rector being found in possession of a sack of sugar when his motor bike broke down and the police went to his aid), as well as a new complexity to married life (a shipbuilder being fined £400 and his wife £200 in spite of his plea that he was busy building ships to save the country, and that his wife alone did the housekeeping).

'Conscience Week'

The spring drive against hoarding in 1918 was enlivened by what came to be known as 'Conscience Week'. Under an order made on February 11th, Food Control Committees were authorized to give an amnesty in respect of all hoarded food surrendered by February 25th; the hoard was to be sold, and half the net proceeds returned to the surrenderer. A certain amount of food was given up in this way, and still more was left anonymously on the doorsteps of public institutions or dropped over their walls. The total effect was disappointing; the value of the scheme, if any, lay in strengthening the case for heavy penalties on subsequent convictions.

Attempts at Evasion

Rationing of course gave many opportunities for evasion, but many who tried evasion found their way to the police court. Retailers who claimed supplies for more customers than had registered with them or failed to collect coupons were apt to be found out. Picture-houses and tea-shops were fined for supplying more than 2 oz of cake at tea. The most exclusive London clubs and the most expensive restaurants were pulled up for over-supplying sugar or fats or meat meals. Householders who claimed ration books for more children than they possessed, or used the books of children or other members of the family away from home, got caught and not infrequently were sent to prison.

One woman found that to pretend that she had burnt the family's ration books and get double rations by asking for emergency cards was not as simple as it seemed; the prosecution pointed out that she had qualified for as many years of imprisonment as the 63 years that she had lived as well as £12,600 in fines. A lady at Brighton who procured cream as for an invalid on a doctor's certificate and used it to fill meringues for a party was fined £20. A Denaby miner who had killed a

Illustrated London News (1910)

13. 'NEW YORK AND BACK IN TWELVE DAYS': in the stokehold of the great Cunarder, RMS *Mauretania* on a record-breaking voyage.

'Women's War Work' (1916)

14. STURDY YOUNG WOMEN such as volunteered in their thousands to fill the gaps in the industrial labour force left by the military call-ups. Top, conveying leather from the dipping-beds in a leather factory; and below, employed in a refuse-collection depot.

pig and sold it to all comers, committing 200 offences, was fined £10, and a large number of women who had bought from him were fined smaller sums. A tradesman who had put a collecting box in his shop towards payment of a penalty of £50 for one rationing evasion, was almost immediately caught again for another £50. Nor was purity of motive any excuse; a Berkshire vicar was fined £20 for aiding and abetting another person to obtain sugar ostensibly for preserving fruit, but really that he might sell it thereafter at cost price to others by way of kindness.

The essential service of rationing, however, lay not in the punishment of wrongdoers but in the security it gave to those who wished to know and obey the law. No doubt much evasion went undiscovered; particularly with butter in the country districts. But desire to evade food regulations was not typical of British temper during the war. More typical was the householder who said: 'Before rationing, when I saw butter or sugar on the table I didn't like to eat it, because I didn't know to how much, if to anything, I was entitled; now I can take my share with an easy conscience, because I know it wouldn't be there unless it ought to be.'

SIR W. H. BEVERIDGE, KCB, *British Food Control* (Carnegie Endowment for International Peace, New York, 1928), pp. 233–43.

2

On and Off the Ration

The foods rationed at present [July 1918] are meat, including bacon; fat, including butter, margarine and lard; and sugar. Definite quantities of these are allowed to each person.

The Meat Ration

Everyone over 6 years of age receives 4 coupons a week for meat. Of these, three only can be used for ordinary butcher's meat. The other coupon, or, if desired, all four coupons, can be used to buy bacon, ham, suet, kidneys, tongue, skirt, sausages, tinned or potted meat, poultry, rabbit, hare, game, or horseflesh.

The weight of each kind of meat which can be bought for a coupon is varied from time to time by the Food Controller according to the supplies. At present, the 3 coupons for butcher's meat allow nearly

7 ounces, including bone, to be bought for each – that is, altogether about 20 ounces per week. The other coupon, or, if desired, all 4 coupons, will each get 8 oz of bacon or 12 oz of ham, or 12 oz of sausage (containing over two-thirds of meat), or 1 lb of sausage (containing less than half meat), or 7 oz of tongue, kidney, skirt, or suet, or 1 lb of venison, or $1\frac{3}{4}$ lb of horseflesh.

One coupon also allows the purchase of a whole fowl up to 2 lb, or a whole rabbit up to $1\frac{1}{2}$ lb. With two coupons a fowl may be bought up to 3 lb, a duck up to $4\frac{1}{2}$ lb, or a rabbit of any weight over $1\frac{1}{2}$ lb. A fowl of 4 lb or a duck or goose of 6 lb needs 4 coupons; and larger geese or turkeys 4 or more according to weight.

The coupons may also be used for getting meat meals at canteens, restaurants, hotels and clubs. Half a coupon gets the meat for one meal as a rule, though sometimes a whole coupon is required . . .

Certain kinds of meat are not rationed at present and may be obtained without coupons. These include some joints of bacon, tripe, sheep and calves' heads, the feet of oxen, sheep, and pigs, and the sausages, brawn and tinned or potted meats made from such kinds of meat; also certain joints of horseflesh, the meat of goats and kids, pigeons, rooks, meat pastes containing less than one-third of meat, and dripping. Wild pigeons and young rooks make excellent pies . . .

Supplementary Rations

An extra meat ration is allowed to all men engaged wholly or mainly on bodily labour, to women doing heavy muscular work, and to boys aged 13 to 18 years. At the present time, these bodily workers, that is, all the men and the women doing heavy work, receive the same extra ration, namely, 2 coupons a week for any meat except beef, mutton, and pork. Most of them will take the extra coupons out as bacon.

Sick folk in hospitals are allowed extra food, also certain invalids and expectant mothers outside hospitals, on a medical certificate.

The Fat Ration

This includes butter, margarine and lard. Five oz of butter and margarine and 2 oz of lard are allowed per head per week to grown-ups and children alike.

Vegetarians may have an extra ration of fat in place of meat. Jews who, on religious grounds, do not eat bacon are also allowed extra fat.

Dripping, olive or salad oil, cocoa butter and other fats and oils are not rationed, and if available may be used for cooking.

The Sugar Ration

Everyone is apportioned half a pound a week. *Milk* is not rationed in the sense that meat, fats and sugar are, and everyone may buy it when it is available; but it should not be used by the general public until those who need it most are supplied. These are infants, children, expectant and nursing mothers, and sick people.

The Foods which are not rationed

Although bread and other cereals are not rationed at present, particular economy is needed in their use. Fish is especially valuable because it can supply the body-building protein instead of meat. Of the vegetables, the potato is by far the most important. Beans, peas and lentils . . . are particularly helpful for meatless days.

Eggs are nutritious and rich in protein, but are expensive at present and the supply is limited. Milk is of course of the greatest value as a food. Cheese is another very nutritious food . . . unfortunately, there is not enough to go round, and it should be left for those who are poorer, and for heavy workers. Fresh fruits are important for health, but their natural food value is not great. Jam, marmalade, and honey are not rationed . . . not more than 3 or 4 ounces a week should be bought for each person.

EDMUND I. SPRIGGS, MD, FRCP, *Food and How to Save It* (H.M.S.O., 1918), pp. 33–9.

3

King George's 'Eat Less Bread' Proclamation

We, being persuaded that the abstention from all unnecessary consumption of grain will furnish the surest and most effectual means of defeating the devices of Our enemies, and thereby of bringing the War to a speedy and successful termination, and out of Our resolve to leave nothing undone which can contribute to these ends or to the welfare of Our people in these times of grave stress and anxiety, have thought fit, by and with the advice of Our Privy Council, to issue this Our Royal Proclamation, most earnestly exhorting and charging all those of Our loving subjects the men and women of Our Realm who have the means of procuring articles of food other than wheaten corn, as they tender their own immediate interests, and feel for the wants of others, especially to practise the greatest economy and frugality in the use of every species of grain; and We do for this purpose more particularly exhort and charge all heads of households to reduce the consumption of bread in their respective families by at least one-fourth of the quantity consumed in ordinary times; to abstain from the use of flour in pastry and moreover, carefully to restrict or wherever possible to abandon the use thereof in all other articles than bread.

And We do also, in like manner, exhort and charge all persons who keep horses to abandon the practice of feeding the same on oats or other grain, unless they shall have received from Our Food Controller a licence to feed horses on oats or other grain to be given only in cases where it is necessary to do so with a view to maintaining the breed of horses in the national interest.

Given at Our Court at Buckingham Palace this Second day of May in the Year of Our Lord 1917 in the Seventh Year of Our Reign.

4

Ways in which Bread and Flour are Wasted

1. One teaspoonful of breadcrumbs saved by each person in Great Britain per day represents 40,000 tons of bread in a year.

One ounce of bread wasted by every person in the kingdom in one week equals 9,380 tons of bread – nine shiploads of bread.

2. Bread is cut for everyone at table, people crumble it and it is swept up and thrown away.

3. Bread is cut before it is ascertained that it is absolutely needed, and each piece cut causes a few crumbs, and these are wasted.

4. Toast is made and the crusts are cut off. They are often thrown away. *If* cut off they should be pounded and used for puddings, 'au gratin' dishes, to thicken soup, etc.

5. In poor houses mothers often give the children a 'slice' to take out and eat in the street, instead of giving them a meal at the table. The little child, if he does not want all of his slice, throws it away, whereas the remnants should have been kept for another meal.

6. In parks nurses and children still feed the birds with large quantities of bread.

7. *Waste of Flour:* It is employed in sauces which should be used with the utmost economy, and not left in large quantities on the plates, as is often the case.

8. *Pastry:* The board, the rolling-pin and the hands are floured. Flour should always be weighed. This checks its lavish use.

9. It is not necessary to eat bread at lunch and dinner when there is

meat or fish and other foods such as rice, butter beans, vegetables, etc. Bread should be reserved for the meals at which it is really needed.

The rich can afford to eat little bread: the poor cannot. The rich should keep well under the ration even including the use of other flours. Puddings made of bread and flour are not necessary for adults who can afford meat, fish and eggs.

Special Constables report that much bread is still thrown away in the gardens of squares, in *cul de sacs* and unfrequented places.

Our Motto must be: *Eat as little* as we can to keep us in health and *Waste nothing.*

Ministry of Food leaflet (1917).

5

Recipe for a War-time Plum Pudding

4 oz flour, 1d. 4 oz soaked bread, $\frac{3}{4}$d. 6 oz chopped suet, 6$\frac{3}{4}$d. $\frac{1}{4}$ teaspoonful of salt and 1 dessertspoonful mixed spices, $\frac{1}{2}$d. 4 oz sultanas, 3$\frac{3}{4}$d. 2 oz mixed chopped peel, 2d. $\frac{1}{2}$ lb apples, 1$\frac{1}{2}$d. 2 oz grated carrot, $\frac{1}{4}$d. 1 egg (dried) 1$\frac{3}{4}$d. 1 gill milk, $\frac{1}{2}$d. 2 oz treacle, 1$\frac{1}{2}$d. Grated rind and juice of $\frac{1}{2}$ lemon, $\frac{1}{2}$d.

Weigh out and measure all the ingredients. Prepare the dry materials and put them in a mixing bowl, stir all well together, then add the egg and milk. When thoroughly mixed put the mixture into two well-greased pudding-basins, cover each with a cloth, and boil or steam for full 3 hours. *Cost,* 1s 8$\frac{3}{4}$d (for six persons). *Average cost,* 3$\frac{1}{2}$d per head.

National Food Journal, November 14, 1917.

6

Menus for a Patriotic Christmas Dinner

The necessity for strict economy in the use of dried fruits has made it necessary to require a departure from traditional Christmas fare in the matter of puddings and mince pies; and on November 2 the Director of Food Economy arranged at Grosvenor House a demonstration of

IO. A LA CARTE

Working Man: 'What's your fancy, mate? Mine's a couple o' sausages.'
Peer of the Realm: 'Well, sir, I was wondering how much saddle of mutton I can get for fivepence.'

Punch (1918)

such cookery as will be patriotic in the circumstances. M. Cédard, the *chef* at Buckingham Palace, with M. Vinet, one of his staff, gave skilled assistance in the preparation of menus and recipes. The menus drafted for Christmas dinners [each for six persons] were suited for various incomes:

1. *Potage Parmentier*, stuffed shoulder of mutton, braised celery, baked potatoes, fruit pie and custard. Cost, 4s 5d.
2. Celery cream soup, braised beef *à la bourgeoise*, brussel sprouts, duchess potatoes, orange pudding. Cost, 5s $9\frac{3}{4}$d.
3. Fish *au gratin*, roast beef, Yorkshire pudding, potato croquettes, savoury cabbage, plum pudding, Cost, 5s $7\frac{1}{2}$d.

In the above recipes the cost is reckoned allowing 4 oz. meat per person, though in each case a larger joint had to be cooked.

4. French rice soup, roast fowl *à la Française*, Parisian potatoes, spinach *au jus*, plum pudding. Cost, 9s $4\frac{3}{4}$d. Filleted haddock *à la paysanne* may be served instead of French rice soup. The cost is then 10s 2d.
5. Herring fillets *à la juive*, braised fowl *en casserole*, stuffed tomatoes, orange and apple mould, mince pies. Cost, 9s $3\frac{3}{4}$d.

The higher cost of these two dinners is mainly due to the inclusion of fowl.

National Food Journal, November 14, 1917.

7

War Bread Dyspepsia

Some foods require more mastication than others. Peas, beans, nuts and lentils, cheese, rice, potatoes, barley, maize, currants, raw fruits, and the present war bread should be most thoroughly reduced in the mouth before swallowing.

Many people complain of 'war bread dyspepsia'. This is due to insufficient mastication. The present bread is of a close texture, caused by the presence of barley and maize, and requires a long mastication to render it digestible. If war bread were completely masticated, 'war bread dyspepsia' would soon disappear.

Food Control Campaign Weekly Bulletin, Ministry of Food, June 6, 1917.

8

Go Careful with the Tea!

Owing to the small imports of tea during the last few months, considerable inroads have been made in the stocks held in this country. On the other hand, the stocks of coffee are high.

Now it is not suggested that there can be any universal substitution of coffee for tea; national habits are the growth of years, and they cannot be altered in a few weeks. But a partial substitution is possible. There are many occasions when coffee can be drunk instead of tea.

Again, much economy can be observed in the making and consumption of tea. Teapots are often sent away with unused tea in them; and at the present time it is much better that a few people should go short of an extra half-cup than that many people should waste a great many cupfuls. Any saving in this direction means the liberation of a considerable quantity of tea, and tea, it must be remembered, is essential for the army fighting abroad.

National Food Journal, September 26, 1917.

9

No Dog Biscuits?

An extraordinary amount of excitement has been caused during the last fortnight by the public announcement that the supply of dog biscuits was on the point of exhaustion.

The position was perfectly simple so far as it concerned the Ministry of Food. All flour fit for human beings must be devoted to the needs of the populace, while the slightly damaged goes to the textile industry. Then come the dogs.

Recognizing the importance to national life of man's best friend, as Kipling has termed him, Lord Rhondda has done his utmost to find a way out of the difficulty, and owners will be relieved to know that enough flour is being set aside to ensure the replenishment of stocks for some months.

One consequence of the recent alarm should be a realization on the

II. UNDERFED

The Working Horse: 'I suppose I don't count.'

Punch (1918)

part of dog-owners that things cannot go on precisely as if no war were proceeding. Some system of rationing will have to be devised by which the store of biscuits can be eked out. That this is practicable is apparent, notwithstanding the limited nature of the meat and fish offals now available. It must be clearly understood, however, that no human food may be devoted to this object.

National Food Journal, May 22, 1918.

10

Never Any 'Serious Hardship'

The popularity of rationing in Britain has to be discounted by the consideration that the limits of consumption imposed by it were not such as to cause serious hardship.

There was never anything in the rationing regulations to compel anyone to go hungry. Bread was always ration free and could be eaten and was eaten to make up deficiencies of other foods. The rations of other foods, though below the average pre-war consumption, were by no means always below the consumption of the poorer classes; this was particularly the case with meat, while, very soon after rationing started, the flood of American bacon gave abundant fat for all purposes, if not always in a palatable form.

Unwelcome changes of dietary, of course, there were. The wealthy classes in particular suffered from the reduction of the meat ration; the poorer classes suffered probably less than they gained by the regularity of work and higher wages.

The rationing system was welcomed mainly as a means of guaranteeing supplies; its efficiency as a means of restricting consumption to a level of real hardship was never tested. There was never anything in this country to compare with the shortages in Germany or Austria, or, indeed, in most of the European countries.

SIR W. H. BEVERIDGE, *British Food Control: 1914–1918*, p. 230.

II

Allotment Idyll

[During the War well over a million men and women of all classes and occupations joined in what Lloyd George called the 'Brotherhood of the Big Potato', and in gardens and allotments made a mighty contribution to the food supply of a hard-pressed nation.]

Harvest on the allotment means, of course, a Show, and we have just had – to quote our programme – 'A Grand Exhibition of Vegetables.' . . . We had nothing to exhibit: not even our marrows had anything distinctive about them. Our neighbour, the 'Family Man', was more adventurous, and sent in 'a bit of spinach' and a marrow which, after the way of marrows, had hidden itself till it had grown to mammoth proportions.

A chief place in the Show was reserved for the potatoes. They were arranged just under the platform, and the band seemed to be playing especially in their honour. They were certainly worth it – blushing King Edwards, British Queens smooth and creamy, Duke of Yorks hardy and rough jacketed. As one 'allotee' met another the question was put, '*Have* you seen the potatoes?' in tones of greatest excitement.

Next to the potatoes the carrots came in for most admiration. The Committee – or someone else – had washed and brushed them till they glowed in all their gorgeous colouring. As they lay in groups of six, tips pointing to the centre, they were the personification of ruddy cheerfulness, like a row of well-scrubbed boys at a prize distribution. Parsnips, despite a tendency to break into little knobs here and there, made a worthy display; the onions were as successful as could be expected in a trying season; and the cabbages as free from the ravages of caterpillars as was possible in a year when caterpillars were rampant . . .

Nominally the harvest is now reaped, but actually it is not so. We are still busy digging our potatoes The cabbages and Brussels sprouts are coming on, and J.'s seedlings are growing sturdily. I cannot induce him to take much interest in my artichokes, but I weed and encourage them and they promise well. We still have a little turf to lift; then the bank at the end, at present but a sorry sight, will be made symmetrical, the rubbish burnt, and our allotment developed into a thing of beauty as well as of utility. With the shortening days comes the close of the idyllic side of our labours. No more will the Family Man drink cocoa as he sits on his turf bank; no more will the Super-Fork Man sit in his bean bower with his wife; no more will the Landscape Gardener pensively pace his pansy-bordered onion beds . . . E. B., *Spectator*, Sept. 29, 1917.

12. KEEP THE HOME FIRES BURNING

Solo by our optimistic Premier

Punch (1917)

CHAPTER 14
KEEPING THE HOME FIRES BURNING

Keep the home fires burning, while your hearts are yearning,
Though your lads are far away they dream of home;
There's a silver lining through the dark clouds shining,
Turn the dark cloud inside out, till the boys come home.

Of all the songs that helped to keep up the morale of the British people in the dark days of the war, perhaps the most popular was this written by the American poetess Lena Guilbert Ford and put to music by Ivor Novello. Everyone was singing it in those days, just as they were to be singing it in that other war some twenty years later. It was in the repertoire of every touring concert-party. Soldiers sang it in YMCA huts behind the lines and sailors in distant seaports; while at home its refrain drowned the clatter of crockery in munition works' canteens. To millions it served as a reminder of happy days that were gone, and a promise of the happy days to come 'when the boys came home'...

'Keeping the home fires burning' was indeed a principal activity of the people in those war-time days. Never easy, it became more difficult as the war dragged on, so that (as is the British way) it was made the subject of bitter joke. Thus in the autumn of 1917 *Punch* published a cartoon 'Keep the home fires burning', showing 'our optimistic Premier' performing as a street musician against a background of shop-fronts plastered with announcements of 'No coal . . . no matches'. But however loud and frequent the grumbles, there was also that hint of a silver lining. How the people managed to 'hold on' and 'see it through' may be gathered, at least in some measure, from the 'documents' that compose this chapter.

(*a*) HOW THEY LIVED THEN: 1914–1918

I

Housekeeping in War-time

Directly after the outbreak of war a Cabinet Committee on Food Supplies began to function, and on August 7th various maximum prices were fixed, such as 4½d per lb for granulated sugar, 5d for lump, 1s 6d per lb for butter, 8d for margarine, 9½d for Colonial cheese and 1s 4d and 1s 6d for Continental and British bacon. These prices seemed high to us then. Later on we should have regarded them as more than moderate.

Luxury foods fell in price owing to the lack of entertaining. English chickens cost 2s 3d to 2s 9d, ducklings 2s 6d to 3s, young grouse 3s a brace, peaches 2s to 3s a dozen, hothouse melons could be bought for 1s 6d upwards and pineapples from 1s.

During that autumn and winter of 1914 we began to suffer from a curtailed supply of fuel and light. The street lamps were dimmed, and everyone was ordered to provide blinds and to keep them drawn at night. Many careless people forgot to do so and were rung up by the police, cautioned and, if the offence were repeated, fined. The maximum penalty for failing to conform to the Emergency Light orders was a fine of £100 or six months' imprisonment.

Life became more and more expensive, and the papers published numbers of articles in which pre-war and war prices were compared. In one, entitled 'Dearer Babies', it was estimated that the cost of maintaining a baby in an upper middle-class home was about £25 a year more than in 1914. The following figures were given: Milk, average consumption 400 to 450 pints: a rise of 2d per quart accounts for 33s to 37s 6d a year. Baby foods up, bottles 33⅓ per cent, wool 33 per cent, soap 33⅓ per cent, toilet powder 100 per cent, and perambulators 25 per cent dearer. Nurses' wages about 33⅓ per cent more . . .

The Cost of Keeping Warm

By the beginning of 1915 the coal shortage was causing such inconvenience that complaints were made with regard to hoarding in private cellars and to profiteering. The poor, who buy in hundred and half-hundred weights, were paying at the rate of 35s to 40s a ton for coal, which it was said then cost 9s 9d at the pit mouth, the rail rate of 6s 3d bringing its price up to 16s. A month later coal was up another 2s per ton, and those who bought by the ton had to pay 34s for best coal and 32s for kitchen coal. Another month went by and brought another increase of 2s per ton. The cheaper coal which cost 34s had a year ago, in February 1914, cost 28s 6d. These prices, however, were trifling in comparison with those paid later.

Before the war ended the coal queue was as familiar a sight as the food queue, and as the country was drained of its men the domestic 'pram' and the soap-box on wheels often took the place of the coal cart in the poorer neighbourhoods. We were to experience such a fuel shortage as made it necessary to regard cinder waste as a punishable offence, and the newspapers published all manner of recipes for making briquettes with clay and sawdust and tar for fuel-saving cookery.

During the winter of 1917–18, October to May, the coal ration was for three to five rooms 2 cwt, six to seven 4 cwt, over twelve 8 cwt per week. The summer rate was half the winter rate, and some extra was allowed for invalids, young children, and lodgers.

Those fortunate people who lived in small houses or flats and had gas cookers and fires and central heating worked by independent boilers which burned coke were indeed fortunate. 'We were very popular,' a friend recalls, 'because we always had hot water. We used to ask people to bathe and dine!'

Keeping to the Ration

It added to the worries of patriotic housewives who were honourably observing the voluntary rations that, as they expressed it, they never knew where they were. One day they were begged to eat potatoes, and potato recipes flooded the country, and the next day they were begged not to eat potatoes, and indeed in many cases could not, because, owing to potato disease the crop failed and only the recipes remained.

In London at one time potatoes were so scarce that a rich man visiting friends to whom in pre-war days he would have brought expensive fruit, flowers or a box of chocolates, appeared with a bag of potatoes.

At one moment rabbits could be procured – at a price – and the price made the would-be buyers so indignant that they demanded that rabbits should be 'controlled'. The Food Controller controlled rabbits, and promptly they disappeared from the market. 'Where *are* the rabbits?' cried indignant women at food meetings, the explanation being that when it was no longer possible to sell a rabbit at a high price its owner preferred to eat it himself, and did.

'Give 'im beans!'

Although we learned to use maize and were thankful to have it, it never became really liked, but continued to be one of those foods which we admitted that people in that vague locality 'out there' might use, but which free-born Britishers would never condescend to in normal times. As for the varieties of dried beans with which we supplemented our lessening supplies of meat, those we frankly hated. When at a cookery demonstration a bean dish was suggested as a substitute for the meat which it was so difficult to obtain, a good lady laughed ironically. 'Give me 'usbin' that muck? Yes, I don't think!' Whilst another added, 'Give 'im beans, an' get a black eye for me pains!'

Sometimes cheese was short and sometimes meat was short, and always fats were short, and mothers were terribly worried when milk was short and threatened to be shorter.

The different regulations which were made regarding meatless days annoyed us and drove the trade nearly frantic, and resulted in putting up the price of fish. Sole rose to 4s a pound, and turbot to 3s, prices to which we were not unaccustomed later, but which horrified us then. There were many complaints that fish was destroyed to keep up the price, and a case of a fishmonger at Folkestone in whose refuse bin were found twenty-two mullet and five plaice gained considerable publicity. In the end it seemed best to leave the public to use what food they could buy to the best of their ability, and the meatless day order was rescinded.

How thankful we were for 'offal', which was not rationed. Offal was the elegant term for liver, oxtails, sweetbread, kidneys, tripe. One begged the kind butcher to let one have a little bit, and sometimes he did and sometimes he did not. As a young married woman writing to a friend expressed it, 'We live mostly on entrails.'

'Tragic Butter Stories'

With scarcity, values changed, and a devoted youth home on leave from Ireland, where food was not controlled, visited his beloved bearing in his hand a pound of butter. Another traveller returning to London brought back some butter. He asked two or three ladies to luncheon, and whispered to the one of his choice that she should remain after the others had left, when he would give it to her. Alas! the

Imperial War Museum

15. 'FLAX-PULLING IN SOMERSET.' Land Girls tying pulled flax into sheaves in readiness for transport to the factory where they will form the raw material of aeroplane wings.

'Women's War Work' (1916)

16. WOMEN 'POSTMEN' starting off on their delivery round (top), and below, loading coal on to a horse-drawn wagon in a railway goods yard.

other guests stayed late, and when the host departed to fetch the precious fat he found that, having put it on the window-sill in the early morning, the sun had reduced it to the state of melted butter.

A still more tragic butter story is told of a lady who hurried home with her prize to find that an observation balloon was hanging in graceful folds from her roof and that its car was in the area. In the agitation of the moment she dropped the butter, and later returned to find that the puppy had eaten it and, with utter disregard for war-time economy, had been sick upon the drawing-room carpet.

* * *

It was during the later part of 1917 that the food shortage became more and more serious, and in consequence control more strict. To throw rice at a wedding became a summary offence, and the sale of luxury chocolates was stopped. No sweetmeats over 2d per oz or chocolates over 3d per oz were permitted, the use of starch in laundry work was restricted, horses and cows and even the London pigeons were rationed; no corn was allowed for cobs, hunters, carriage horses and hacks, most of which had by then been commandeered for Army use. The amount of bread or cake which might be sold at tea shops for afternoon tea was reduced to 2 oz. It became an offence to adopt and feed stray dogs; these innocent victims of war had to be handed over to the police.

Local food controllers were appointed, butchers were ordered to display price lists, and bakers were forbidden to bake any but Government regulation bread. This bread was compounded from various ingredients, including barley, rice, maize, beans, oatmeal, and in October 1917 bakers were permitted to add potato in the proportion of 1 lb to 7 lb of flour.

The public, especially members of the Labour Party, demanded fixed prices. When the price of any particular food was fixed, it mysteriously vanished from the market. Food Control Committees had a hard battle to keep even with the retailer. Grocers would not sell to people who were not registered with them for sugar, and, it was said, insisted on other purchases being made in addition to sugar, which resulted in the appearance of comic advertisements such as, 'Will the lady who overheard salesman refuse to supply a mackerel unless lady bought six pairs of lisle thread stockings or ear trumpet, kindly communicate with the Food Controller, Grosvenor House?'

That winter the world was the poorer for the disappearance of the muffin. The muffin-man, carrying his baize-covered tray upon his head and ringing a bell, was no more seen, and we consoled ourselves for our muffinless, crumpetless state by owning gloomily that when we had neither butter nor 'marge', of what use to us was the muffin?

As Christmas drew near the Ministry of Food planned a patriotic Christmas dinner for us, which consisted of French rice soup, [or] filleted haddock, roast fowl and vegetables, plum pudding, caramel custard. This, it was said, would cost 10s 2d for four people. It seems difficult to believe this statement, considering that a fowl then – in any large town, at all events – cost at least 10s.

The poor old souls in Maidstone workhouse were ordered cornflour instead of Christmas pudding, but at Epsom the more kindly authorities added a trifle to the Christmas dietary. Those who wished to include a dish of oranges in the Christmas bill of fare noted with dismay that the *wholesale* price of the first consignment of Valencias was 4½d each. They were sold retail at 6d each.

By that time we were in receipt of sugar tickets. Milk was the first item of our dietary to be controlled, and sugar the first for which ration cards were issued.

Food Queues

By now so great were the discomfort and ill-feeling caused by the food queues, and the suspicion that the rich were obtaining more than their fair share of eatables, that the demand for compulsory rations became more and more insistent.

Anyone who penetrated the poorer neighbourhoods became familiar with the queue. In the bitter cold and rain of that depressing winter of 1917 women and children waited outside the shabby shops common to the poor districts of all towns. They carried baskets, string bags, fish basses, bags made of American cloth, and babies, and stood shifting their burdens from one arm to another to ease their aching. Often, in spite of cold, rain and weariness, there was a flow of wit. Sometimes a late-comer would try to sneak in at the head of the line, and then there would be trouble, promptly allayed by the policeman or Special Constable, or in some provincial towns the policewoman.

In the early winter of 1918 a queue of thousands of people waiting to obtain margarine caused considerable comment, and about the same time a photograph appeared in the press of Smithfield meat market with all the hooks empty.

Women used to go from shop to shop trying to find one at which they could buy meat or margarine, tea and possibly a little extra sugar. The rich escaped these unpleasant tasks, partly because they could send servants to shop for them and partly because the customer who bought on a large scale could still have his goods delivered at his house, though by now the cart or motor was generally in charge of a woman and women had taken the place of the younger men both in butchers' and grocers' shops. Notices were displayed in shops and stores asking customers to carry their own parcels whenever possible, and roomy baskets and bags became fashionable adjuncts to the toilette. The master bakers begged customers not to waste the time of their employees by chatting to them when they delivered goods.

The conduct of certain tradespeople who at this time shut their shops to the general public and sent out meat and other goods to favoured customers via the back door infuriated the people, and occasionally luckless butcher boys were held up and the contents of their basket looted. The knowledge that some well-to-do folk were hoarding food also caused discontent. It was these annoyances which made local authorities adopt rationing schemes before national compulsory rationing came into force. One of the first cities to do so was Birmingham.

After February 1918 veal was no longer on sale, and it became impossible in London and the six home counties to buy butter, margarine or meat without cards. The allowance generally procurable was 1½ lb of meat per head for adults, for children under ten 10 oz, butter or margarine 4 oz, and sugar 8 oz. By the end of April 1918 the national rationing of meat came into force, and everyone was required to register for bacon also. Owing to the scarcity of meat, fancy prices for offal and poultry were charged, and in some places butchers' shops opened only for about one hour each day. The rations of the Home Army were reduced, and it became legal to inflict a fine up to £400 for hoarding.

Many were the grumbles of the charges made by hotel and restaurant proprietors. At a hotel at Torquay a visitor, receiving a tiny portion of meat without any potato and a mere scrap of cabbage, on asking if she could not have a little rice or maize with it, was assured that she could not, as the vegetable cook did not know how to cook them!

Our difficulties and discomforts were added to by the prevalence of influenza, which in many cases developed into pneumonia. It was difficult to obtain nurses or drugs or sufficient nourishing food for invalids. Charwomen were not to be had.

By the end of July 1918 the public knew that all fear of starvation owing to the German blockade was ended, but that supplies must continue to be limited and prices remain high. Considering the suffering and discomfort due to these causes, to the shortage of fuel, overwork, personal unhappiness and general mental strain, the people as a whole remained wonderfully calm. They grumbled, but their grumbling was chiefly an emotional outlet. Directly they understood the position, though they might still grumble, there remained the determination to 'stick it', to do their 'bit' and to win the war.

MRS C. S. PEEL, *How We Lived Then: 1914–1918* (The Bodley Head, 1929), pp. 54–8, 90–104.

2

'Economy Programme' in a Middle-Class Household

When war broke out in August 1914 my wife and I were convinced it was going to be a long business. So we drew up our 'war programme' and we signed it. Here is the document:

1. The servants must take 25 per cent less wages.
2. We must have no guests to stay in the house.
3. No casual entertaining; no theatres; no outings for pleasure costing over 2s 6d each; no taxis; only third-class travelling.
4. No wines, spirits, or cigars.
5. Neither of us must have one single new article of dress for at least a year.
6. No newspapers except *The Times* and one feminine weekly.
7. If any golf, no caddies; and only on the home course.
8. No Christmas, birthday, or wedding presents.
9. Rigid economy in food: no soups, entrees, sweets (i.e. crystallized fruits, etc.) or fruit except from our own garden; only joints, plain puddings, and simplest food.
10. Strict economy in coal, gas, and electric light.

That was our programme; and for more than eighteen months we have done our best to live up to it. It has not been possible to follow it to the letter in every detail, as, for instance, in regard to having no guests staying in the house. This clause has been waived in favour of guests coming to us from outside Great Britain.

We have violated the provision which limits the cost of outings to half-a-crown per head, but only rarely. For it is surprising, when you abjure taxis and travel 3rd class, how much can be done on half-a-crown.

In the matter of Christmas presents, again, we have spent several pounds less in each of the last two years than we had spent at any Christmas for some years before; but, as each winter has come on, we have found ourselves less churlish than we had hoped to be.

Casual entertaining, again, is a thing which it is not possible to abstain from altogether; but now our guests must have precisely what we would have had if we had been alone. If the clause in regard to wines has been taken to read that it only means that we will open no wines for ourselves, it is extraordinary how much gratification there is in contemplating the pyramids of bottles which have now had nearly a year and a half added to their age when, but for the war, at least one-half of them would be empty long ago.

On the other hand, in some particulars we have improved on the programme. We found, for example, that the easiest way to comply with our regulations as to food was to abolish late dinner altogether and to substitute for it what is sometimes supper and sometimes high tea. We enjoy that meal enormously. At breakfast we have come to a sort of Continental breakfast with porridge and marmalade added. Only on Sundays do we now make the acquaintance of the friendly kipper or eggs and bacon.

A curious thing in connection with this was the behaviour of the servants. My wife made no suggestion to them, and for a couple of months after we had abandoned everything like meat or eggs or fish at breakfast they continued (for the cook orders as she pleases for the kitchen) to have the same morning meal as before. It meant an expense of 9s or 10s a week; and after two months we imagine that the cook grew ashamed of seeing that weekly item in the household books, and without a word being said it disappeared.

And what has been the result? In the first place, the fortnightly cheque for housekeeping is, on the average, in spite of something like a fifty per cent rise in prices, about £2 less than it was before the war. But the real economy is not in the housekeeping books, but in the miscellaneous expenditure. Pocket-money for my wife and myself is always drawn in cheques of £5 each to 'cash' and, with curious punctuality, three £5 cheques now last as long as five cheques did before.

A Correspondent, *The Times*, February 2, 1916.

3

The Passing of the Servant

Long before the war began the domestic servant problem was becoming acute. . . . In the past sixteen months things have grown much worse; and if they go on as they are going the domestic servant will be as rare as breakfast bacon in Germany.

The conditions of war have opened up to women a hundred new avenues of work, nearly all of which offer free evenings, much intercourse with the world, and good wages. The chief of these is perhaps munitions work; but women are now acting as chauffeurs, conductors of tramcars, messengers, doorkeepers, pages, waiters in clubs and restaurants, and in a number of other capacities usually confined to men and boys.

This shifting of occupations has even invaded the servants' hall. The butler has enlisted or been 'put down', and the parlourmaid is doing his work (and doing it very well too) at higher wages than he had before. Never again will she stoop to act as 'house-parlourmaid'. Should she desire a change, what she will do is to go as waitress in a good club or hotel. Many a servant too has left her place to marry a good fellow who has joined the Army, and was anxious to have his sweetheart comfortably off with a nice little separation allowance before he faced the guns. And a third cause is the tide of prosperity that has left very few of the humbler homes unblessed with its refreshing waters. What with pay and overtime allowances for the head of the family, there is no need, at any rate just yet, for the girls to go out to work; let them live 'like ladies' while they have the chance.

The offer of higher wages proves of little use. Already the old 'general' at £16 to £18 a year is a thing of the past. The employment of women of gentle birth as domestic servants has been suggested and to some extent tried; but for the most part it does not work out very well. Ladies too often take places knowing nothing about the work; they are apt to make difficulties, to object to doing the heavier work, to refuse to wear servants' dress, to demand higher wages and to expect an impossible amount of consideration. Most women of gentle birth would rather be companions or 'useful helps' at £18 and live with the family than be domestic servants at £25 to £30.

The Times, December 8, 1915.

4

What Made the People Grumble

At a very early stage in their investigations it was forcibly borne in upon the Committee that the question of food prices was the most general, if not indeed the most important present cause of Industrial Unrest.

The high prices of staple commodities have undoubtedly laid a severe strain upon the majority of the working classes, and in some instances have resulted in hardship and actual starvation. It is no doubt true that in some instances wages have risen to such an extent as largely to compensate for the increased cost of living, but there are workers whose wages have been raised very slightly, if at all, and some whose earnings have actually diminished, and on these the high food prices have borne heavily.

Joined to the sense of actual hardship, there is undoubtedly a deep-seated conviction in the minds of the working classes that the prices of food have risen not only through scarcity, but as the result of the manipulation of prices by unscrupulous producers and traders, who, it is alleged, owing to lack of courageous action on the part of the Government, have succeeded in making fabulous profits at the expense of the consumers. It is alleged that importers have made unfair use of cold storage accommodation, and also that the scarcity of certain essential foods, such as sugar, has been accentuated by inequalities of distribution . . .

Report of Commission of Inquiry into Industrial Unrest, No. 1 Division: North-East Area, Cd. 8662 (1917), p. 2.

5

The War and the Workers' Cost of Living

The immense numbers of men, who have been embodied in the Naval and Military Services in all branches, left great gaps in the ranks of industry generally. At the same time the expansion of all industries connected with the equipment and supply of the Forces, including shipbuilding, the erection of new factories and the enlargement or adaptation of old ones, called for new supplies of labour, skilled and unskilled. These new wants have been supplied, partly by the transfer of persons from trades, the activity of which has been curtailed by the war, partly by the promotion of the unskilled to skilled work, partly by enlisting persons, who before were either not engaged in industry at all, or who, owing to age or other causes, had ceased to seek employment. . . . By the operation of these and similar causes unemployment in the country at large has almost disappeared. Short time also is now very exceptional.

'Few out of work'

There are trades, of which Cotton-spinning may be cited as the best-known example, where a very different account has to be given, and we are not unmindful of the hard cases of many individuals. The statistics, however, relating to unemployment generally show that in the main few wage-earners are out of work. According to the Trade Union percentages of unemployment at the end of June 1914, it was 2·4 per cent; at the end of July 1914, 2·8 per cent; in 1918 it has been, at the end of June, 0·7 per cent; at the end of July, 0·6 per cent; at the end of August, 0·5 per cent.

There have been corresponding changes also in the occupations themselves. Thanks to the magnitude of the orders placed, to the uniformity of the work in hand, and to the usually full supplies of material, little time is lost in waiting, and those working at piece rates make a full use of their opportunities. The cessation of voluntary limitation upon output has been a very important matter. Repetition work and the extended use of special machine tools also have their effect in increasing earnings, while overtime and night work, though varying greatly in amount between one trade and another, carry it still further. Many who would normally be learners now earn an adult man's wage, and many who in ordinary times would be employed on quite unskilled work are now enabled to do work of a semi-skilled character, and have risen to a higher grade of remuneration.

Some attendant drawbacks must be noticed. Overtime imposes a strain on the system, and nature requires the compensation of more food and of more nourishing food in consequence. The same is true of Sunday work. Night shifts and abnormal overtime tend to disorganize the household, with the result of some increase of expense. . . . Still, after full effect is given to such matters, there remains a most substantial counterweight to the increase of the cost of living in the improvement of employment generally.

Increased Family Incomes

The increased demand for labour directly affects the households of all workmen who come under its influence in increasing the employment of the principal worker, and has an additional effect on those households where there are one or more young persons over school age or a second adult worker. The popular idea that in a great number of working-class households before the war there were to be found unoccupied persons, who have now been drawn into industry, is exaggerated, for it was quite exceptional to find boys or girls over school-age who were not at work; but during the war some, it is clear, have been withdrawn prematurely from school, while a certain number of young women, and probably a larger number of married women in the working classes have gone to work, who would normally have confined themselves to household duties. We are not here taking into account the employment of soldiers' wives.

Under war conditions these recruits to industry, and the boys and girls who would normally be occupied, are fully employed, and they obtain work and wages on a much higher scale than before. Some who could not formerly have paid their parents the full cost of keeping them and providing for them at home, are now fully able to pay; some are well able to do much more, and, without stinting themselves, to make an actual contribution to the family exchequer. To what extent this is done must depend on the conditions of each household; it is incapable of statistical estimation, but it is reasonable to suppose that the result of this counterbalancing factor is very substantial. The influence of the parents over their children and the affection of the children for their parents naturally lead to such a result. On the other hand, many young persons have left their homes to work at new industrial centres, and to some extent their assistance is withdrawn from the household.

Tribute to Workers' Patriotism

We desire, not merely lest otherwise we might be supposed to have overlooked it, but from a sense of justice, to pay our tribute to the patriotism, which has in so many cases enlisted workers in tasks to which they are unused and might well have thought themselves unequal, and has stimulated them to efforts which might not have been put forth merely for the sake of an enhancement of earnings. The fact, however, remains that, economically speaking, higher employment, fuller employment, and more profitable employment do result in improvements of the worker's position under war conditions which, in turn, accrue largely to the collective benefit of the family, of which the worker forms part.

There is a group of other matters, which although interesting in themselves and important in the aggregate, fall very far short of the considerations as to employment above set out. In many cases uniforms or overalls are provided which protect and save the workers' clothing. Canteens and national kitchens, when established, often enable better value to be got for a given outlay on food than when it has to be brought ready cooked from home. The inconvenience and extra expenses often experienced by those who have to be absent from their homes for many hours at a time, can be reduced and sometimes obviated in these ways, but to such persons average conclusions are not altogether applicable . . .

Allotments

Allotments again are a special and important feature of the activities of the industrial population in time of war. They have very greatly increased in number, and in this way many thousands of acres are estimated to be under intensive cultivation. Those who have exerted themselves have been actuated by patriotic motives, and have performed a genuine national service. They have materially supplemented the national food supply, and have substantially helped to steady and to standardize the price of garden produce.

Families that were better fed

We have found, on the evidence of the budgets of working-class expenditure, that in June 1918 the working classes, as a whole, were in a position to purchase food of substantially the same nutritive value as in June 1914. Indeed, our figures indicate that the families of unskilled workmen were slightly better fed at the later date, in spite of the rise in the cost of food.

This conclusion is more than confirmed by the reports we have obtained from the Medical Officers to the Education Authorities in the great cities. From London it is officially reported, after inspection of all the children entering school, that 'the percentage of children found in a poorly nourished condition is considerably less than half the percentage of 1913'. A similar improvement is shown by the figures furnished by Birmingham, Bolton, Bradford, Bristol, Glasgow and Nottingham.

Fewer 'necessitous children'

The general impression, especially of the poorer children, is favourable. And the view that parents are now better able to give their children the necessary food is borne out by the information we have received as to the number of meals provided to 'necessitous children' by the local education authorities. It is only in very exceptional cases that education authorities are supplying anything like as many meals as before the war; in most places the number has fallen to about half . . . and in some places it is hardly necessary to provide meals at all. The last available figures for England and Wales, those for 1917, compared with the estimated number in 1914, show a decline by about four-fifths in the country as a whole.

With regard to the other necessaries for children it is not so easy to get information; but London contains so large a proportion of the population of the country that it cannot but be significant that the 'clothing cupboards', from which exceptionally necessitous children used to receive garments before the war, are no longer resorted to, and, on the other hand, that parents who pay into the numerous school boot-clubs are found to be at least as well able to pay the sums necessary to obtain boots at the present high prices as the much smaller sums required before the war.

Decline in Pauperism

Finally, it cannot be out of place to refer to the remarkable decline in pauperism which has taken place during the war, and is still going on – a decline which has brought it much below what it has ever been before. Alike in the Metropolis and in the other great urban areas, it had fallen by July 1918 to two-thirds of what it was in July 1914. Pauperism, of course, touches only the fringe of the working population, but its extent is so largely affected, directly and indirectly, by the industrial situation that it has always, and properly, been regarded as one of the best available indications of the general state of the country.

Report of Working Classes' Cost of Living Committee (1918), Cd 8980, pp. 8–9.

6

Food Prices (Maximum Retail): September 1918

	s	*d*		*s*	*d*
Bacon, Ham, and Lard, per lb			Fish, per lb		
Back, streak, etc.	2	4	Cod	1	10
Gammon hock	1	8	Haddocks	1	1
Ham	2	0	Herrings, fresh		7
Lard	1	8	kippered		11
Beans, coloured haricot, per lb		5½	bloatered		9
Beer, imperial pint		5	Plaice	1	8
Bread, 4 lb loaf		9	Salmon	3	0
Butter, per lb	2	4	Soles	3	2
Cheese, Government, per lb	1	8	Flour, per lb		2½
Chocolate, per oz		3	Jam, per lb	1	2
Cocoa powder, per lb	3	2	Margarine, per lb	1	1
Coffee, roasted or ground per lb	1	6	Marmalade, per lb	1	0
Condensed milk, per tin	1	2½	Meat, per lb		
Dried fruits, per lb			Beef, topside	1	8
Sultanas	1	2	Rump steak	2	2
Currants	1	2	Minced beef	1	6
Figs		8	Mutton, leg	1	7
Persian dates		6	loin chops	1	5
Dripping, per lb	1	10	neck	1	2
			Suet	1	2
			Pork, leg	1	8
			Veal cutlets	1	10
			Milk, imp. gallon	2	8

	s	d		s	d
Poultry & game per lb			Sugar, per lb		7¾
Fowl	2	8	Sweetmeats, per oz		2
Duck	2	3	Syrup, per lb	2	8
Turkey	2	8	Tea, National Control,		
Goose	1	8	per lb	2	8
Rabbits, wild, per lb		9½	Whisky, per gill, etc.	2	6
Rice, ground, per lb		4½			

From a typical Table in *National Food Journal.*

7

Average Prices of Clothing Ordinarily Purchased by the Working Classes in 1914 and 1918

MEN'S	1914 s	1914 d	1918 s	1918 d	WOMEN'S	1914 s	1914 d	1918 s	1918 d
Suits	28	6	60	0	Costumes	44	0	80	3
Overcoats	27	4	46	8	Dresses	8	0	15	11
Shirts (union flannel)	4	6	8	2½	Underwear	3	2	6	0
Underwear (Union)	2	11	5	5	Corsets	4	0	6	11
Hosiery (Union)		10	2	1	Hats	10	7	19	2
Boots	10	10	21	7	Stockings	1	8	3	8
Hats	3	0	6	2	Aprons	1	4	2	3
Caps	1	5	2	7	Boots	11	6	22	4
Collars		5		7	Shoes	9	6	21	9

YOUNG CHILDREN'S

	1914 s	1914 d	1918 s	1918 d
Frocks	4	4	8	3
Pinafores	1	10	3	4
Underwear	1	1	2	7
Socks		9	1	10
Shoes	3	0	4	7

Average Increase: Men's clothing, 94%; Women's, 90%, Children's 89%.

Cd. 8980 (1918), p. 21.

13. WHAT THEY WERE WEARING ON ARMISTICE DAY
Daily Mail, 12 Nov., 1918

(*b*) 'ENJOYING THE WAR'

I

A Crop of Dances

During the past two days we have been deluged with a flood of letters, from all classes of readers and from every quarter of the country, about 'the crop of dances' which were said by a Sunday newspaper to have taken place last week.

We have refrained from publishing these letters solely because we are satisfied by investigation that the facts, so far as detailed facts were given, were inaccurately stated. But we have also satisfied ourselves in the process that there are whole circles of society, both in London and elsewhere, in which the spirit of sacrifice is utterly unknown, and 'pre-war-time conditions' still flourish without the smallest regard for the exhortations of the Prime Minister and the Food Controller.

The more exalted the position of the offenders, the greater the difficulty of instilling economy into those well-paid industrial communities which are said to be 'enjoying the war'.

But it is a matter of nothing less than life and death to this country that there should be no exceptions to the rigorous rule of self-denial which has been willingly undertaken by the great mass of our people. If nothing but the pillory will bring these thoughtless spendthrifts into line, then the pillory it must be. We shall not hesitate to expose them wherever the facts are beyond dispute.

The Times, February 28, 1917.

2

Oysters and Champagne

Perhaps the most flagrant product of this spirit of callous self-indulgence, so far as it prevails in the wealthier grades of society, is the public or semi-public dancing-supper, which has for one of its results, and perhaps of its objects from the standpoint of those who provide it, an unnecessary consumption of food.

There are many private dances given in London which are quite in keeping with the times. The hostesses are content to hire a room, a band of three or four musicians, and a light snack supper. Almost without exception the men who attend these dances are men who are serving in the Army, and many of them are only enjoying a little relaxation after a spell in the trenches. Little or no frittering away of food or money is involved . . .

There are, however, dances of an entirely different type which do involve a reckless waste both of food and money. Such dances are held nightly in some of the big London hotels for the express purpose of promoting the consumption of expensive and unnecessary meals. The dancing, in fact, serves as an excuse for the eating and drinking.

There is no absolute obligation on those who dance to take the supper, but the fact that the management provide the dancing facilities creates a virtual obligation to requite the management by taking supper in the restaurant. The meal, though limited as to the number of courses, is unlimited as to quantity of food consumed or prices charged. All through the evening the tables in the restaurant are crowded with people who in most cases have dined in the hotel a few hours before and are therefore in no need of nourishment.

Even worse from a national point of view is the new type of pseudo-private dance which is being held in certain halls and galleries. There appear to be a number of people who are determined to keep alive by every means open to them the 'gay' whirling life which had its vortex in the night-clubs, and which has been checked by the liquor restrictions and the compulsory closing at half-past twelve.

The method adopted is this. A leading member of this set, or perhaps a group of them acting together, hires a hall, orders early in the day a large supper of food and liquor, invites friends and acquaintances and as many of the principals and chorus of the *revues* as can be induced to go, and gives a dance and supper party which, being ostensibly a private

14. HOW TO LOSE THE WAR AT HOME

Punch (1917)

entertainment, is subject to no regulation as to hours or consumption of liquor.

At a dance of this kind recently in a London gallery, an unlimited supply of champagne was provided. There was a smart supper set at a bar off the dancing hall, and underneath the hall was a set supper with many small tables. The menu would compare favourably with any of pre-war days. There were oysters for each of the hundreds of guests, and salmon and lobster mayonnaise. Fowl, quail, pheasant and other game were to be had in unfailing supplies. The proceedings, which began at 9.30 p.m. and continued without a break until after 5 a.m., were marked as the night wore on by scenes of the most disgusting kind . . .

The Times, March 5, 1917.

3

New Clothes and Taxicabs

Wilful extravagance takes many shapes, and no class of society can be wholly acquitted of indulgence. The middle classes are by no means blameless. Among them, it is true, are many households which have found it hard to adapt a fixed income, or a reduced income, to soaring prices, and no class has made more ungrudging sacrifices. But there are middle-class families to whom the War has meant gain, and gain [of] luxuries unattainable before.

The Spring number of the *Drapers' Record* (a production of nearly 250 pages, which, according to an editorial note, 'appears in a somewhat attenuated form this year, owing to the restrictions on paper') speaks of the trade in nightdresses and similar apparel: 'Most retailers have been experiencing exceptional demands on their stocks by those who have hitherto only been able to cast longing eyes on fascinating garments beyond their purchasing power.' Again, while expensive luxuries are very little bought, 'cheap' i.e. low-priced luxuries continue in great demand. In other words, some middle-class women, as well as some working-class women, finding themselves with more money to spend, spend it on clothes.

Some of the leading West End firms made considerably larger profits last year than in 1915, and this year's outlook is regarded as promising. The immense popularity of furs probably helped to pile up the profits . . .

Nor in some circles is the taxicab habit any the less persistent. In spite of tubes, omnibuses, and tramways, many people think nothing of hiring a taxicab for any journey, short or long, whether for business, shopping, or pleasure.

The Times, March 13, 1917.

4

'Extravagant' Wage-earners

Among the wage-earning classes there are thousands of families who are stinting themselves of many things for the sake of the country. . . . But there are others who are unwilling to deny themselves anything which is in their power to buy, not because they have always been accustomed to it but for the exactly opposite reason. Fur coats have come to be known as 'munition overalls'.

Take a visit to a typical industrial district of London, and ask the bakers whether their sales of bread have fallen off since the appeal of the Food Controller. They will tell you that many of their customers have entirely ignored the appeal, that some of them are now buying even more bread than they did before the war. Walk along a busy shopping street, thronged with buyers, and consider how it comes that seven butchers' shops can exist and show every sign of flourishing trade in a space of less than a hundred yards. Watch the business going on in shops of every kind – provision dealers, furnishers, drapers, jewellers, and the rest – and try to find any indication that any of them have felt the slightest pinch . . .

Nor is this the only form of extravagance of which wage-earners are guilty. It is not without significance that pears are displayed in a fruiterer's shop in Walworth Road at 3d apiece and grapes at 5s a pound. But it is also significant that every picture-palace is crowded night after night, and that some people visit different halls three or four times a week.

The Times, March 5, 1917.

5

Mrs D's Fur Coat

Mrs D, who worked and most efficiently, at munitions for many hours a day during the War, and who, in common with women of all kinds has been in the habit of gazing into shop-windows, suddenly found herself with the wonderful new possibility within her grasp, not only of looking but of buying.

She bought a fur coat. She had never had one before, and the joy of walking about in it must for the moment have been the very crown of existence. It was extravagant of her, no doubt; it was foolish. But she bought a fierce rampant joy with it all the same.

What about Lady F? She has worn a fur coat when the weather was cold enough ever since she grew up. But, all the same, does not she look into shop-windows – and go in at the shop door?

In 1917, at the very height of the War, a well-known house of business in the West End followed its usual custom of sending round circulars to its clients and announcing a display of fashionable clothing worn by *mannequins*, i.e. young women who processed past, for which show numbered and reserved seats could be obtained by payment. At the time these circulars were issued there was much disapproving talk about the young women working in war factories, who with their means suddenly doubled and trebled, were buying effective clothes, and even jewellery, worst of all, for the first time in their lives. It is not every one of us who, having a sudden windfall, puts all of it at once into Government funds instead of expending it on some 'treat' not dictated by wisdom.

LADY FLORENCE BELL, 'Women at the Works – and Elsewhere', *Fortnightly Review*, December 1919.

(c) HOLIDAY SNAPSHOTS

I

Along the South Coast

From Hastings to Bognor . . . the hotels and lodging-houses are full; indeed, they are fuller than in most years. People are spending their money, too, pretty freely; perhaps not quite so lavishly as of old, but fast enough to keep the row-boats and the sailing-boats and the motor-boats, the touring cars and the flies [horse-drawn hackney carriages], and the beach donkeys comfortably busy. There are bands playing, and singers singing; the theatres and cinematographs are doing well, and every place has its little troupes of Funs or Drolls or Merries, giving open-air entertainments.

But holiday-making on the South Coast is full of subtle differences from the holiday-making of most years. Many of the visitors are people who in normal times go abroad for their summer holiday; many others are people who would have gone to the East Coast but felt for their safety . . .

The long front at Eastbourne is crammed with people who in ordinary times would have avoided Eastbourne as dressy and dull. At Littlehampton you may see gowns and hats that look as if they were made for Trouville . . . Brighton is very full – but for Brighton very quiet. It is at Brighton that the spectator will remark with more surprise than at Bexhill or at Eastbourne what an enormous number of women and children there are in the world. There are men about in these places – perhaps one in ten; they are not young; they are obviously appurtenances of the women and the children.

Where are the young men? There are a few indeed at Brighton. But even here a real 'nut' is a thing to stop and look at; and the poor 'noisette' in her white muslin or her gay knitted coat, must hang about in bunches of three or four of her own sex, since there is no male hand to gather her. She looks cheerful, but she is quiet. The nut of nuts is probably somewhere in the trenches; and she sits writing long letters, or knitting, and her favourite male escort is a wounded soldier.

On the pitch-dark sea front at night, the voices are low, and there is none of that shrill laughter in which girlhood blows off its high spirits.

At Brighton and everywhere else the crowd is quiet, all except the children. To them, whatever forts have fallen, a sand-castle is a sand-castle. Mother, seeing them happy, is content to sit in her deck-chair, sewing or reading or writing to their father, who is maybe somewhere over the water, or in London, 'taking no holiday this year', or only running down for a day or two to see that all is going well with the family.

The Times, August 18, 1915.

2

A Holiday by the Sea?

A few of my friends tell me that they will not be taking a holiday this year. 'The times,' they say, 'are out of tune with holiday-making; all the men and women are wanted at their posts; money must be saved; the seaside is the only holiday that is recuperative – and the seaside is unsafe . . .'

We have worked 'overtime' these last eleven months past at our trades, businesses, and professions. All of us have worked 'overtime' at our emotions. The doctors have a tale to tell of ill-helath in the country, and any observant watcher of the faces in streets and trains can see black Care's haggard signs for himself. The only cure for tired bodies and tattered nerves is the seaside.

The 'week-ender' knows how even two days at places like Whitby, Clacton, Margate, Ventnor, Bournemouth, Torquay, Aberystwyth and Blackpool store his mind and body with a sort of elixir for many days afterwards.

The chief reason that makes people hesitate at a seaside holiday is the fear of air raids. . . . London is believed to be the coveted goal of the raiders. But I have not yet met one single person living in London who admits any personal tremor; I do not know a man or a woman who sleeps the less soundly of nights. And I cannot see why one should sleep more soundly in London than in, say, Clacton or Skegness. I cannot believe that the air raiders – even Hun air raiders, for the German is an economist – will waste their bombs on Staithes or Bournemouth.

And what of the children? Can they do without their seaside holiday this year? Ask them.

A City Worker, *Daily Mail*, June 19, 1915.

3

Lord's in War Time

At moments it was almost possible to imagine it was not war time. The turf had its traditional smoothness and greenness. The usual sparrows hunted for insects careless of a ball that might come spinning along the carpet. Hot sunshine poured down upon ten thousand spectators; there was a crowd in the Pavilion, and a scramble for lunch and tea at the buffet outside. There was the right sprinkling of muslin frocks and gay parasols, and of knowing urchins in grey flannels and club colours who instruct fathers and uncles in the points of the game. And when the dramatic moment arrived, and the file of white figures came from the Pavilion to take up their positions in the field, followed by two famous bats who were to make, or not make, their century each, the usual cheers broke out, and when they had subsided there was the usual hush as the expectant crowd settled down to that enjoyment which is not less intense because so decorous.

The match being one between England and the Dominions, the latter consisting chiefly of Australians, it was to be expected that Colonial exuberance would have triumphed handsomely over etiquette. But decorum had its way. There were no long-drawn 'coo-ees', no partisan shouts, no caustic pleasantries as are associated with the friendly critics from overseas . . .

The men from overseas in khaki, or the pathetic blue of the hospitals, looked on, smiled satirically or encouragingly from under their slouch hats, commentated in low voices, and when England was all out for 98 lounged off with the rest of the crowd . . .

There were moments, as has been said, when it was possible to forget that it was war cricket, but the moments were few. There was the hospital blue in the Pavilion, in those reserved balconies, and sprinkled among the crowd in all directions. Khaki was prevalent. Special constables, wearing the star of long service, patrolled the green. A band played, thus accentuating the fact that the match was for charity – for whoever heard of a test match at Lord's being accompanied by a band?

But in truth it was only necessary to look down the scoring-card to know that England was at war. Only one name had not a naval or military prefix. Privates, gunners, corporals, sergeants, Lieutenants, Captains, Majors, Commanders – such is the list of players for a game at Lord's in the summer of 1918 . . .

E.B., *The Spectator*, July 6, 1918.

4

Bank Holiday on Hampstead Heath

The crowds who went yesterday [August Bank Holiday Monday] to Hampstead Heath, to the Zoo, or the parks in a steady, never-ending stream were quite unlike any crowds before or since the war.

Good clothes and general prosperity have had an extraordinary quieting effect. The noises of the old pre-war days were almost unheard. Everyone was well dressed; in the morning, when it rained, pretty working girls in their hundreds, and sometimes in their thousands, poured along the great highways in neat waterproofs cut in trench-coat fashion. But the plentifulness of money was even more evident when the sun came out and the waterproofs came off. The clothes that silenced the loud laugh and stopped the 'linking' of the traditional Bank Holiday 'Arriet were well made and becoming, if not exactly durable. The long velvet coat, the imitation sable stole, and the feathered hat were replaced by pleated georgette, pleated silk, white coats and skirts or the 'golfer', bright of hue and neat of make, and its suitable skirt. While fox furs, fashionable from Belgravia to Bethnal Green, from Mayfair to Hampstead, proclaimed that there is a new equality in the expenditure of pin-money.

The feminine holiday-makers were well hatted and well shod, well gloved and neat of hair. When you have a neat little turban hat and the newest kind of frock, and transparent silk stocking in your high-heeled shoes, and a white fox fur or a couple of yards of tulle round your neck, it is difficult to make a chain of arms across Hampstead High-street and sing the old songs.

The children were equally well dressed. Some of them looked as if they were going to a party with their white muslins and pink bows;

and others again, trotting by the side of fathers and mothers obviously of the working classes, had neat little overcoats that West End mothers could not have bettered. Many of them had their hair done 'Buster Brown' fashion, and long, tortured, curl-paper ringlets were no more.

Food was brought to the park in despatch-cases, and though many families had no 'head' with them, still 'mother' appeared to manage very well. Where father was present he was proudly displayed in khaki or navy blue, and there was competition to hold his hand and trot along beside him. Sometimes he carried the most tired member of the party, and had a little head, in its new hat, sleeping on his shoulders.

Hampstead Heath had, however, lost some of its glories, for though there were swing-boats and a merry-go-round for the children the grown-ups had not the usual 'horses'. But the pedlars seemed to be more numerous. Sellers of penny buttons and paper feathers, crowing cocks and coloured balls, lined Heath-street, and carnations and roses were sold out at 3d each. Oranges varied in price – threepence, 'tuppence-'apenny, and tuppence', but the biggest trade of all was done by a man with a huge metal bath of lemonade, with half-lemons floating on the top to show that it was genuine, into which he dipped tumblers at 1d a time. Saucers of shell-fish, sweets, apples, and tomatoes were eaten indiscriminately and the little restaurants with their lunches and teas did well. Some of the hawkers had wound stripes, and many of them displayed discharge badges.

The Times, August 6, 1918.

(*d*) GOING TO THE PICTURES

At the beginning of the century the Cinematograph was hardly more than a fair side-show, but by 1914 there were few towns of any size in which there might not be found an establishment variously styled cinema or kinema, bioscope, odeum, electric theatre, movie theatre, picture-house, etc. Some of these were palatial, rivalling in garish splendour the largest music-halls, but towards the bottom of the scale the projectors flickered in converted shops and disused chapels that were often very appropriately known as 'flea-pits'.

After the outbreak of war cinema-going (which up to then had been regarded as rather 'low') became the most cherished pleasure, the blessed anodyne, of millions. It was indeed a most happy coincidence that it was just then that a young Londoner named Charles Spencer Chaplin became the most popular 'star' in the American films that largely monopolized the screen, and from then on his unique combination of comedy and pathos made an irresistible appeal to all and sundry.

But the very popularity of the new form of entertainment aroused the suspicious concern of the (often self-constituted) guardians of the public morals. The Cinematograph Trade took alarm, and in 1916 the Exhibitors' organization invited the National Council of Public Morals to conduct 'an independent enquiry into the physical, social, moral, and educational influence of the cinema, with special reference to young people'. A Cinema Commission was thereupon set up, and from its report, issued in 1917, the following 'documents' are taken.

I

The Poor Man's Theatre

The picture-house is the cheapest, the most accessible, and the most widely enjoyed form of public entertainment. . . . Roughly speaking, half the entire population, men, women, and children, visit a cinematograph theatre once every week.

The cheapness of this form of entertainment has created what is really a new type of audience. Over a half of the visitors to the picture-theatres occupy seats to the value of 3d or less. In the main, the vast majority of picture-house patrons were not in the habit of attending any other places of amusement. The picture-house is emphatically the poor man's theatre, and, it must always be remembered, is the only organization which *systematically* provides amusement for children.

2

What the Cinema Means

There are a good many picture palaces in the district [East End of London]; they are very well attended and the level of behaviour maintained is good. The audiences comprise many mothers with their children – not so many fathers since the war – but many soldiers on leave and others who have been wounded attend them. The factory lads and lasses attend in great numbers. I consider the entertainments are a great improvement on the old penny gaff, the old music-hall and club entertainments, particularly in view of the fact that no drinking is permitted.

There is a large population of children in the district, and nearly all the boys and girls go out to work at the age of fourteen. The average home conditions are bad, and, in some parts, very bad. . . . Just imagine what the cinema means to tens of thousands of poor children . . . to families living in one house, six or eight families under one roof. For a few hours at the picture palace at the corner they can find breathing space, warmth, music (the more music the better), and the pictures, where they can have a real laugh, a cheer and sometimes a shout. Who can measure the effects on their spirits and body?

To be able to make the poor pinched-faced, half-clad and half-nourished boys and girls in the crowded slums in cities to forget their pain and misery and their sad lot is a good thing, and the pictures do it.

MR JOHN MASSEY, Court Missionary and Probation Officer of Old Street Police Court, London.

3

'Indecent Behaviour'

The charge has been brought against the picture-house that the darkness encourages indecency, especially where there are boxes, and that the promenade or the standing room at the back, where such exists, affords opportunities for improper conduct.

In 1915 there were only two prosecutions for indecency in connection with the cinema brought under the notice of the London Branch of the Exhibitors' Association. . . . A probation officer of 25 years' experience stated that he had known of only one indecent assault in a cinema; and another that during four years one charge of indecent assault had been made ('I think it was only an attempt to put his hands up a little girl's clothes'), and that there were far more charges of indecency in open spaces.

Mr F. R. Goodwin, representing the Exhibitors of London, asserted that in many cases the charge should never have been made. 'When investigation is made it is usually found that the alleged misconduct is nothing more than the privileged manifestation of affection between the sexes. Most unmarried couples sitting in close proximity at entertainments will hold hands, or link arms, or even an occasional arm will be found round a waist, this under the strongest as well as under the very much diminished lighting.'

4

A Good Place to Take a 'Bird'

Most of the children [in the East End of London] are tailors or cigarette-makers, and the work is no great strain on them mentally, so they have plenty of time to think and talk of things, and in the evening when they have finished their work they feel they must have some excitement . . .

The next point is that the cinema is a dark place, and if you have a young lady it is very convenient to go there. It is also a convenient rendezvous for family parties, but the elder children do not go with their parents; they go with their 'bird'. The expression down there is that you take your 'bird' to the pictures.

I notice that the couples go for the love stories. The children are always in the cheapest seats, which are under the exit lights, whereas the couples go where it is darker. . . . If a couple are sitting with their arms round one another they can fairly easily manage anything they want to . . .

MRS BASIL HENRIQUES, in charge of youth clubs in St George's in the East.

5

All the Boys Like Charlie Chaplin

Four schoolboys, two aged eleven and two thirteen. They lived in the Bethnal Green neighbourhood, and two of them attended cinemas on Saturday night and two on Saturday afternoon, only going once a week.

The Chairman (Bishop of Birmingham). What do you like best at the cinema? – All about thieves. The next best? – Charlie Chaplin. And you? – Mysteries; and then Charlie Chaplin. And you? – Mysteries, and Charlie Chaplin. What do you mean by mysteries? – Where stolen goods are hidden away in vaults so that the police can't get them. And you? – Cowboys; and then Charlie Chaplin second . . .

Do you sit among the girls? – Sometimes. What do you pay? – 1½d and 2d.

Have you ever seen the boys behave roughly to the girls? – Yes. What do they do? – Aim orange peel at them. Do they pull the girls about? – Yes, their hair. And do the girls pull back again? ? No; they seem to enjoy it.

6

Love Stories Bore the Schoolgirls

Three South London schoolgirls examined together.

The Chairman: What do you like best? – Pretty pictures about dancing and horses. . . . I should like a good drama, but not a love drama. There is too much fooling about in them . . . it is a lot of silliness. I do not think it would happen in real life.

What do you like the least? – The topical budget . . . Love stories . . . I think the same: love stories.

The Cinema: Its Present Position and Future Possibilities, being the Report . . . of the Cinema Commission of Inquiry instituted by the National Council of Public Morals (1917), pp. xiv, xxv, 5–6, 83, 198, 209–10, 239–40.

CHAPTER 14

'SEX' IN WAR TIME

Notwithstanding some loosening of convention in the Edwardian Age, what may be called 'Victorian morality' survived virtually intact right up to the outbreak of war in 1914. Then the sudden transformation of the lives of millions gave rise to problems such as had never been encountered before.

In those great military camps, that sprang up almost overnight in close proximity to centres of population, were hosts of men – young men for the most part, vigorous, in the prime of life, with a good deal of leisure on their hands and nothing much to do in it: what deplorable situations might arise when they mixed with the flocks of giddy young girls who hung about the gates at all hours of the day, and night! It was out of this fear that the first women's police organizations came into being.

Great numbers of men, too, were billeted in private homes throughout the country, and it was not unreasonable that parents should be worried about their impressionable daughters.

Thus the first of the 'scares' gained currency, that of a host of 'war babies' fathered by soldiers who were here today and gone tomorrow. As will be seen from one or two of the 'documents' given here this scare turned out to be greatly exaggerated, but there were plenty of others.

Young people were marrying in haste, and turning the deafest of ears to warnings that they might repent at leisure. And who could have it in his heart to blame them, when (the casualty lists being as long as they were) they might have no tomorrow in which to 'repent'? Then there were the women and girls, hundreds of thousands of them, who left the homes in which, as likely as not, they had been living reasonably sheltered lives, and went away to work in munition factories in places at a distance, where deadly boredom and a desperate loneliness might make them welcome a sexual adventure. Finally, mention should be made of 'V.D.' (still generally referred to in books and newspapers as the 'hidden scourge' or by some other euphemism), the spread of which had led to the appointment of a Royal Commission just before the war, whose reports made most alarming reading.

These were the most important of the sexual problems brought into prominence by the war that (as shown in the 'documents' quoted here, taken in the main from the columns of *The Times*) exercised a most disturbing influence on public opinion.

'SEX' IN WAR TIME

I

War Marriages: the Pros and the Cons

A 'war marriage' is not of course any marriage which occurs in war-time, but only a soldier's marriage. Further, it must be the marriage of a soldier immediately going to the Front, or, better, returned on leave in order to get married and go off again. This is the true, the authentic war marriage; it has the requisite hurry and hazard about it.

Perhaps to be perfect it ought to be the sort of marriage that in dull times of peace it would not have been, by the parents or the middle-aged people generally, considered 'prudent' to contract. 'Hadn't you better wait a year or two?' 'Wait a year, and see how it looks then.'

Now, with happiness everywhere threatened, the middle-aged generally and the parents in particular, have not the heart to refuse anything to the young, who in their turn are refusing nothing, risking everything in this war. So, if it must be part of his leave, or part of his preliminary training before going abroad that he should marry, why he must; for what would be their elderly remorse did he go unhappy away, refused, baulked, of the wish most dear to him? He shall be denied nothing, not even marriage. He marries . . .

'Married in haste' then? No; married because the war has made it possible. Before the war it was impossible, because, frankly, there wasn't enough money. Before the war, his mother told the youth – he is only 22 – that when *she* married, her father was earning a thousand a year. . . . That was in peace-time. But war changed the perspective of both young and old. Instead of advising him, his mother went diplomatically to his father and 'made it all right'. Very well; rapture for a while in the families involved.

And now he has returned to France, and she is staying with his parents, and getting on, let us admit, sufficiently well, since all this household agree in thinking only of him. It all seems to have been miraculously easy now it is accomplished. Why, then, are peace marriages so beset with objections? Why are war marriages as easy as joys achieved in dreams?

That question you shall answer after the war. Then shall you see him (as we all hope) safely returned as a hero. It must be very beautiful. But then also shall you see him necessarily subject of that sometimes painful process they call 'settling down' . . .

R.J., *The Times*, April 30, 1915.

2

The New Social Problem: Unmarried Mothers

The problem of the large number of unmarried girls and women in this country who are expecting to become mothers is being widely discussed. A great wave of emotional nonsense has been set in motion, and much that is being said is subversive both of the principles of morality and of the foundations of the State.

'These poor girls have so little to give, and they gave their all,' is a sample of the explanation that is being offered. Such apologies, if they gained general currency, would ultimately do more mischief than the harsh treatment which is equally to be deprecated.

Nor must the problem be obscured by fanciful misrepresentation. The babies that are expected are only in a very few cases the children of 'the men that fought at the Marne and Mons'. We shall not arrive at the truth by talking rubbish about 'the children of our dead heroes'. The Regular Army had little to do with this situation, and the Navy, which was mobilized when war began, practically nothing at all. The acknowledged unmarried dependants of our sailors and our Regular soldiers were quickly provided for. Most of the men responsible for the miserable position of these girls and women belonged either to the Territorials or the new armies. A large proportion of these have not up till now fought anywhere, or have only gone to the front quite recently.

Some of the remedies now being proposed are at variance alike with law and common sense. It is impracticable to 'legitimize' children in cases where the father is either not known or where the alleged paternity is not admitted. Something might be done by passing a general law legitimizing children born out of wedlock, in cases where the parents marry after the child is born; but such legislation cannot be lightly or hastily undertaken, for it would strike at the basis of our present laws of inheritance. The real stigma of bastardy is social, and it cannot be removed by any legislative declaration, as some people seem to suppose.

The further question of State aid to these prospective mothers is equally difficult. If every girl who is with child by some unknown male whom she says is a soldier is to be provided with a State allowance, we shall . . . be saying in effect that every future war is to be the signal for an outburst of indiscriminate licence and the State will pay the cost.

Such remedies as are devised must imperatively be voluntary. The first thing necessary is the cultivation of a more charitable and more compassionate public opinion. Parents who have cast off their daughters should be reasoned with and when possible be induced to take them back. The various societies which have this matter in hand should be assisted by voluntary subscriptions and personal aid. The State might support societies by grants. . . . Men who acknowledge their responsibility might be induced to marry, and possibly an Act could be passed prescribing legitimization for children already born in such cases out of wedlock. We must deal with the situation broadly and compassionately...

The Times, April 19, 1915.

3

'War Babies'

The Committee on Illegitimate Births during the War, of which the Archbishop of York is chairman, has considered the report of Mrs Creighton's sub-committee who undertook to investigate the allegations of a large prospective increase of illegitimacy owing to the quartering of troops in camps and billets throughout the country. The Committee accepts and endorses the sub-committee's conclusion that 'the rumours which have been circulated proved beyond doubt to have no foundation in fact'.

The sub-committee made special enquiry in 62 towns and districts through branches of the National Union of Women Workers, the Women's Patrol Committees in large military centres, and other agencies possessed of special local knowledge, and by a skilled lady investigator. In no case has any confirmation been obtained of the rumours which have been circulated.

We were told that in many places the Local Government Board were making large additions to the lying-in wards of the infirmaries. Not a single new bed has been ordered. We were told that in a well-known maternity hospital preparations were being made to add fifteen new wards, and that 56 beds had been placed at the disposal of our informant. We learned that the additions being made to the hospital were begun in 1913 and that it had received no more illegitimate births than usual.

In a northern city, where the wildest statements had been made, enquiry at a manufactory employing 3,000 girls showed that there was only a single case among them, and that a doubtful one. In another place, where it was said that five hundred cases were known and that two hundred had already been received into homes, investigation has shown that there are not more than three.

Of those individual cases reported to us, very few are under 16, and many are girls known as having already borne a bad character and as having had illegitimate children previously. Place after place reports 'nothing abnormal', 'no increase expected', 'no appreciable increase'.

The general conclusions we have arrived at, therefore, about the reports that have been circulated as to the large numbers of 'War Babies' is that they are without foundation, and reflect unfairly on the characters of our soldiers and our girls. We do not mean to deny that there has been grave cause for anxiety on account of the prevailing low moral standard, as well as on account of intemperance, often the result of thoughtless treating, nor that there has been much giddiness and foolish excitability among the young girls leading often to most undesirable conduct. . . . But we feel that the way in which the subject has been treated in many quarters is likely to do incalculable harm.

The Times, June 18, 1915.

4

'Sexuality' in the Music-Hall

From the play-bill to the stage the appeal to sexuality is constantly emphasized. The wall-poster, which is exposed to the public as the best possible indicator of the attractions offered, will usually bear the figure of a woman, not naked but as nearly so as public opinion will permit, her limbs extended in an unconventional attitude, and freely displayed, while nothing else in the picture matters. Sometimes, as in the case of a London West End music-hall poster, which was withdrawn after protest, the head and upper part of the body of the woman are omitted, leaving only the lower part, greatly magnified.

The word sexuality is not necessarily an evil word, but the tone and atmosphere of the music-hall tend to make it an evil thing. Love, as between the sexes, on the music-hall stage frequently becomes lust. Peaceful domesticity becomes a butt of cynical jest, and while harlotry is condoned, honest matrimony is represented as a thing full of pitfalls, delusions, troubles and tricks, normally chequered with unfaithfulness, on the part of husband or wife, or both.

From time to time efforts have been made to make the pendulum swing the other way, as Mr Harry Lauder has done, or as Mr Chevalier successfully did with 'My Old Dutch', the sentiment of which is indicated by the lines:

> We've been married now for forty years, and it doesn't seem a day too much:
> There's not a lady in the land I'd swop for my old Dutch.

But this kind of thing, however highly appreciated by the East End costermonger and his wife, for whom it was originally intended, is entirely out of place in a modern *West End* revue. The basis of at any rate one type of *revue* is fleshly indulgence, eating, drinking, dress, flippancy, and fornication . . .

JOHN COWEN, 'Music Halls and Morals', *Contemporary Review* November, 1916.

5

'Open sewer' at Waterloo

The Waterloo-road and its purlieus, which have for many years had a bad reputation as a centre of immorality, have been brought into prominence during the last few days by the campaign for the cleansing of London from impurity.

Night after night the short stretch of road between Stamford-street and the 'Old Vic' is thronged by women who are unmistakably pursuing the traffic of prostitution. Some of the most shameless of them openly accost soldiers as they walk along the street or loiter at the corners. The writer two nights ago saw a flagrant instance of solicitation outside the doors of the Union Jack Club. A young woman, fairly well dressed, walked up to a soldier, who stood on the kerbstone aimlessly watching the traffic in and out of Waterloo Station entrance. She spoke a few words to him, and he turned away. Unabashed, she moved a few yards along the road, and made her appeal to a second soldier, who was whiling away his time at the edge of the pavement. He also rejected her overtures. A little farther on she offered herself to a third man, and again she was rebuffed. In each case as she moved away she flung back a taunt at the soldier. In the third case the writer caught her words, uttered in rather shrill tones, 'Well, what are you standing there for?' Presently the woman was seen to accost another soldier, and this time, apparently, she found a victim, for the two remained talking for some time and finally disappeared into one of the side streets.

Solicitation can be practised in other ways than by the spoken word, and in those other ways it goes on continuously in the area immediately outside Waterloo Station. The whole district is so infested by prostitutes that no one can walk a hundred yards from the station in any direction without passing scores of them. There is ample evidence that the back streets which spread like a net between Westminster Bridge Road and Blackfriars are honeycombed with 'houses of accommodation' and shebeens.

Here is the statement made to our representative by a level-headed and experienced businessman who has been giving his time lately to social work among soldiers in the neighbourhood of Waterloo: 'If you describe the Waterloo-road and the back streets as an open sewer you will be somewhere near the truth. Not a day goes by, and sometimes not many hours go by, without bringing to me some soldier who has been waylaid and robbed by the creatures who pollute this part of London. Three nights ago two young fellows came to me within a few minutes of each other and told me the same story, of how they had got into bad company, and, after leaving the public-houses, had gone away with women, who rifled their pockets during the night and were gone when they awoke in the morning.

'One of them, an Australian, said that he picked up a girl and went with her late at night to a stable, paying the night-watchman 3s for shelter there. In the morning he found that the girl had disappeared with every penny of his money . . .'

To a considerable extent, the men themselves are to blame, for in most cases they admit that they had been drinking freely and were not altogether aware of what they were doing at the end of the night. I was told on very good authority that there is a great deal of touting carried on in and about Waterloo Station by young boys who go up to the soldier when he has just arrived as though they were asking for cigarette-cards, and say, 'You want a drink? My mother will get you one; she lives just round the corner. I'll show you . . .'

The Times, February 22, 1917.

6

Girls in Evidence

I do not think anyone who has known the London streets for the last 20 or 30 years could avoid being struck by the fact that whereas 20 or

25 years ago the streets of the West End between 8 and 12 o'clock were full of women, professional prostitutes but women of considerable age, well over twenty-five, now I should say there are far fewer of those regular professional prostitutes and many more quite young girls, whom you did not see in the old days; at any rate, they would not be there alone. (Sir E. Blackwell, Under-Secretary of State, Home Office.)

* * *

These girls are getting better wages, they dress themselves rather more flashily, and use powder on their faces. One can hardly go down a street without seeing girls of 13, 14 or 15 with powder on their faces and rouge on their lips. (Mr Neville, MP.)

* * *

There are a great many young girls in the streets. They talk with soldiers. A great many do not take money at all if they go wrong. They are simply out for a lark. (Miss MacDougall, Lady Assistant, Metropolitan Police.)

* * *

I do not think it is the case, that a considerable amount of the girls falling is owing to young men and women being employed together in large works. . . . I think the more boys and girls work together upon equal terms in factories or offices the less they are inclined to have sex dealings with each other. They respect each other more, and get into a better frame of mind as regards their treatment of the opposite sex. (Cecil Chapman, London Police Magistrate.)

Report of Joint Select Committee on the Criminal Law Amendment Bill and the Sexual Offences Bill, No. 142 (1918), pp. 8, 38, 39, 102.

7

'Much exaggerated'

It is obvious that the condition of the streets in the centre of a place like London at present must be very different from what they are in peace-time. You have vast numbers of soldiers on leave, and you have very large numbers of young women living a much more independent life than they were in peace-time.

I would like to say that I think that the representations that have been made in some quarters with regard to the condition of the streets are very much exaggerated. I mean to say that we are constantly having streets watched, and it is very surprising to me to read the kinds of things that are said in the newspapers about them. I think that those who raise these criticisms are apt to forget that the public is entitled to use the streets as a promenade, and that it is not the duty, and should not be the duty, of the police-force to interfere with that use of the streets unless it is of a disorderly character.

Lord Muir Mackenzie (Chairman): I think that one might ask you whether your view is, as it is, I think, of many people, that the general manifestations of mutual regard are less reserved than they used to be before the war? – Undoubtedly. There is no doubt about it at all.

HON. TREVOR BIGHAM, Assistant Commissioner of Metropolitan Police, No. 142 (1918), p. 36.

EPILOGUE: AFTER THE WAR

Lloyd George became Prime Minister towards the close of 1916, when the war was going badly for Britain and her allies and looked as though it would go worse. As indeed it did do. Between the day of his 'kissing hands' as the King's chief minister and the ecstatic clamour of Armistice Day there lay nearly two years of most dreadful war. Yet he never wavered or weakened in the 'will to win', any more than did the great mass of the people. There may have been some faint-hearts in Whitehall and at Westminster, but there were precious few among the munition workers, the miners, the shipwrights and engineers, the farm workers. Nor were the women any less resolute than the men.

1917 was a bad year, what with Passchendaele and the U-boats. 1918 opened with a solemn appeal from the Prime Minister to the people: 'The road of duty and patriotism is clear before you; follow it . . . and it will lead ere long to victory' – and as though to make a mockery of his words, within a matter of weeks the German armies had smashed the British front and were going hell for leather for the Channel ports. Somehow or other, however, the enemy onrush was halted, the gap filled, the disaster repaired. July saw the beginning of the turn of the tide, and from August there was no longer any doubt which way it was flowing. September's news was good and October's better. And then, at 11 o'clock on November 11th, the armistice was concluded that brought to an end the fighting in what Lloyd George was to describe a few hours later in the House of Commons as 'the cruellest and most terrible war that has ever scourged mankind'.

In retrospect, this moment, when he was being acclaimed on every hand as 'the man who won the war', may be seen as the high-water-mark of Lloyd George's achievement as a statesman; equally, as the climax, the triumphant culmination, of the 'era' to which we have appended his name.

At the time, there were few who saw it in that way. Lloyd George most certainly did not. He had another of his dazzling visions, this time of returning to the work of social reform from which he had been dragged away in 1914. Already Fisher's great Education Bill had reached the Statute Book, and very shortly large numbers of women would be enjoying the parliamentary franchise. Now in the general election campaign that followed immediately upon the Armistice, while Lloyd George went along with those of his followers in the Coalition who played on war-torn nerves with such clap-trap phrases as 'Hang the

Kaiser!' and 'Squeeze Germany dry till the pips squeak!', he insisted on including in the Coalition's election manifesto 'domestic reform in all spheres'. In a speech at Wolverhampton on November 25 he put the rhetorical question, 'What is our task?' and made reply, '*To make Britain a fit country for heroes to live in!*'

No doubt at all, he meant it; and his plea found an echo in countless hearts and minds. The Coalition won a tremendous triumph at the polls. But as the first of the post-war years dawned it was very soon made apparent that this was a very different Britain from the one that had gone to war in the eager idealism of 1914. For a few months there were boom conditions in industry, as war gratuities and savings were splashed in a glorious spending spree. But before long the jazz fever subsided. Great numbers of men who had noisily clamoured for immediate demobilization in order that they might hurry back home to reclaim the jobs that had been theirs before they enlisted or were called up, found themselves on the unemployment 'dole'. During the war years there had been no praise too high for the women and girls who had answered their country's call and gone to work in munition factories and workshops, but now they were roughly told that a woman's place was in the home, and if they delayed they were thrust out with ruthless speed on to the scrap-heap of unemployment. Now that the war-time ban on strikes had been lifted, hosts of sullen or angry workers militated against the pressures on their standard of living, and revolutionary undertones were detected in unemployed demonstrations outside the Houses of Parliament and on the Clyde. As for Lloyd George, he was so completely occupied in 'peacemaking' in Paris that for weeks at a time Westminster saw him hardly at all.

This, then, was Britain 'after the war' and, in its own very different way, the picture is as depressing as 'before the war' was found to be – even more depressing, perhaps, since now there was disillusion and foreboding where in the earlier picture there had been 'indications on the horizon of a brighter tomorrow'. So it happened that the 'Lloyd George Era' that had seen the foundation of the Welfare State and victory in the Great War, moved to its close in a squalid confusion of political bickering, class antagonism, labour disturbances and social distress.

LLOYD GEORGE'S EIGHTY-TWO YEARS

1863	(January 17) Born in Manchester; son of William George, an elementary school teacher, of Welsh peasant-farmer descent.
1864	Death of his father; brought up by his mother and her brother, Richard Lloyd, village shoemaker, at Llanystumdwy, near Criccieth, North Wales.
1866–76	Attended village (Church of England) school.
1879	Articled to firm of Solicitors in Portmadoc.
1884	Started practice as Solicitor in Criccieth.
1888	Married Margaret Owen, daughter of a farmer near Criccieth.
1890	Elected Liberal M.P. for Caernarvon Boroughs; held the seat without a break until elevation to peerage.
1899–1902	Leading (and most unpopular) critic of the Boer War.
1905	President of the Board of Trade in Campbell-Bannerman's Liberal administration.
1908	Chancellor of the Exchequer in Asquith's administration.
1909	Introduced his first Budget ('People's Budget').
1911	National Insurance Act.
1915	(May) Minister of Munitions in Asquith's Coalition.
1916	(July) Secretary of State for War.
1916	(December 7) Prime Minister heading a Coalition ('Win the War') administration.
1917	Ordered adoption of Convoy system for merchant shipping.
1918	(November 11) Announced conclusion of the Armistice.
1918	(December) General Election; overwhelming triumph of the Lloyd George Coalition.
1919	Peace Conference at Paris. Signed Treaty of Versailles (June 28).
1921	(December 6) Concluded treaty for establishment of Irish Free State.
1922	(October 19) Fall of the Coalition; resignation of Lloyd George.
1926–31	Leader of the Liberal party; instituted inquiries into Land use, Coal and Power, Britain's Industrial Future, etc.
1931–34	Writing *War Memoirs*, mostly at Churt, Surrey, where he had a farm of 750 acres.
1940	Invited to join Churchill's War Cabinet, but declined.
1941	Death of Mrs Lloyd George.
1943	Married Miss Frances Stevenson, his secretary for more than 30 years.
1945	(January 1) Created Earl Lloyd-George of Dwyfor.
1945	(March 26) Died at his home at Llanystumdwy; buried beside river Dwyfor at Criccieth.

INDEX

INDEX